The Theological Papers
of
John Henry Newman

The Theological Papers of
John Henry Newman
on
Biblical Inspiration
and on Infallibility

selected, edited, and introduced by
J. Derek Holmes

CLARENDON PRESS · OXFORD
1979

Oxford University Press, Walton Street, Oxford OX2 6DP

OXFORD LONDON GLASGOW
NEW YORK TORONTO MELBOURNE WELLINGTON
KUALA LUMPUR SINGAPORE JAKARTA HONG KONG TOKYO
DELHI BOMBAY CALCUTTA MADRAS KARACHI
IBADAN NAIROBI DAR ES SALAAM CAPE TOWN

British Library Cataloguing in Publication Data

Newman, John Henry
  The theological papers of John Henry Newman on
  Biblical inspiration and on infallibility.
  1. Popes – Infallibility 2. Bible – Inspiration
  I. Title   II. Holmes, James Derek
  220. 1′3′08   BX1806   78–41118
  ISBN 0-19-920081-5

*Set, printed and bound in Great Britain by
Cox & Wyman Ltd
London, Fakenham and Reading*

Contents

Introduction

THIS volume comprises the drafts and outlines of two works projected by Newman on biblical inspiration and papal infallibility. Although tentative and incomplete, Newman's papers contain valuable insights on these two subjects which continue to be of crucial significance. Professor Bruce Vawter for example has commented that Newman was concerned with and wrote about scriptural problems all his life long, and that much of his best writing on the subject has never been fully published to this day.[1] The controversy over the nature and extent of inspiration was occasioned by the publication of *Essays and Reviews* in 1860. At this time, Newman was able to argue that the issue did not affect Catholics so directly or severely as other Christians, because Catholics had a sufficient basis of faith in an infallible Church and did not depend on Scripture alone. As he told Malcolm MacColl,

The religion of England depends, humanly speaking, on belief in 'the Bible and the whole Bible', . . . Now the plenary inspiration of Scripture is peculiarly a Protestant question; not a Catholic. We indeed devoutly receive the whole Bible as the Word of God, but we receive it on the authority of the Church, and the Church has defined very little as to the aspects under which it comes from God, and the limits of its inspiration.[2]

Newman did not consider that a belief in biblical inspiration caused any particular difficulties for a Catholic until the First Vatican Council defined the notion of inspiration more precisely than before and considerably restricted the freedom which Catholics had previously enjoyed in dealing with biblical questions. It was as a result of these restrictions that Newman later felt obliged to turn his attention to another aspect of inspiration, which he did in 1884.[3]

Nevertheless, even during the early 1860s, Newman was not prepared to reject the findings of science or history either in the case of the Bible or the theological claim of papal infallibility. He knew that Catholics must be prepared to face up to the issues involved and he appreciated the need for intellectual honesty in dealing with the problems as they arose. Although he never experienced any difficulty in reconciling the scientific evidence in favour of evolution, for example, with scriptural claims, he was also aware of the

---

[1] B. Vawter, *Biblical Inspiration*, London 1972, p. 136.
[2] *The Letters and Diaries of John Henry Newman*, edited by Charles Stephen Dessain, London 1961 ff., XIX, p. 488.
[3] J. H. Newman, *On the Inspiration of Scripture*, edited with an Introduction by J. Derek Holmes and Robert Murray S.J., London 1967; see also 'Newman's attitude towards historical criticism and biblical inspiration', *Downside Review*, vol. 89, 1971, pp. 22–37. J. Seynaeve, *Cardinal Newman's Doctrine on Holy Scripture*, Louvain 1953, pp. 53* ff., reproduced the earlier notes on inspiration, but not always satisfactorily.

force of biblical criticism; as he later wrote to H. P. Liddon, 'It is clear we shall have to discuss the question whether certain passages of the Old Testament are or are not mythical. It is one of the gravest of questions, and we cannot spend too much time in preparing for it.'[4] Meanwhile, he was also conscious that the claim to papal infallibility was a matter of fact and 'facts are facts from the first.'[5]

However, by 1863, Newman felt under the 'arbitrary, military power' of Propaganda which acted like a man of business with a civil service. The solution of contemporary difficulties such as biblical inspiration demanded 'elbow room — but this was *impossible*'. The attitude of Propaganda made any attempt to solve contemporary problems like fighting '*under the lash*' or with a chain on the arm.[6] Furthermore, the *Munich Brief* and the *Syllabus of Errors* were clear warnings from the ecclesiastical authorities that they were unlikely to have much sympathy with theological discussions which did not reflect the prevailing ultramontane opinions in the Church. Newman interpreted 'recent acts of that authority' as 'tying the hands of a controversialist' and 'a call to be patient'.[7] He was beginning to learn that

Those who would not allow Galileo to reason 300 years ago, will not allow any one else now. The past is no lesson for them for the present and the future: and their notion of stability in faith is ever to be repeating errors and then repeating retractations of them.[8]

To turn now to the second subject considered in this volume. Early in September, 1865, Newman received a copy of E. B. Pusey's *Eirenicon*, an attack on Catholic devotions to the Blessed Virgin, and although Newman recognized his friend's sincerity and genuine desire for unity, he also considered that Pusey's attack was less than fair. Newman's *Letter to Pusey* criticized not only the latter's misunderstandings, but also the exaggerations of the extreme ultramontanes which had given rise to them. Originally, Newman also intended to deal with another question raised by Pusey, that of infallibility, but he was involved in other projects, feared dividing English Catholics even more, and, perhaps most important of all, was convinced that although he had been successful as a check on the extremists, it would be unwise and imprudent to antagonize them any further. In any case, the need to publish his opinions on papal infallibility was superseded by the subsequent controversy between W. G. Ward and H. I. D. Ryder.[9]

Newman then did not use his notes at this time, though they illustrate how his mind was working and show how he would have approached the issues

---

[4] *Letters and Diaries*, XXVI, p. 66.
[5] *Letters and Diaries*, XXIV, p. 334.
[6] *Letters and Diaries*, XX, pp. 391, 447; XXIV, p. 120; XXVI, p. 27.
[7] *Apologia pro Vita Sua*, edited with an Introduction and Notes, by Martin J. Svaglic, Oxford 1967, pp. 235–6; see also, W. Ward, *The Life of John Henry Cardinal Newman*, London 1913, vol. I, pp. 640–2; *Certain Difficulties felt by Anglicans in Catholic Teaching*, London 1907, vol. II, pp. 276–98.
[8] *Letters and Diaries*, XXVIII, pp. 71–2.
[9] *Letters and Diaries*, XXII, pp. 166–8, 178, 187, 191–2, 203; see also, D. McElrath, *The Syllabus of Pius IX, Some Reactions in England*, Louvain 1964, pp. 153 ff.

under discussion. He did of course use some of his earlier insights in his *Letter to the Duke of Norfolk* during the controversy over W. E. Gladstone's attack on *The Vatican Decrees* in 1875. Newman himself, however, had already clarified his attitude to the definition of papal infallibility in a letter written to Ward in February, 1866; 'I have ever thought it likely to be true, never thought it certain. I think too, its definition inexpedient and unlikely; but I should have no difficulty in accepting it, were it made.'[10] Newman's important letter to J. S. Flanagan explaining his attitude to papal infallibility is included in this volume for convenience and provides a suitable conclusion to his notes on infallibility.

Newman himself arranged the order of the documents on inspiration 'on putting aside these attempts' and this order has been followed. He also indicated which documents were partly or almost completely superseded and these are either quoted or referred to in the footnotes when they are of any importance. The documents on infallibility are published in what seems to be the chronological and logical order.

Some passages which Newman erased have also been included because of their interest. These are noted as they occur, but it should not be forgotten that nearly all the papers are unrevised and unprepared for publication, though much more ready for publication than most of the *Papers on Faith and Certainty*. Newman's alternative readings are inserted in angle brackets, and his marginal notes and corrections are also in angle brackets and are usually placed where they appear to belong. Newman's own brackets are always printed as round ones, square brackets being reserved for editorial additions. Newman's paragraphs and punctuations are reproduced, except that single quotation marks are printed throughout, and double ones for quotations within them. Further, a parenthesis or quotation which he began with the proper mark, but failed to complete, or completed, but failed to begin, is supplied. All other punctuation marks supplied by the editor are enclosed in square brackets. Newman's abbreviations, except in the case of proper names, are printed out in full. Oddities of Latin here have not been corrected.

I am most grateful to the late Father Charles Stephen Dessain and to Mr. Gerard Tracey for their generous help in preparing this volume.

J. DEREK HOLMES

Ushaw College,
Durham

---

[10] *Letters and Diaries*, XXII, p. 157; 'Cardinal Newman and the First Vatican Council', *Annuarium Historiae Conciliorum*, vol. I, 1969, pp. 374–98.

Part I   Papers on Inspiration

July 23, 1861   *On putting aside these attempts*

A   is the rude sketch of the whole subject under the two heads of inspiration and interpretation. On the second head I have done nothing but what is here — and it is in brief confused *notes*. [later note in pencil: 'September 29 1861 I have written these out fair today'] pp 5, 6 also are unused relating to the argumentative view of inspiration which is begun in B § 4

B   The three first § of B are nearly superseded — as the pencil lines of erasure show — some pencil notes etc. may be important. Fasciculus 1 upside down (p. 25 back) has not been used, and belongs, I suppose, to B § 4
    Portions of fasciculus 3, and the whole of fascicules
⎡torn pieces⎤ the final copies of the (inchoate)
⎢of mss.   ⎢ view.
⎣missing ⎦

C   was intended for a last and fair copy! the Introduction *is* finished pp. 1–69 — whether it is expedient or prudent at all is another question.
    § 3 pp. 97–127 on the Scripture argument
    § 4 pp. 127–171 on the dogmatic definitions of the Church
    § 5 pp. 173–205 on the habit of *requiring* dogma for faith are the only copies which I have written on their respective subjects.
    § 6 is *worked up* otherwise in Latin MSS (e.g. E) but all the *matter* is not elsewhere used.

D   was the re-writing of C § 2 — but is superseded by E almost entirely — but there are *notes* to be looked at in it.

E   is the final copy of C § 2; it [contains? torn piece of mss. missing] also the *Fathers'* view of inspiration.

F   is a proposed remodelment of [piece of mss. missing]
        [This fragment was attached to A]

I   Preliminary Remarks on the Problem of Inspiration, 1861

April 6, 1861   A

It is not very wonderful that such reports as you mention about me should be spread. It is the consequence of words which I have spoken passing through a number of mouths and naturally in suffering without any one's fault from the memory or the apprehension of successive recipients, for written words one can be answerable; but what is spoken (though 'volat irrevocabile,'[1] it is not immutabile ⟨irreformabile⟩) (it would be well, if it were volat immutabile ⟨irreformabile⟩ as well as *irrevocabile*) 'volat' mutabile ⟨variabile⟩ as well as 'irrevocabile'. Two years since, feeling that it would be charitable in me to speak in explanation of various religious points, I began to do so in ⟨by⟩ the pages of a periodical. Kind and good friends, speaking with authority, prevailed with me to change my intention. They urged that in the few cases in which my words were necessary, it would be well to address them to the ear of the individuals calling for them, and confine them to his definite need ⟨necessity⟩. But as the event has proved, such a course only provides for the misrepresentation not the privacy of what an adviser ⟨a man⟩ says. Those who have ears, have voices, and thus at length public rumour speaks instead of him ⟨for me⟩ as if his ⟨mine⟩ what is its own, and no blame to any one; it is from the nature of the case. But this is not all. Overzealous persons two years ago took offence at what I actually wrote. They decided on their own judgment, without asking from me any explanation that what I said was of an heretical character.[2] As to my own feelings on such a charge, I may well be understood by those who recollect ⟨gathered⟩ from the story told of a holy hermit, who, silent when slandered ⟨accused of other sins⟩ indignantly broke out with a denial when accused of a sin against faith, because, he said, it was to the dishonour of his Lord. One of them brought the matter before Propaganda. Propaganda did not take the matter up. I say all this, because here also, I think words written such as those I now put down better than vague, and exaggerated, unauthenticated, whispered rumours. And because I had rather tell the whole truth now while I live, than leave it to be made falsehood of when I am no more.

So much by way of clearing the ground. And now, as to what I am going to say. I understand of course that I take on myself the whole responsibility; I

---

[1] Horace, *Epistle* I, xviii, 71.
[2] See Newman's Memorandum, 14 January 1860, *The Letters and Diaries of John Henry Newman*, London 1961 ff., XIX, pp. 279–83.

take on myself the responsibility of any proposition which is logically deducible from it; of every proposition, if there be any, which I knowingly imply, though I do not state it. I have a perfectly clear conscious [sic] that I am speaking nothing in what is to follow inconsistent with any article of Catholic faith. Yet I submit every one of my words to the Church's judgment, which I believe in religious matters to be infallible. If the competent authority tells me, that any thing I say, or that I logically involve, or knowingly imply without stating, is wrong, I recant it by anticipation both outward and by internal *act* ⟨acquiescence⟩ of my mind

If the competent authority tells me to be silent, I am silent; but I will not yield to any judgment short of that of the competent authority unless I feel it to have a personal claim on my deference.

NB The above is almost a challenge to Ecclesiastical authority to speak and pronounce — so I must take a new beginning.

Thus

A periodical issue of Disquisition, (say) incorporated in or bound up with the Rambler, or separate and bi-monthly, called

'Stationarius'.

'In urbe maneo. Haec mea sedes est, haec vigilia, haec custodia, hoc praesidium statutum'. Cic. Phil. xii[1]

by J. H. Newman D D

No. 1   No. 2   No. 3 —

Perhaps numbers one and two — on 1 the bigotry and meddling of men of science, as illustrated by the 'Plurality of Worlds'[2] controversy — and 2 the classics as represented by Plutarch's Lives, or by Aristotle, Sophocles, etc.

[1861   Paper A   Essay on Inspiration]

One of the characteristics of the day is the renewal of that collision between scientific men and believers in Revelation, or rather of that attack ⟨interference⟩ on the part of Science with the statements of Scripture and of that perplexity in consequence and scandal on the part of the religious portion of the community, which first occurred in the 16th century. At the latter date it was Copernicus and Galileo, or at least the conduct of their adherents, who roused the jealousy of good Catholics; and now we feel alarm at the discoveries and speculations of the geologist, the ethnologist, or the linguist. The jealousy of astronomy ran its course, and resulted ⟨terminated⟩ in the Brief? of Pius VII, which gave toleration and liberty of speech to the Newtonian

[1] Cicero, *Philippics* XII, x.

[2] D. Brewster, *More Worlds than one in the creed of the Philosopher and hope of the Christian*, London 1857, and W. Whewell's work first published anonymously in 1853, *Of the Plurality of Worlds: An Essay. Also a dialogue on the same subject*, London 1855; both these editions are to be found in Newman's room. See also, I. Todhunter, *William Whewell, D.D. An Account of his writings*, London 1876, vol. I, pp. 184–210; Baden Powell, 'The Plurality of Worlds', *The Unity of Worlds and of Nature*, London 1856.

System in Catholic Schools;[1] and we have accordingly *the* reason to expect a parallel termination in our present controversies, nay, and that the more, inasmuch as the principles implied in the Pope's toleration of astronomy provide us with a safe refuge ⟨retreat⟩ and defence of our faith and refuge from the interference of all other secular ⟨human⟩ sciences, such as those which are mentioned above.

This is a consideration which ought at this time to teach moderation to the assailant, and equanimity to the assailed; to enforce it, and to strengthen it with collateral suggestions shall be the object of the following pages.[2]

We find then at the present day a number of powerful minds, pursuing each his own subject, in good faith, and, for the most part, without any intention whatever, of shocking the received belief, and ultimately reaching conclusions which are antagonistic to those doctrines ⟨opinions⟩ on physical subjects which are generally considered to be Biblical and therefore Divine. Thus M. Agassiz is said to hold that the present race of man has originated, not in one progenitor, but from various local centres [in pencil: ⟨Whereas Scripture says⟩]. Mr Darwin's speculations are said to point to the conclusion that the first man was formed, not of the mud or dust of the earth, but came of organized matter [in pencil: ⟨Whereas Scripture says he was limus⟩] M. Bunsen, ⟨who is more of a theologian than the great⟩ however, cannot be said to be without some intention of a theological teaching, has claimed a period of many thousand years to the ancient Egyptians; [in pencil: ⟨Whereas the Scripture chronologies, Samaritan — etc⟩] and others have drawn similar inferences from the study of antiquities, or languages, or comparative! anatomy [in pencil: ⟨which are or seem to be opposed to the Sacred text.⟩] No one can say that the theories, of which these are specimens, have been proved; (most men or at least) many men, who have from their attainments a right to speak, [say] that they have not, and never will be. But many others anticipate or apprehend or have misgivings that they are in the way to be proved. Let us then for argument's sake, and on behalf of ⟨for the sake of⟩ those who lie under this misapprehension, let us suppose that this is the case. Let us, for argument's sake, suppose that they are in the way to prove, that the seven days mentioned in Genesis i and ii were not seven days literally; or that there was a pre-adamite race, now extinct, rational, but purely natural from its beginning to its end, without external aids of any kind or degree, religious or social, natural or supernatural, and omitted in the Mosaic record of the Creation, as the Angels are omitted; or that the *limus* terrae, out of which Adam was formed, was an organized, not a rude elemental *limus*; or that the deluge, which destroyed the whole race of Adam did not cover the whole surface of

[1] On 25 September, 1822, Pius VII approved a decree to this effect.
[2] Marginal note: Important. April 17. Two points
1. to have a basis of *de fide*, not the word of man
2. to *throw oneself* into that de fide. Canonical. sacred. which ensures more [illegible] perpetual jugglings or admissions?
[in pencil]: 1. must bona fide throw himself with the Church
   2. must take what she says as something [illegible].

the earth; or that the race of Adam has lasted ten thousand years; or anything else, for which arguments are adducible of whatever weight, and which, though not at the very first blush and directly, incompatible with the Creeds of the Church and the decrees of Councils, — Origen? (vid treatises on Terrestrial Paradise etc.), yet certainly *are prima facie* at variance with the sacred text of the Old Testament. Let us ask ourselves whether they are really opposed to that Scripture text in any other way than the Copernican system is opposed to it, which was once thought to be opposed, as these opinions are thought now, but has at length been acknowledged not to be opposed at all.

But here some one will tell you — Well, if so, it saves me trouble ⟨may interrupt me with the remark⟩ that such suppositions are simply impossible, because though not directly contravening any article of the Creed or decree of Council they are virtually and really against the faith. If so, absisto totus; I have not another word to say. If it be against the faith, then, however strong ⟨well⟩ appearances may look for these theories ⟨suppositions⟩ being proved, proved they never will be, but will wither and fall, ere they come to perfection, as blossom ⟨leaves⟩ upon a tree. Then too we need have no alarm whatever, however plausible they look; they are to be contemned as absurdities, or to be guarded against as temptations; but any how they are fallacies and fictions — on the other hand, we ought to be very sure that they are thus directly opposed or inconsistent to the definitions of the Church, for so was thought the doctrine that the earth was not the centre of the universe but a mere satellite of the sun, not overarched with a solid firmament, but circling through empty ⟨open⟩ spaces. Yet it is not granted to be a doctrine perfectly consistent with the whole Catholic dogma. For myself, I have not found any sure ground for saying so; and therefore I do not consider it superfluous to inquire whether these theories, true be they or false, are incompatible with the written word, considering that, rightly or wrongly, many minds just now are perplexed at what seems to them the contrast presented between the book of Genesis and some ⟨the⟩ modern deductions of science.

I have no intention at all here of doing, what Galileo is accused of doing in his own matter, of asserting and proving that the certain particular statements of these sciences are reconcilable with the statements of Scripture, nor of saying that the former are proved to be true. But, on occasion of the misgivings and anxieties of various people, I shall attempt to inquire whether there is any cause of apprehension lest as time goes on of the revealed word of God coming into collision with scientific points, demonstrated to be true.

In cases in which the Church has not authoritatively decided the sense of Scripture in particular passages, there are two points to be considered by those who are perplexed by those passages viewed in the light of scientific speculation — one of them is, what is the right *interpretation* of ⟨is to be given⟩ them; and the second, are they guaranteed to us by *inspiration*. I commence with the latter of the two.

6

Inspiration —

The first question is, supposing for argument's sake, that it is demonstrated by science that the earth is a globe, a satellite upon the sun, and revolving round it, and supposing the Old Testament states that earth was made first, and the sun after it in order to be a measure of time for the use of the earth, which was immovable and in the centre?, are we to say that in so far as these physical statements are concerned, the Old Testament was divinely inspired. In other words does the inspiration of Scripture extend to all statements ⟨matters⟩ of fact, or only such as directly or indirectly belong to the 'matter of faith and morals'.

A (It is apparently too sanctioned by Amort, a great authority from his intimacy with Benedict xiv. He writes as follows: (vid in Chrismann [pp. 44–5])

'Communem nunc esse apud cordatiores Scripturae interpretes et theologos sententiam, non omnes libros Scripturae in eo sensu esse sacros et canonicos, quasi omnia verba, aut *omnes sensus* essent inmediate dictati a Spiritu Sancto; sed arbitrantur ad constituendum librum sacrum et canonicum sufficere, quòd scriptor ex speciali motione, seu inspiratione divina motus se applicuerit ad ea scribenda, quae vel ex libris fide dignis, vel *ex ratione idoneorum testium,* vel *ex ductu rationis* cognoverat, ita tamen, ut Deus speciali suâ assistentiâ caverit, ne in eiusmodi scripto irrepserit error, *specialiter in materia fidei et morum'.*)

About the meaning of the word *falsitas* vid Canus p. 85.[1]

The practical difficulty in the latter solution is that of drawing the line between those facts which are in materia fidei et morum, and those which are not so. Where are we to stop, if once we grant that a sacred writer is not protected from error in any one of his statements? If it is a mere human statement that 'Phaleg lived after he had begotten Reu two hundred and nine years', why is it not a human statement that there are ten generations from Shem ⟨Sem⟩ to Abraham? And if so, why is it not a human statement that 'all flesh of birds, living things ⟨beasts?⟩ and reptiles of the earth were destroyed by the flood?' And if so, why is it not a human statement that Eve was taken out of the side of Adam? And if so, why not a human statement, that Adam was formed de limo terrae? And how shall we separate these later statements from those of the trial and the fall of Adam? Salmeron illustrates this [Vol. I] p. 6, col. 1. That Scripture is the 'word of God' is acknowledged by all

---

[1] The following is found in the margin at this point: For the *distinct ways* in which the Holy Ghost operates in different persons *vid omnino* Canus p. 85. [*De Locis Theologicis*, II, xviii, fin.]

Supposing as true the theory of a plenary inspiration extending throughout the whole volume and every part of it, but operating only there for religious objects, just as a lamp ⟨light⟩ might illuminate a surface, without now imparting to it warmth. I will ⟨for arguments⟩ then take the hypothesis to mean that inspiration has breathed or diffused religious truth ⟨light⟩ over the whole sacred text without its operating for its historical infallibility or *accuracy*; but even then the difficulty I speak will be found. NB This should be drawn out, and it shows that this even admits *verbal* inspiration. Scripture *one whole*. Salmeron [Vol. I] p. 3 ol. 1.

7

Catholics; this is a substantial and a sacred truth; nothing must be said to weaken or disparage its substantial truth; now since Scripture contains a multitude of facts which in their substance belong to human history, but which it viewed in a religious light and in one way or other connects with the miraculous and providential operations of the Almighty God, how is it possible that we can allow the possibility of error in statements concerning them without infringing the inspired teaching, weakening the argument for its doctrines, its interpretations of human affairs, and its vehicle of divine appointments ⟨operations⟩? It is often said, as an argument for the truth of the miracles, that they cannot be separated from the context of Scripture, without rendering the historical narrative incoherent etc and tearing it to pieces, so that the history is a sort of guarantee for the miracles contained in it, and that in contrast to the prodigies of Livy etc; consequently ⟨but⟩ if the context is to be given up as possibly erroneous, what becomes of the miracles?

Important as this argument is when drawn out in detail, there is a further consideration to which it leads which increases its force. We must consider, not only what the Sacred Writers say, but in *what manner* they say it. If they worded those statements which are of a cosmological or ethnological nature in a different tone from that in which they convey what is of faith and morals, an opening would be made for a distinction between the two as regards their inspiration; but it is undeniable that Moses, for instance, speaks as authoritatively in the first chapter of the Genesis as in the third; and in the first his solemn announcement 'In principio creavit Deus caelum et terram', which is surely a dogma of faith, is not more dogmatical in its tone than that in the 7th verse, 'Fecit Deus firmamentum, divisitque etc'. It follows that, if we suppose that the divine assistentia did not secure him from error in his cosmology as well as in his theology ⟨vide Calmet's Treatise on Inspiration⟩, it has to be explained which [why] he adopted so confident a tone in reporting that which was not divinely guaranteed to him as true, and whether such an inaccuracy or exaggeration, as we may call it, would not ⟨does not⟩ destroy the impressiveness of his revelations which are of a directly religious character. And accordingly, we may reverently conclude ⟨expect⟩ that the Divine Authority of the Scriptures, would have guarded its writers against leaving on the reader the impression ⟨that they were,⟩ there were aspects or relations in which the sacred volume was not to be considered inspired.

Moved, I suppose, by such considerations, which are of extreme importance, the received teaching of theologians is in disapprobation of this distinction between historical fact and religious truth in determining the inspiration of Scripture, and in favour of the doctrine that the inspiration of Scripture, though it need not be considered to extend to the words themselves, is such that not even the lightest error exists as regards the matters which it relates and its statements.

Again we must recollect there are those who unable to draw the line, will give up the whole if they have or given up a part. [In pencil: ⟨Again, *love and reverence* for the sacred writers'⟩]

Again, if in *science* things may be true which are (not against but) beyond the text, so also in dogmatics — e.g. state of heathen, natural virtue, etc.

Thus Canus in the second book of his de Locis, draws out the obvious-argument, which I have already insisted on, in proof of his doctrine that the inspiration of Scripture extends to its minute historical statements; speaking of the opposite opinion he says: 'Is error quam sit impius, illo primo argumento demonstro, quod sacrarum scripturarum magnâ ex parte labefactatur auctoritas, si haec opinio vera est'. He then quotes St Augustine who says 'Si in sacro quovis libro unaquaeque falsitas reperitur, totius libri certitudo interit'. [p. 73] He ends by saying 'Nulla in sacris litteris levis, sed gravis esset (falsitas) per quam scripturae auctoritas elevaretur'. And by the exhortation, 'Hos quidem ab hoc sermone removeamus, qui erronea sententiâ omnem Scripturae et vim minuunt et elevant auctoritatem. Ipsi vero fateamur singula quaeque sive magna seu ⟨sive⟩ parva, à sacris auctoribus, Spiritu Sancto dictante, esse edita. Id a patribus accepimus, id fidelium animis inditum et quasi insculptum est; id itaque et nos, et ecclesia praesertim ipsa magistra et duce, retinere debemus'. p.75

The same protest against the doctrine disowned by Canus, is found in theologians of the present day. F. Perrone says 'Illud in primis profitemur, rejicere nos laxiores eôrum sententias, qui non nisi adsistentiam Spiritûs Sancti, quam negativam vocavimus, adsciscunt, qua fieret ut inmunes tantummodo servarentur ab errore Scriptores sacri . . . Multo vero magis Holdenii, si tamen id docuit aliorumque commentum respuimus, qui ita Spiritûs Sancti adsistentiam coarctant, ut ad graviores tantum errores declinandos idoneos effecerit scriptores sacros etc'. t. 2. [p. II] p. 66 . . . Sit igitur propositio 'Jure merito concilium Tridentinum docet unum Deum esse librorum canonicorum utriusque Testamenti auctorem, seu eos esse libros sacros, utpote, Spiritu Sancto afflante, saltem quoad res et sententias, conscriptos'. [p. 71]

Mgr Bouvier says to the same effect 'Notandum in libris sacris tria distingui posse, videlicet, res, stylus et voces. Constat, ex dictis, inspirationem admittendam esse quoad res, id quoad facta et sententias vocibus expressas; sed probabilius videtur eam non extendendam esse, saltem ordinarie, ad stylum et voces'. t. 2. p. 32.

Archbishop Dixon says 'As to Catholics, we may say that all are agreed thus far: that it cannot be admitted that the sacred writers fell into any, the least, mistake or error in their writings . . . Many have considered even the verbal inspiration of Scripture clearly proved, both by the manner in which the Holy Fathers express themselves regarding inspiration, and by the way in which the Scriptures have been ever viewed in the Church, viz. as containing the inspired language of the Holy Ghost; nor does it appear that any insuperable difficulty can be brought against this opinion. Yet, with St. Alphonsus

Liguori we consider it more probable that, *generally* speaking, the *very* words have not been inspired . . . It is more probable that in *some* places the very words were inspired etc.' vid. [I] pp. 5–9.

I suppose I am not wrong in saying that there has been in the last three hundred years a growing tendency in divines to abandon the doctrine of the verbal inspiration, and to acquiesce in an inspiration quoad res et sententias, without any tendency whatever to allow the errability of the sacred writers in any [of] the most minute facts of physics, history and other human sciences.

What is the universal sentiment has ever a claim upon our reverence and submission; and I for one am not bold enough against such authority, and against that intrinsic difficulty of the hypotheses on which I have already dwelt, to hold that any error whatever, however slight, is admissible in the sacred writers. However, what this age may hold, or what I may hold, is not the question in the present inquiry, but what the Church declares dogmatically. I want to know what I am to think of the threatened invasion ⟨encroachment⟩ upon certain ⟨the⟩ Scripture statements; am I to say, I need not take any trouble whatever, am I to prophesy to others that nothing will or can come of the menace ⟨prospect⟩, however formidable, for God's infallible word is pledged, as it was to Ezechias then the prophet, that Sennacherib never should see the walls of Jerusalem, much less enter into the city; or must I take another line of argument, as being ⟨am I⟩ destitute of such assurance, and then must say to others, Science may possibly prove things contrary to the Scripture narrative, and therefore I forewarn you not to care for it, for so far as statements ⟨things⟩ in Scripture are upon mere matter of human science, they have not been subjects ⟨matter⟩ of inspiration? It is not enough to tell men what the prevalent sentiment of theologians is, at this time, unless I am guaranteed that that sentiment has been defined by the Church, or faithfully represents the tradition on the point from Apostolic times.

'It *need* not mean so and so,' this *has* a right sense.

It is some times objected ⟨said⟩ that it is a cold and grudging way to believe only what you are obliged to believe, and that in Scripture praise is given not to those who believe only what they are obliged to believe, but to those who with a generous faith embrace what comes on good authority without asking all evidence which could be given. I have *expressed*, and I sincerely ⟨certainly⟩ hold this sentiment myself, but it does not enter the present question. The question is *what* is to defend me against the plausible conclusions of science? nothing but the infallible voice of God — *where* is the infallible voice of God? in the Church, who has the keeping and dispensation of the Apostolic tradition, both written and unwritten, and both values and interprets each for us?

I can bow my reason to faith in God's voice, but to nothing but that faith. I am as strong as a hero. I am armed to the conflict with an irresistible weapon if I know I am on God's side. But the opinion of theologians of one particular century or age, is not necessarily God's voice, it is but the voice of fallible men; it does not arm me to the Conflict. I think there is a great deal of sense in the question, which is asked by the inquiring youth in Loss and Gain, whether the doctrine of the eternal punishment is de fide etc. etc. Has the Church pronounced that Scripture is verbally inspired? has she pronounced it to be so inspired as to have not the smallest error in its statements of human fact? has it said one word about inspiration any where? No. These are the questions to be asked.

It is safer to hold the stricter side; but its being safer does not make that side speculatively true ⟨certain⟩. It only leads to this, that a person should say 'I will believe it, *if it turns out* to be de fide'; I withhold my assent with the reservation that the Church shall not ask for it — I will withhold it with an implicit reference under correction to the Church's decision.

About 'safer' look at the condemned proposition. It applies to joining the Church — does it apply to taking *each article* for what *is* safer there?

Accordingly it is not wonderful that ⟨Now first it is certain that⟩ various writers from time to time have taken that view which the present day does not take, and though their opinion ⟨they⟩ have been disapproved and disowned by theologians, no one has called it heretical⟨?⟩ Caietan is a name of offence to almost all theologians since his time, but not as the name of a heretic. God has not pledged himself that what Caietan said about Holy Scripture is false ⟨not true⟩; or the whole world would have called Caietan a heretic. Yet he said that Quetif et Echard. t. 2. p. 17 etc. [and p. 18] 'Has in sacra Scriptura expositiones Ambrosius Catharinus noster, eum in multis erroneas vel etiam hereticas et saltem hereticis faventes, facultati theologicae Parisiensi denunciavit, et ut, quae in Evangelio sunt, censurâ notarentur obtinuit'. 'Alphonsus a Castro, Ord. Min. et Gabriel Prateiolus, Caietanum inter hereticos recensuerunt, sed ambos recivit Index Expurgatorius Inquisitionis Hispanae' Pallavicino. t.1. p. 240. [']Qui Caietanum ex editis in Sacras Literas commentariis aestimat perinde sese habet, ac qui non ex pennis, sed ex pedibus pavonis pulchritudinem aestimat.[']

'Mitto hic singularem, ne quid amplius dicam, Holdenii sententiam'. Rabaudy ap. Zacc. Thesaur. Suppl. t.1. p. 471.

Again Holden is commonly considered to have taught leviores errores in Scriptura are compatible with inspiration; some have doubted whether his words mean it, but no one said that his supposed opinion was a denial of any thing to which the truth of God was pledged. His words are these [Quotation not inserted. See Holden, Divinae Fidei Analysis, I, v, and II, iii.]

Bergier again in his theological dictionary uses words which imply, if they do not express, at least do not disown ⟨prohibit⟩ the same doctrine.

'On doit donc tenir pour certain: 1. que Dieu a révélé immédiatement aux Auteurs sacrés, non seulement les prophéties qui'ls ont faites, mais toutes les vérités *qu'ils ne pouvaient pas connaître* par la seule lumière naturelle, ou par des moyens humains. 2. que, par une inspiration particulière de la grace, il les a portés à écrire, et les a dirigés dans le choix des choses qu'ils devaient mettre par écrit. 3. que, par une assistance spéciale   de l'Esprit Saint, il a veillé sur eux, et les a preservés de toute erreur, soit sur les faites *essentiels*, soit sur le dogme, soit sur la morale ... Il n'est pas besoin que Dieu ait dicté à ces écrivains vénérables les termes et les expressions desquelles il se sont servis'. [II, p. 331]

What is remarkable is, that even Amort, the intimate friend of Benedict xiv does clearly separate his decision from the judgment at present so commonly received and does *not* clearly separate his judgment from the opinion which is considered by most theologians so inadmissible. He says A) [Newman here refers to p. 7 above]

And it will be observed that Fr Perrone (in his de Inspiratione, above quoted, only speaks of his doctrine (as a *deduction*, and) as an *opinion*. He says, 'Viam mediam ineuntes, illam inspirationis notionem amplectimur quam tenuit', (not, Ecclesia Catholica, but) 'cl. Marchini'. And so in like manner, in the proposition which I have quoted he first professes to give the Council's words, and *then* his own explanation of them. 'Concilium Tridentinum docet unum Deum esse librorum canonicorum utriusque Testamenti auctorem, *seu* eos esse libros sacros, (and then he adds de suo) eos esse libros sacros, *utpote* Spiritu Sancto afflante, *saltem quoad res et sententias* conscriptos'. [II, ii, pp. 69 and 71]

Now Mgr Bouvier fully allows that his doctrine is not part of the dogma of faith, and laying down the proposition Libri V. et N. Testamenti vere fuerunt inspirati and adds, Haec propositio est de fide, 'non solum ad praecipuas, sed ad omnes partes scripturarum ab auctoribus sacris exaratas extendenda est (inspiratio⟨?⟩)' he observes after all, Quia sacrum concilium ipsâ voce *inspirationis* non utitur, propositio nostra, licet certissima, non est de fide catholicâ. [II, pp. 25 and 28]

In truth, nothing has been defined on the subject of the inspiration of Scripture and nothing on the subject of their historical fidelity in smaller points. In early times the Gnostics denied that the God and Father of Our Lord Jesus Christ was the author of the O.T. Accordingly, St Irenaeus and other Fathers, are earnest in enforcing and proved the contrary. He says [quotation not inserted]

Taking up this confession, the ordo of consecration puts this among other questions to the *consecrandus* (vid in Perrone p. 72).[1]

Adopting this article from the Ordo, the Council of Florence says [quotation not inserted. See Denzinger, 1334.] and the Council of Trent

Sacro Sancta .... Synodus .... orthodoxorum Patrum exempla secuta, omnes libros tam Veteris quam Novi Testamenti, cùm utriusque *unus* Deus sit auctor, necnon Traditiones ipsas, cùm ad fidem tum ad mores pertinentes etc ... pari pietatis affectu ac reverentiâ suscipit et veneratur ... Si quis

---

[1] Perrone, II, ii, p. 72, quotes the question asked of the bishop about to be consecrated, in the *Pontifical*: *Credis etiam Novi et Veteris Testamenti, Legis, et Prophetarum et Apostolorum, unum esse auctorem Deum ac Dominum omnipotentem?*

autem libros ipsos integros cum omnibus suis partibus, prout in Ecclesiâ Catholicâ legi consueverunt, et in veteri Vulgatâ Latinâ editione habentur, pro sacris et canonicis non susceperit, et traditiones praedictas sciens et prudens contempserit, Anathema sit. [Denzinger, 1501, 1504]

But it may be urged, that the judgment of the Holy Fathers, and again that of doctors of the School is definite and distinct, and therefore binds our faith, since what they testify must come from Apostolical tradition.

As to the Holy Fathers it is certain on the one hand that the Holy Fathers cannot together ⟨at the same time⟩ all err in a question of dogma, and therefore if they one and all declare anything about the inspiration of Scripture, we must accept it by faith as coming from the Apostles; and on the other hand, when there is a difference of judgment among them and though the many are on one side[,] some are on the other, then we can deduce no conclusive argument from their testimony.

As to the school, I would lay down on the one hand that to contradict the judgment of all theologians ⟨doctors⟩ when it is one and the same, in a matter of faith, is very near heresy; but on the other hand there is no obligation to assent to it, if even theologians of weight ⟨a few⟩ are dissentient from the decision of the majority.

Now in the present case either the Holy Fathers or the Schola are concordant and then they prove too much for the view advocated by the theologian of this day; or on the other hand they are not concordant and then the argument from them avails nothing.

If they agree, they agree in maintaining the verbal inspiration of the Scriptures. I have not met with any one who appeals to the Fathers as being unfavourable [to] verbal inspiration; I meet with many who appeal to them as favourable to it.

Billuart says: 'Probabilius videtur ad rationem Scripturae Sacrae requiri, quod non solum sensus et sententiae, sed etiam singula verba sint a Spiritu Sancto dictata. Est communior, quam fecit suam Academia Lovaniensis in sua censura contra Lessius. And presently he quotes, for the Fathers, St Chrysostom, St Augustine and St Gregory. de Fide T. 2. p. 38, 9.

vid Valentia who takes the strict view,[1] Suis manibus Deus. Aug. de cons. Evang. 1 cap. ult.[2]

Rabaudy (Zacc. Thesaur. Suppl 1. p. 472) says 'Scriptura sacra sacris scriptoribus fuit inspirata, nedum quantum ad omnes sui partes, et res omnes quas continet, sed etiam *quoad singula verba*'. Presently he says (p. 473) Sancti Patres eidem veritati aperte favent.

Perrone p. 68 says that these who are for the 'latior' view of inspiration explain the testimonies of the Fathers which are against them 'commode', and

---

[1] *Quare dubium esse non debet, quin omnes et singulae particulae Scripturarum sint Spiritu sancto dictante exaratae.* Gregory of Valentia, III, p. 331.
[2] *non aliter accipiet quod narrantibus discipulis Christi in Evangelio legerit, quam si ipsam manum Domini, quam in proprio corpore gestabat, scribentem conspexerit.*

oppose to them others, in which the Fathers seem to teach as they do, such as one of St Augustine's and another of St Jerome's. However St Jerome says the very syllables and letters⟨?⟩ in the divine scriptures are full of mysteries, and speaks as to St Paul in his Epistles speaking of every thing, of Christ speaking in him. Rabaudy.

However else where St Augustine ⟨Ep. 14⟩ says that Scripture not only speaks truth, for so might, ⟨would⟩ a man's work, but its *words and phrases* are the Holy Ghost's who dictated them. St Augustine and St Gregory (Perrone [p. 73]) call the Bible the Epistle of the Almighty God to his creation. St Ambrose says that 'the Divine Spirit ⟨Holy Ghost⟩ ministrated the fertility ⟨abundance⟩ of words, of all things'. (Rabaudy) And St Gregory as St Augustine speaks of His dictating it. St Chrysostom says (Billuart) that there is not a syllable in Scripture without a profundity and says Perrone that it is written by the Holy Ghost. And Theodoret says that the tongues and hands of the sacred writers are the very pens of the Holy Ghost. [Perrone, p. 73]

Now observe the position of those who take the view common at this day. They cannot claim the Fathers for their opinion viewed as a body of testimony. They cannot say more [than] that the proofs from them in favour of the verbal inspiration *need* not be proofs, and may be otherwise explained. Now I ask, is not the process of *accommodating* the fathers to a theory one of the very faults which we impute in ⟨to⟩ the case of heretics? And are ⟨is⟩ there any doctrine, any joint testimony of the Fathers to a doctrine but might be cavilled at as not satisfactory or ⟨and⟩ decisive; if we are at liberty to say the same of the witness ⟨testimony⟩ they bear to verbal inspiration.

And further why could not the opinion which I have mentioned above be not able to appeal to the testimony of the Fathers quite as well. This opinion does not exclude verbal inspiration. It can freely adopt all the strong words of the Fathers about syllables and letters ⟨points⟩ — it professes that the *whole* of Scripture is inspired, not some parts, left without a supernatural influence — that inspiration is *plenary* — But it says that this inspiration is everywhere directed to an end, one end and no other, that is, for the publication of the Gospel faith and morals — that it is inspired every where for that object, and not for any other such as a mere fact of secular science or history, in writing which, they, as well as other writers, however honest, may err. The advocate too of this theory may say, 'we are not called upon, there is no *need*, of believing that the Fathers are against us — we explain their strong statements *commodè* and *benignè*, and we have passages, as St Basil's, which seem, as far as separate writers will avail, to recommend our hypothesis.'

But there is another consideration behind, which now must engage our attention. We are told of a *rigidior*, and a *latior* or *liberalior* teaching on the inspiration of Scripture, the former is that of verbal inspiration, the other excludes verbal — Now what is the meaning of these words? it is not obvious. Why should it be rigid to insist on verbal inspiration? I hardly know what answer to give except this, that teaching is the more rigid which limits in a greater measure our freedom of speculation upon a subject in question, and which calls for (not greater, but) a more complex act, or more numerous acts of faith. And by liberalior must mean a teaching which leaves more to private judgment. I so determine from the use of the words in Moral Philosophy, in which they are applied to decisions which are respectively more unfavourable or more favourable to liberty of action. But are they terms which are usual in the treatment of dogmatic theology? Are they terms ever applied to truths of Apostolic Tradition? The Apostles delivered a point of faith; this allowed of development; and this process of development resulted in a teaching on the point more or more 'rigid'. By development I mean the process by which what is at first implicit in an article of faith becomes explicit. That our Lord is perfect God and perfect man is a point of faith transmitted from the Apostles, and witnessed by the earliest Fathers; that His soul ⟨He⟩ has the utmost knowledge that man can have, is a doctrine implicitly contained in this Apostolic doctrine and one with it, and has been determined in the 5th⟨?⟩ century to be of faith too. Before that it was so declared some ecclesiastical writers ⟨Fathers⟩ implied that He had not this perfect knowledge from the first ⟨experimental?⟩ but grew in it. That is to say that, till the dogmatic definition of the 5th? century their liberty was in possession and they used it. They used it to say what was *untrue*; this is strange kind of liberty; and the dogmatic judgment of the 5th century may [be] more rigid than the decision (say) against the Apollinarians in the 4th, which was liberalior. This is strange rigidity, strange liberality — I prefer the rigidity, but it is nothing more or less than a greater knowledge. I can understand it to be rigid, to *oblige* your private judgment to accept my private judgment but I think it is only a divine privilege ⟨mercy⟩ if I am able to *learn* on divine *authority*, that what supersedes both your judgments and mine. If then we do not use these words rigid and liberal in the doctrine of our Lord's divinity, why do we not use it in the case of inspiration? I suspect the use of those words betrays that there is *no* divine revelation in the matter of inspiration at all, any more than in the matter of Indulgences — that it is more a matter of private judgment, and ever will be and that whether I take the rigidior view or the latior view I may indeed be committing scandal, or I may show a bad turn of mind, or I may give accidental tokens that I shall soon say something of my own on what is *not* a matter of private judgment, but I am not opposing any dogma of faith.

I am confirmed in this view by the question ⟨doctrine, instance⟩ of the divine decrees. Here perhaps the words rigidior and liberior may be used respectively of the doctrine of St Thomas⟨?⟩ and St Alfonso, Francis of Sales as to the question of praevisa merita; but here in matter of fact there seems to have been, as modern theologians seem to grant, no tradition on the subject. The theologians of the four first centuries ⟨Ante-Nicene Church⟩ took the liberior view; St Augustine the rigidior; and it was transmitted through St

Gregory, St Anselm, St Thomas, and their schools down the 16th century; since then there has been a re-action till most writers of this day will be found to be allowed to be as Ante-Nicene or Nicene on the subject as they will, saving the necessity of guarding against Pelagianism. Here is a further instance in point, for no one would call the Anti-pelagians in teaching of the Church rigidior than the vague or confused expressions of the earlier centuries.

But here we are brought to an argument a fortiori — When the Jesuits, St Francis de Sales, St Alfonso, Fr Morin took the conditional⟨?⟩ view of the Divine decrees, at least they could appeal to the very first ages of the Apostles as agreeing with them. They appealed emphatically to Apostolic Tradition. But can the 'latior' doctrine received on the question of inspiration now make a similar appeal? Certainly not; where is that doctrine that inspiration belongs to the things and sentiments only, not to words, in primitive times? where was it found for 1600 ⟨1500⟩ years? Nothing but a more 'rigid' doctrine prevailed for 1500 years. To give up verbal inspiration is a clear innovation. You have given it up — Well then if there is no Apostolic tradition on the subject, if you may oppose the opinion of the Fathers, why may not another ⟨I⟩? If you refuse their distinct statements to the effect that inspiration is verbal, why may not another refuse their statement that it embraces all subjects. The latter's departure ⟨my innovation⟩ from them is not greater than yours. I do allow verbal ⟨literal⟩ inspiration in matters of faith and morals and you do not. I disallow inspiration in pure secular matters and you do not.

But you say that the Fathers *need not* mean the more *rigid* sense? do you actually *quote* them for that *liberalior* sense which you adopt — not at all, but by your mode of speaking you imply that they are against you. Then what do you mean by '*need* not'? This, that you are determined to have your own opinion, and determined that the Fathers shall not *mean*, what from not *foreseeing* that you were to examine them, they did not state to a demonstration. It is only what your Protestant antagonist says, when a case is made out against him. *I* in like manner might quite as well say that the patristical proof is not such as to compel me to believe that nothing in the Scriptures is purely human. St Basil's words will be to the point. [quotation not inserted]

And now in concluding this part of the argument I will say personally that for myself, I — while I protest against the limits of faith being determined by private authority, never will think of advocating the liberior view which I have here been bringing out, till I saw my way to draw the line so distinctly between what is merely secular and what not, as to secure me from doing irreverence and invalidating the authority of what is divine — next that I submit what I have said absolutely to what the Church may determine. I take her word to be ⟨as⟩ the word of God; but I will not confuse that word with the judgment of some casual theologian who cannot be fair to my meaning or who has read me through the medium of an incorrect translation.

Interpretation   [in pencil: transcribed Sept 29 1861]

Some one, Father or divine, says that the Evangelists spoke of things as the persons around them did. This goes very far.

St Jerome says that the Evangelists sometimes express the opinions of the populace. Canus 81.

vid Chrysostom in Hebraeos Tom. 18 [12] or ⟨on⟩ St Paul quoting from Gamaliel in Heb. ad init. [p. 1]

Jacob and Abraham both dissemble, yet in God's intention prophesy. Canus p. 8, 9.   Therefore Moses may mean one thing, and the Holy Ghost another.

If the future may be expressed allegorically, why not the past? Bellarmine says de V. D. iii, 3, [p. 137] that Papias etc erred in assigning a *literal* sense to the Apocalypse, why then may it not be an error to assign a simply literal sense to the seven days of creation, especially when it does not go so far as allegory?

on the obscurity of Scripture, vid Bellarmine

profundity Ambrose Ep. ad Constant. 44

on literalibus figuratis lectionibus August. lib. 3 de doctr. Christian.

More than one literal sense Aug. Confess. xii, 26 de Civ. Dei. ii, 19 de doctr. Christiana, iii, 27   Salmeron makes several literal senses.

NB. 'Ex solo *literali* sensu peti debere argumenta — *nam,* eum sensum, qui ex verbis *inmediate* colligitur, *certum est, sensum esse Spiritus Sancti'.* Bellarm. V. D. 3. iii, [p. 137]

Sensus spirituales, non semper constat, an sint a Spiritu Sancto intenti. ibid.

An efficax argumentum, *not* from the spiritual sense. Canus p. 48 and so Bellarmine, who says that always there is *one sense* intended by the Holy Ghost.

Papias, who ought to have taken the literal *figurative,* and did not. ibid. Vid Hieron. Praef. lib. xviii in Isai, in Ezech. xxxv; Augustine Civ. Dei. xx, 7.

As to the *mystery* of the *seven* days, and of *ten* patriarchs etc. Canus p. 82 allows that Moses may have been led by the sacred *number* to make ten.

From what Canus says p. 53, the giving up the original Greek and Hebrew must have been very unacceptable in his time.

No one can interpret Scripture without a special gift, Canus p. 65 How then dare you dogmatize upon the meaning of Genesis i?

Many things in Ecclesiastes ex opinione vulgi. Bellarm. p. 21. [p. 13]

A bit of history without a material ⟨literal⟩ sense in Maccab. Bellarm. p 69 [p. 47?] and Canus.

St Jerome in Eccles. cap. ult. says that the Proverbs have not their meaning on the surface, yet it is a *literal* meaning — Why then the first chapters of Genesis?

Did the sacred writer know always the full sense of the Holy Spirit in prophetical passages? If not, a DOUBLE SENSE, one the writer's, one the Holy Ghost's, is unavoidable. This *against* the objection of the Westminster etc., that the notion of a double sense is an evasion.

[End of Document A.]

[The conclusion of the first three parts of Document B.]

I conclude from all these various considerations that the words 'sacred and canonical' applied by the Church to the books of Scripture, as a matter of faith, do not necessarily involve the idea of divine dictation or inspiration, or absolute immunity from incorrectness ⟨imperfection⟩, whether ⟨as⟩ of style and grammar, or ⟨so⟩ of historical statement.[1]

One other consideration may be added. It is observable, that Fr Perrone, when discussing the subject of Inspiration, speaks of a *rigidior*, and a *latior* or *liberalior* teaching as regards it. Of these the *rigidior* maintains ⟨is⟩ the verbal inspiration or dictation of Scripture, and the *liberalior* denies it. Now why should these words be used to express these views respectively? Why should it be 'rigid' to teach ⟨hold⟩ that inspiration extends to the words? Why 'liberal' to confine its range or dilute its sense? Are we to explain the words as used with reference to freedom of speculation, and say that that doctrine is the more rigid which limits private judgment, and that more liberal which favours it? Such is the meaning which the words would bear, if interpreted according to the analogy of the use made of them in moral theology; there they mean respectively the teaching which gives more, or which gives less scope to liberty of action; here they will mean what gives more or gives less scope to liberty of thought. Yet the words surely are not ordinarily found in dogmatic matter, and, to tell the truth, they are not natural or even intelligible when so found. What is there rigid in holding that the Divine Spirit has given us in Holy Scripture a more wonderful gift, what more liberal in holding that the gift is less wonderful? What more rigid in the announcement that we have the warrant to speak very definitely about inspiration, what more liberal in determining ⟨laying down⟩ that more little is known about it? Is it even thought a hardship that tradition tells us much upon an important point, and a favour and indulgence that tradition has told us but little?

Take a parallel case: We know, for instance, that the Apostles have delivered to the Church the great dogma, that our Lord is God and man. The question arises, had He two wills or but one? This point was not defined till the [7th] century; what [was] its definition an act of rigour? would any of the holy men who were concerned in it say to the heretics who denied it, 'we are very sorry that it is our duty to abridge your liberty; and (we are very sorry that we cannot) indulge you on this point; but, as an act of penance allow us to be rigidiores who would, if left to ourselves, be latiores and liberiores'? A

---

[1] In the second fascicule of Document B, Newman had concluded: 'On the whole then, I consider that I satisfy all that the Church requires of me, if I believe that the Holy Ghost moved the sacred writers to write the books of both Testaments, the law and the gospel, the prophetic, evangelical and apostolical teaching, the salutaris veritas and morum disciplina and preserved their writings from error in that great subject matter, that is, in faith and morals; and that in consequence these writings are sacred, canonical, and objects of veneration. But I consider a Catholic ⟨myself⟩ at liberty to hold if he will that their inerrancy does not extend beyond that subject matter, and, though sometimes the direct result of the inspiration of the writers even to the very words which they use, sometimes on the other were no work of inspiration at all whether in themselves or their writers, but the work of human diligence altogether.'

strange sort of rigour and liberality! I prefer that rigour which makes revelation tell us more, than that liberality which makes it tell us less — such rigour is bountiful, such liberality is parsimonious. If indeed revelation has said nothing, and I am merely forcing my private deductions upon you, and oblige your private judgment to submit to mine, then I can quite understand the use of the words, but ⟨and⟩ then only. Otherwise, we ought to adopt the same at this day as regards free thinkers generally; it is rigid [to] hold our Lord's divinity, it would be liberal to leave it as an open question; it is narrow to be zealous for the atonement, and would be broad to deny it; it is severe to uphold the law of faith, and it would be kind to give out that we may think and speculate just what we will, or at least to avow that we are very sorry that we cannot. How is it a boon ⟨privilege⟩ to have to grope by my own reasons for conclusions, while it is an evil that a revelation should dispense with my anxious investigations and tell ⟨give⟩ me the real matter of fact?

There is something so incongruous in this, that I am led, from the very fact of the use of these two words in a dogmatic ⟨this⟩ question ⟨subject matter⟩, to conclude of necessity that the resolution of it cannot be ⟨subject matter in fact is not⟩ dogmatic, for the very reason that they are used. I am led to think they would not be applicable and would not occur for introduction in such a matter, unless that matter was in the province of private judgment, and the propositions maintained, not matters of faith or of the nature of faith, but of the greater and less probability, rigorous or liberal according as they obliged us or not to curtail our liberty on grounds short of a divine decision. That the books of Scripture are sacred and canonical, is a truth which the Church has had the means of determining; that they are all inspired, or ⟨and⟩ inspired to the same extent, or for what purposes, are questions determined by no Apostolic tradition, but only answered variously by various doctors.

But the thought which we are pursuing leads to a further remark. It is the nature of a dogmatic truth, to become clearer as time goes on, than it did at first to our perception. Just as meditation impresses it more vividly ⟨sensitively⟩ on the affections ⟨heart⟩, so does a steady contemplation of it make the image of it clearer and more exact to the intellect. It never makes it less so. The more I think of Almighty God, the more vividly indeed I may see how much ⟨feel that⟩ I do not know about ⟨of⟩ Him, but the more vividly I shall hold what can be known. Catholic teaching then, in the course of ages, may and will become more precise and minute, or what has been in this particular case called 'rigidior'; it never can become 'latior'. For instance, as regards our Lord's divinity, the teaching of the Nicene Creed is 'rigidior', more exact, than that of the Apostles'; and, as regards the Holy Trinity, the statements of the Symbolum *Quicumque* are more rigorous, that is more scientific or theological, than those of the Nicene. But on the other hand, as regards the doctrine of Inspiration, for 15 centuries was the 'rigidior' teaching in possession; for 15 centuries more was taught about it than afterwards; for 15 centuries the general effect of the teaching was to identify it with dictation, to place it in each separate word, and to extend it to every subject introduced into Scripture; since that time, there have been various schools of thought on the subject, and most of them speaking more vaguely and less decidedly. Nay further, the vague, indistinct views on the subject have more and more driven out or tended to drive out the others. We never had less confidence in the exact views with which Bellarmine⟨?⟩ or Canus opened the later period than we have now. Inspiration was a supernatural dictation; but has successively come to be considered *not* a dictation, *not* a positive assistentia, *not* a supernatural motio or prompting Amort p. 110 col. 1; not more than a natural providence and an after ex post facto supernatural sanction. There never was less believed about it among Catholics than now, and it seems probable that soon less will be believed still. Meanwhile the communications of the Church to us instead of being protests and instructions [with ?] later condemnations of propositions were as barren on the subject of ⟨as to⟩ inspiration at Trent, as they were in Carthage. The subject is not introduced into the Creed of Pope Pius. They do not explain the words 'Auctor utriusque testamenti'; they do not assign the ground on which Scripture is sacred and canonical. All this is so contrary to the general nature and history of dogma, that it is a strong reason for saying that there are no materials for a dogma on the subject of Inspiration at all as there is none for Indulgences, and that we are left to private judgment, the judgment of particular divines and schools of divines, when we would say more than that the two Testaments are ⟨it is⟩ from Almighty God as its author, that the books in which they are recorded ⟨and is⟩ sacred and canonical. Let us now then go on to consider what arguments and what conclusions are the best exercise of private judgment in this matter.

§ 4.   [of Document B]
On the Argument from Grounds of Reason
     The Bible has two aspects; it is both the work of God, and the work of man. As the work of God it is the record of supernatural truth, in which (include religious truth generally, for the object and subject-matter of natural religion is supernatural); as the work of man it accidentally, sometimes necessarily, contains much statement of a natural, human, secular, kind. As the work of God, teaching supernatural truth, the Scriptures proceed from inspiration throughout, from beginning to end, and they may in such sense be said to be dictated by the Holy Ghost, that it is scarcely safe to assert ⟨be determined⟩ what part of them is not so dictated. They have a divine significancy and purpose even in their wording, so that the most trivial half sentence, provided the text be sound, has a religious use. On the other hand they are also the writing of man, and in this second aspect they relate to mere human facts or doctrines, whether secular or scientific, and have just that authority which any other book would have, written under the same circumstances, and are to be believed more than other books, because their writers, even as men,

and not as Evangelists, have greater claims on our faith than other writers. Thus, for instance, that Emmaus is 60 stadia from Jerusalem is the statement of a natural fact; and it is to be received on the authority of St Luke as a human historian; but such a resolution ⟨this⟩ does not interfere with the ⟨it still has its⟩ religious aspect of the passage, which besides the geographical fact is capable of mystical meanings or moral inferences ⟨deductions⟩ which vindicate for it the prerogative of a divine origin. And this might be the case, and even in the divine intention, though there were reasons (whereas there is none) to doubt of St Luke's accuracy.

It seems to me as if this view combined the acceptance of what Father Perrone calls the rigid view of the Fathers with the latior and liberalior of Bonfrère, or rather the latissima of Holden.

On the whole then, Scripture is only inspired in that Almighty God does nothing in vain. He does not do that by miracle, which can be done by ordinary means. If he uses extraordinary means, it is for an extraordinary end. If the Scripture is inspired, it is for the sake of teaching what is supernatural; and in that sense it is inspired, and inspired in every part of it.

This commends itself to the reason; but it may be expedient to draw it out more at length.

Christianity is a supernatural Revelation, made directly by the Creator to His creature, of truths, (bearing on his eternal interests), which he could not otherwise know, and involving necessarily the recognition and confirmation of other truths (of a similar kind), in the natural order, which he could otherwise know. This revelation is known by the emphatic title of the Verbum Dei.

The questions which rise immediately on this account of it, [are] what are the channels of the Verbum Dei ⟨revelation⟩, what is its object, and what its subject-matter or contents. In one word, its object is the eternal salvation of the human race; its subject-matter is God Himself as the author of that salvation, or Emmanuel, the Word Incarnate; and its channels or instruments are the Prophets, Evangelists, and Apostles.

But the Prophets and Apostles have long departed this life; how can they now be channels of the Verbum Dei? They are still the channels of the Verbum Dei, first by what they said and have delivered to us, next by what they committed to writings, (wrote and have preserved every age to ⟨this day⟩) bequeathed to posterity and lastly by the existing hierarchy, which, as representing them, has the office of preserving and explaining both their words and their writings.

The question of the Church is not before us, nor how it is in one point of view divine, in another human, according as its word is Verbum Dei or not*,

* [note by Newman] as for instance the Acta Conciliorum are not the Verbum Dei, (but the definitions in which they issue are;) in the matter of faith and morals in a Pope's ex cathedrâ Bull (is commonly received as the Verbum Dei, but) his reasonings, illustrations, individual statements of facts, etc., are not.

N.B.: We have the Scripture in our hands — three questions arise. 1. as to the sense — 2. as to the (correctness of) text — 3, as to the autograph.

nor of Tradition, or how what is the Verbum Dei ⟨apostolical⟩ in it is at first sight intermingled and embedded with what is not so; but of Scripture, viz., in what sense it is the Verbum Dei or canon or rule to us under the magisterium of the Church.

At first sight then it would appear that, as Verbum Dei, which the Church has committed to her lies in the matter ⟨matters⟩ of faith and morals, and in such matters as are directly or indirectly connected with it, but in no other, and as tradition does not convey to us any Verbum Dei except in the same matter, so is it with Scripture also. Its object, as that of the Verbum Dei generally is that and that only of the salvation of the soul; its subject is Emmanuel, and in the fulness of that immense idea it is acquiescent and exhausted; and accordingly that it is a canon of faith and morals, but of nothing beyond them

The spring cannot rise above its source; to the Prophets and Apostles was committed the Verbum Dei; whatever is in Scripture of authority has its authority as being a portion of that Verbum Dei. If then the Verbum Dei in the Prophets and Apostles lay simply and only in the matter of faith and morals, and what thence follows necessarily though but indirectly in other matters, so much more is it with Scripture. It is the Verbum Dei, and thereby is a Rule in the province of faith and morals, and in that only.

To enlarge upon this representation:- The object, I say, of Revelation is the salvation of mankind; its subject (matter) are ⟨is⟩ the truths necessary for that salvation; its instruments are certain supernaturally endowed persons, Prophets, Apostles, Evangelists. Let us suppose these gifted men to speak; whatever they speak, as whatever they do, and however they look and carry themselves, will breathe of heaven and excite the interest and veneration of beholders; but still all that they say will not be of equal preciousness ⟨value⟩. It is not that there are degrees in their inspiration, and that at one time they are more inspired than at another; but that inspiration having an object, there will be more scope for it in one speech than in another. They will always have the habit of inspiration; not always will they stand in need of its acts. There will be more scope for their inspiration in answer to the question 'What shall I do to be saved? or when speaketh the Prophet thus?' than to questions about their native country, their citizenship, the hour of the day, and the length of a journey. We should at all times listen to them with a religious curiosity, but in religious subjects with faith and awe. If they spoke on matters foreign to their mission, on the fine arts, on the state of trade, on military matters, on scientific

---

1. It is from the consent of the Fathers, and correct *quoad fidem et mores*; (vid Canon of Trent).

2. It is from transcribers and is correct is guaranteed, *quoad fidem et mores*; (Ex-Charmes, p. 7, 8).

3. It is the Verbum Dei. (Now as to the autograph.) Distinguo, accordingly as it is the Verbum Dei immediately or mediately. 1. If immediately, the penmen being mere instruments, is true and perfect every word. 2. If mediately with human writers, it is (by analogy) quoad fidem et mores.

truths, we should not expect much more than from other men; but if they spoke ex cathedrâ on points of faith and morals, we should feel every word to be full of divine ⟨sacred⟩ life, and we should drink it in syllable by syllable, as proceeding from the very throne of God. On every subject they would speak nothing but what was good; but what they said on religion we should receive on our knees and kiss their feet in acknowledgement.

Now transfer this from their speech to their writings If such a gifted person wrote ex cathedrâ, as for instance an epistle to a Church, we should cherish it as something of inestimable value; as more valuable than their speech, for this reason, that it was revealed, and we have the ipsissima verba of the Apostle. On the other hand, if it were a letter to a private friend about some private matter, though we should be sure it would contain tokens of the writer's sanctity, and implicit ⟨indirect⟩ enunciations of doctrine, and precedents for conduct, yet we should not feel in the same way as if it began 'Thus saith the Lord,' and professed to be formal and authoritative. Thus it is impossible that we should not pay to St Paul's Epistle to the Hebrews a veneration greater than we pay to his Epistle to Philemon; not that we pay less veneration to him, the writer, in one case than in the other; not that he was more inspired in one Epistle than the other, but that he has larger opportunity for exercising his gift. And in like manner in writing to St Timothy, he did not cease to be a man because he was an Apostle, nor to be a friend because he was the Doctor of the nations. Hence there is more place for inspiration to act in his prophecy of the coming evil times in his Second Epistle, than in his notice of Titus, Luke, and Mark, and his directions about his cloak and parchments, and there was more of miraculous power in his healing the cripple at Lystra than in his tent making, though he never was without both the one gift and the other.

And so in like manner, if there were a company of prophets, as Samuel's school might be, they would be all of them inspired men, but, though they would all speak from God and what He meant them to say, and what therefore was authoritative, yet according to the subject they wrote about, whether about the coming destruction of Babylon, or the past fortunes of the Jews in the reign ⟨court⟩ of Ahasuerus, there would be more exercise of inspiration in the one writing than in the other.

If indeed the Bible was one whole book, or assemblage of systematic treatises, or a code of laws, or an extended creed or digest of canons de fide, the case would be otherwise; but it is beyond dispute a miscellaneous collection of books written independently of each other, one in the intention of Almighty God, but great part of it in every human respect accidentally written, in good part at least and accidentally preserved. So far is it from being the case that all of them say, 'Thus saith the Lord,' that one of them does not contain the name of God in it, and the writer of another apologizes for his style of writing. In a case when they have a direct opportunity of writing as inspired men, they would not be writing in this manner. Their writing then, as their speaking, is sometimes from actual inspiration, sometimes from habitual.

The sacred writers then are one as far as this, that Almighty God has employed them for a supernatural object, and has inspired them and made them infallible in their speeches and writings in all things which bear upon it; but in many, or all other respects they differ. They write in human language, and various languages, in various styles, some hardly grammatical, others correct and elegant. One has more delicacy and refinement of intellect than another; one shows more secular learning than others. None of them are men of science, or critics, or astronomers. Nor should I ever be scandalized by St Paul, if I found him thinking, gifted as he was, that the sun went round the earth; nor by the prophet Isaias, though he had heard nothing of the contemporary foundation of Rome, or of the history of Alba Longa, or of the Etruria. I never should think of confusing the two functions ⟨states of mind⟩ together, nor fancy that a herdsman or fisherman, sent by a divine command to prophesy or to preach, would on that account be an antiquarian or a savant. Surely we may let little things take their course, when we have the presence and substance of what is great and momentous. Whether they compose without skill, or narrate without science, what is that in the face of their stupendous mission of reconciling souls to their Maker? They can afford to be little in little things, when they are so great in the greatest. They can be content to have the treasure in earthen vessels, while that treasure they have.

And if they are immeasurably above other writers in their mission and credentials, what shall we say when we dwell upon the subject-matter of which they preached and have written. That subject is in one word Emmanuel, the Eternal God in human nature and the circumstances and history of His taking it upon Him. To such a thought I cannot do justice without changing the character of my composition, and making it a sermon or meditation. Of this great theme the whole of the canonical Scriptures are full; it is to be found every where, pervading every part of it. Those very passages, which at first sight bear ⟨have⟩ an human aspect, have this divine aspect also. Those very sentences or expressions which are wanting in scientific or historical precision ⟨exactness⟩, have a higher meaning in which they are sacred and authoritative. To illustrate this point, I must enter upon the subject of Scripture interpretation, which is not yet before us ⟨me⟩, but I am only throwing a particular interpretation, adopted by St Augustine into the form of a principle, when I say that in Scripture historical fulness and exactness are ⟨is⟩ distinctly made subordinate to the higher purpose of inculcating divine mysteries. He accounts, as I shall show in the proper place, for a certain representation, which is short of exact, on the principle of its inculcating, when thus defective, a religious lesson. This being taken into account as a principle, it will follow that there may be many parts of Scripture which are not exact in the letter, and no part of Scripture, but conveys ⟨has⟩ a larger supernatural truth that is a final authority in some point of faith and morals; and, while this prerogative holds even of those books or portions of books which are secondary ⟨do not arrest attention at first sight⟩, it has an emphatic fulness as regards the length

24

and breadth of what Prophets, Evangelists and Apostles have written. This portion, it is not too much to say is really dictated by the Holy Ghost, and inspired in the very letter; so that we may take phrases and words, and use them and deduce from them as containing most rare and precious information. Who can limit the fulness and the precision of theological meaning contained in the Psalms, in the last 26⟨?⟩ chapters of Isaias, ⟨such passages as the beginning of St John's⟩, in St John's Gospel, or in the Epistles to the Ephesians or Hebrews? And surely, if this be so, we are not wanting in reverence to a special gift of God, to say that He has not revealed to us scientific truths or historical facts, when He has revealed to us the Gospel of Our Lord and Saviour, the way to please Him, and the way to attain to heaven.*

Without saying that Salmeron could accept every word that I have said, for he certainly would not, I conceive that I am following the spirit, not to say the letter, of some of those eloquent passages on the dignity and authority of the Holy Scriptures, with which he introduces his comments upon the New Testament.[1] A portion of these shall here be freely translated. He insists on the overwhelming authority of the Holy Scriptures, as arising from 'their principal subject, or the argument which they handle.' This is nothing short of Emmmanuel, Him who is God and man, explicitly in the New Testament and implicitly in the Old. God, he says, is one and three; it treats especially of the Creator ⟨Him⟩, not of the creature of things created *only in their reference to Him*, and of the Redeemer, and not of His redeemed except as they relate to His glory. He illustrates this by secular compositions. Caesar, he observes, wrote commentaries, but this in reason that he might be his own hero, and others take their place as bearing upon him. When Aristotle again wrote the history of animals, it was not for the sake of those animals themselves, but to enlarge and perfect man's knowledge of them. Hence Our Lord says in the Gospel, 'If you believed Moses, surely ye would believe Me, for he wrote of Me;' and 'search the Scriptures, for they testify of Me.' Again, 'in the head or sum-total of the book it is written of Me.' And He Himself, beginning with Moses and the Prophets, expounded to the two disciples in all the Scriptures the things concerning Himself; and shortly after, all things must needs be fulfilled which are written in the Law of Moses, the Prophets, and the Psalms, concerning Me. And St Paul says that Christ is the end of the Law. Scripture, he continues, contains *nothing else* than the precepts of faith and conduct; the end of man and the means to the end, the Creator and creature, love of God and man, and all these things are contained in the one idea, Christ. He is the exemplar of all virtues, our ⟨the⟩ way and our ⟨the⟩ goal; the way when we start, the truth while we journey, the life when we have reached the end. Scripture, if Christ were not in it (Christo vacans), would have nothing great

---

* [Note by Newman] NB Wording. The inspiration of St Luke does not oblige us to believe de fide. that the enrolment took place first when Cyrenius was Governor of Syria.
[1] Newman first wrote: '. . . . . . passages like the following in his introduction to the N.T. p. 4 col. 2'. These Newman proceeds to quote.

or worth our study. It would be a scabbard without the sword, a husk without the grain, a cask without wine; 'ita plane Scriptura sacra quae Christum *aliquo modo* non complectitur, quasi cadaver est, animae et spiritûs expers;' if in some way or other Christ be not its subject, it is a mere corpse. He alone fills the Scriptures, He alone enlightens them with His divinity, as the sun lightens the universe ⟨world⟩, and the soul vivifies the body.

(On the Application of the above view of Inspiration)[1]

What I have been advocating is this: that Scripture, as far as it teaches religion, is inspired; but, as far as it speaks of merely natural and secular matters, of matters of science and history, in which religion does not enter, it is not inspired, but the work of human writers. And in saying this, I do not mean to say that one integral⟨?⟩ portion of Scripture is inspired, and another not; but that since as a whole it is religious, as a whole it is inspired in its relation ⟨as far as it relates⟩ to the supernatural.

Two limitations or rather safeguards 1. That since it is a religious work (the work of inspired men), any particular passage or verse must be assumed to have in some respect or other relation to religion, and therefore correct, unless it is demonstrated to be otherwise. 2. That in every part, even such passages which present critical difficulties of fact or science (if the text be sound) must be supposed to have a religious use since they are subjects of ⟨written in⟩ habitual inspiration, and 3. *all this comes under Interpretation.*

Thus Scripture in the aspect of its supernatural or religious matter is inspired; in relation to history or science it is not inspired. The narration about Paradise and the fall of man is inspired, because it relates to super-natural occurrences. The first book of Samuel is one of human history, though its drift, lessons etc., are inspired, because supernatural. *What protects any part of Scripture from scientific and historical criticism is the profession or the claim to be religious ⟨supernatural⟩.*

To say what is the supernatural truth and therefore inspired sense in each passage, and what is the merely human, when there is such, would be to enter upon the subject of the Interpretation of Scripture, which I reserve for another chapter. Here, however, in order to illustrate what I would mean, I will take two instances, without implying what the real view of them is.

For instance St Matthew reckons three times fourteen, or forty generations from Abraham to Our Lord. They are not all the generations which actually intervened. This arrangement may be ascribed to the writer, not as an Evan-gelist, but as a human writer; and it would seem as if by insisting on these fourteens that he drew up the genealogy in this way in order to make it easy to the memory or for neatness and precision, the Holy Spirit thus allowing him this range of private purpose. But this will not at all interfere with the divine intention ⟨religious motive⟩, which is recognized by Fathers and spiritual writers, viz that by forty might be represented mystically the present life, the time of labour and penance, and preparation for the world to come.

[1] See also, Seynaeve, *Newman's Doctrine*, p. 143.*

For another instance take the book of Judith. Considered as history, it falls under the aspect of what is human and not inspired. Now I do not say nor insinuate that it is not a history, but a representation; but suppose it as an hypothesis. Granting it, for argument's sake, to be so, still this would not breach the fulness of its inspiration, whether historically true or not; for the spiritual and moral benefit from it is the same in both cases. But here I am brought, as I said, to the line of thought proper to the next chapter.

§ 2 [of Document B which Newman referred to at the beginning of Document A as belonging to Chapter 4]

In an inquiry such as this, we must be sure of two things, that we observe our duty towards Scripture, and towards the Church.

1. As to Scripture, we must recollect, on the one hand that it was not simpliciter necessaria, Salmeron p. 2, and even now, supposing it to be miraculously removed from the world, our faith and hope would not die with it. Here we are otherwise placed than Protestants.

2. It has on the other hand a depth of instruction, consolation, and strength for us, unlike anything else, (enlarge on its ten thousand gifts). It is ever to be the object of our supreme reverence as the Word of God — and everything which interferes with the fulness of this confidence and veneration is to be put aside.

3. But the question arises whether this sacredness will not be kept up more simply in our minds by believing that it *has nothing to do* with physics, instead of always being in an attitude of *reconciling* it with science.

4. As to the Church, we must not grudge her our faith — we must throw our minds into her real meaning — and not stickle about the letter.

5. but on the other hand we may fairly and religiously and dutifully stand upon *what she has said* — and resolve that we will not equal any truths, though, what are called, certissima, in comparison of those which are distinctly *de fide*, — and that because faith ALONE (and we cannot give FAITH to the word of man although certissimum) can sustain the *weight* of some doctrines, which to the natural imagination are so startling, as that of eternal punishment.

II   Newman's Revised Introduction
1861

May 24 1861

Introduction[1]

One of the characteristics of the day is the renewal of that collision between men of science and believers in Revelation, and of that uneasiness in the public mind as to its results, which are ⟨is⟩ found in the history of the 17th century. Then Galileo raised the jealousy of Catholics in Italy; and now in England the religious portion of the community, Catholics or not, is ⟨are⟩ startled at the discoveries or speculations of geologists, natural historians and linguists. Of course I am speaking, in the case of ⟨as regards⟩ both dates, of the educated classes, of those whose minds have been sufficiently opened to understand the nature of proof, who have a right to ask questions and to weigh the answers given to them. It was of such, we must reasonably suppose, that the Father Commissary was tender in 1637, vid Tiraboschi Biographie t. 8 p 1.2. p. 171, and to such he alluded in his conversation with Galileo, as he took him in his carriage of the Holy Office. 'As we went along,' says Galileo, 'he put many questions to me, and showed an earnestness that I should repair *the scandal, which I had given to the whole of Italy*, by maintaining the opinion of the motion of the earth; and for all the solid and mathematical reasons which I presented to him, he did but reply to me, "Terra autem in aeternum stabit", because "Terra autem in aeternum stat", as Scripture says.'

There could not be a greater shock to religious minds of that day, than Galileo's doctrine, whether they at once rejected it as contrary to the faith, or gave ear ⟨listened⟩ to the arguments by which he enforced it. The feeling was strong enough to effect Galileo's compulsory recantation, though a Pope was then on the throne who was personally? friendly to him. Two Sacred Congregations represented the popular voice, and passed decrees against the philosopher, which were in force down to the years 1822 and 1837.

Such an alarm never can occur again, for the very reason that it has occurred once. At least for myself, I may say, that, had I been brought up in the belief of the immobility of the earth, as though a dogma of revelation, and had associated it in my mind with the incommunicable dignity of man among created beings, with the destinies of the human race, with the locality of purgatory and hell, and other Christian doctrines, and then for the first time had heard of Galileo's thesis, and, moreover, had had the prospect held out to

---

[1] Newman later noted:–February 18 1863   The commencement, *after* Introduction, if there is to be any, is at p 245 [and] NB 36 of these pages make nearly 20 of the pages of my Parochial Sermons. Or one page of the latter takes 1 4/5 of these; and one page of these is 5/9 of the printed.

me that perhaps there were myriads of globes like our own, all filled with rational creatures as worthy of the Creator's regard as we are, I should have been at once indignant at its presumption and frightened at its speciousness, as after that history I never can be, (now that the whole transaction ⟨his life⟩ is a matter of history,) at any parallel novelties in other human sciences, bearing on religion; no, not though I found probable reasons for thinking that the first chapters of Genesis were of an economical character, that there was a pre-adamite race of rational animals, or that we are now 20,000 years from Noe. For that past controversy and its issue have taught me beyond all mistake that men of the greatest theological knowledge may firmly believe that scientific conclusions are contrary to the Word of God when they are not so, and pronounce that to be heresy which is truth. It has taught me that Scripture is not inspired to convey mere secular knowledge, whether about the heavens, or the earth, or the race of man; and that I need not fear for Revelation, whatever truths may be brought to light by means of observation and experience out of the world of phenomena which environ us. And I seem to myself here to be speaking under the protection and sanction of the Sacred Congregation of the Index itself, which has since the time of Galileo prescribed to itself a line of action, indicative of its fearlessness of any results which may happen to religion from physical sciences. Many books has it placed ⟨have since that time been placed⟩ upon its ⟨the⟩ prohibited catalogue, the works of (humanly speaking) distinguished men, the works of Morhof ⟨since?⟩, Puffendorf, Brucker, Ranke, Hallam, Macaulay, and Mill; but I find no one⟨?⟩ there of physical celebrity, unless such writers as Dr. Erasmus Darwin, Bonucci, Klee, and Burdach are so to be accounted. This ⟨One great⟩ lesson then surely, if no other, is taught by the history of theological controversy since the 16th century, moderation to the assailant, equanimity to the assailed, and that as regards geological and ethnological conclusions as well as astronomical.

But there is more than this to give us confidence in this matter. Free speculation in Astronomy two or three centuries ago created a scandal among the Catholics of Italy, as if leading ⟨it led⟩ to conclusions contrary to the faith. High and revered authorities felt themselves constrained to take it up (the matter); the works of Copernicus, Kepler, and Galileo were prohibited in their existing state, and all other publications 'docentes idem,' 'donec corrigantur.' Such a repression or extinction of irreligious books has been a usage in the Church from the very time of St Paul, when the converts at Ephesus, 'qui fuerant curiosa sectati, contulerunt libros et combusserunt coram omnibus.' It has ever been a solemn religious act. I do not dream of questioning the right, in this matter, of those exalted tribunals. But what I may without presumption question, is the expediency of the particular measure to which I am referring. I have no duty of deference to acts of past centuries, which have been reversed by the very authorities which enforced them.[1]

[1] Newman later scribbled a pencil note which seems to read: This has ever been acknowledged, if any names of former times are sacred it is the names of Popes — Yet Rinaldi — Cardinal Pacca Baronius? Ciacconi Orsi? Palma?

And then again expedience is not a matter of dogma; it varies with the age; a later day has the materials for judging of the proceedings of an earlier day. 'Exitus acta probat;' the facts, which experience accumulates are common property, which private individuals are quite able to appreciate and pronounce upon.

Consider then the case before us: Galileo on his knees abjured the heresy that the earth moved; but the course of human thought, of observation, investigation, and induction, could not be stayed; it went on and had its way. It penetrated and ran through the Catholic world as well as through the nations external to it. And then at length, in our own day, the doctrine which was the subject of it was found to be so harmless in a religious point of view, that the books advocating it were taken off the Index, and the prohibition to print and publish the like was withdrawn.

But the course of investigation has gone further, and ⟨done⟩ is now even doing some positive service to the cause which it was accused of opposing. It is apparently in the way to restore to the earth that prerogative and preeminence in the creation which it was thought to compromise. Together with the doctrine of the earth's revolving round the sun the conjecture naturally was made to which I alluded above, of ten thousand satellites revolving round a thousand suns, in the regions of infinite space, and each of them peopled with intelligent beings. This had been a great increase of the difficulty which the new astronomy seemed to be inflicting upon faith, for, if the rational creation was to be extended and multiplied into so vast a series of habitations, why should the race of Adam be singled out from among them all for the incommunicable privilege of supplying a created nature to the Creator, (of having the Almighty God of their own flesh and blood), and of becoming kindred to the Eternal and Immaterial? How should not Galileo sap the foundation of the Christian Creed that the Son of God had become the Son of man? Yet it was so plausible to argue that, if creation was to be allowed to suggest to us any ⟨a⟩ final cause at all, its material extent and variety (were provided into order to) pointed to a corresponding exuberant yield of intellectual natures, that (it was soon taken for granted without proof in those new schools of thought which rested our knowledge of a God mainly and supremely upon the argument from design). In England certainly it has become almost a religious belief, and doubting on the subject has been scouted as profane, and a man of great scientific eminence lately has maintained it in an Essay with the remarkable title, 'More worlds than one, the *Creed* of the philosopher and the *hope* of the Christian.'[1]

However, the spirit of scepticism which showed no reverence for the philosophy of the theologian, is not likely to make much account of the theology of the philosopher; men of science must learn to bear what they had inflicted; and if dogmatism is undefensible even in the province of dogma, what is it but ⟨it is⟩ simply offensive, shocking and disgraceful in the province

[1] See footnote above on p. 4.

of free inquiry. It is preposterous for ⟨in⟩ science to talk of its religious 'Creed;' it is a piece of impertinence in it to pronounce anything about ⟨of⟩ 'the hope of a Christian.' The question is one of dry fact depending on observation and consequent reasoning (upon it). Are there proofs, and if so, what, for believing the existence of intelligent beings besides mankind? What has observation and reasoning to say to ⟨to do with⟩ religious antecedent probabilities or analogies? This has at length been felt in some quarters where greater depth and independence of thought exists than in the ordinary literature of the day; and, now that ⟨when⟩ time has gone on, and at length observation and reasoning, so far from corroborating the conjecture of a Plurality of worlds, has even damaged it, signs have appeared ⟨shown themselves⟩ of a reaction in scientific circles, and an incipient return to that more sober view of the intellectual portion of the universe, which from the time of Galileo had been rejected.

An anonymous Essay has appeared within the last half dozen years, in which the question has been raised whether after all there is any (other) globe in our system but our own inhabited by intellectual beings, and again whether there is any other system than ours at all. It has been answered in various? quarters; but the result ⟨upshot⟩ of the controversy seems to be at least this, that there are (more?) physical probabilities against? this hypothesis and not any ⟨than⟩ for it. Thus investigation, which Catholics would have suppressed as dangerous, when (it has run), in spite of them, it has had its course, results in conclusions favourable to their cause. How little then need we fear from the free exercise of reason! how injurious is the suspicion entertained of it by religious men! how true it is that Nature and Revelation are nothing but two separate communications from the same Infinite Truth!

Nor is this all; much has been said of late years of the dangerous tendency of geological speculations ⟨researches⟩. Well, what harm they have done to the Christian cause, others must say who are more qualified than I am to determine; but on one point, that is, the point before us, I observe it is acting on the side of Christian belief. In answer to the supposed improbability of there being planets without rational inhabitants, considering that our globe has such, geology teaches us, that, in fact, whatever our religion may accidentally teaches us [sic] us to hope or fear about other worlds, in this world at least, long ages past, in which it had either no inhabitants at all, or none but those rude and vast brutal forms, which could perform no intelligent homage or service to their Creator. Thus one order of physical researches bears upon another, and that in the interests ⟨service⟩ of Christianity; and, supposing, as some persons seem to believe in their hearts, that these researches ⟨they⟩ are all instruments in the hands of the enemy of God, we have the observable phenomenon of Satan casting out Satan and restoring the balance of physical arguments in favour of Revelation.

Now let us suppose that the influences which were in the ascendant throughout Italy in 1637 had succeeded in repressing any free investigation on the question of the motion of the earth. The mind of the educated class would have not the less felt that it *was* a question, and would have been haunted, and would have been poisoned, by the misgiving that there was some real danger to Revelation in the investigation; for otherwise the ecclesiastical authorities would not have forbidden it. There would have been in the Catholic community a mass of irritated, ill-tempered, feverish, and festering suspicion, engendering general scepticism and hatred of the priesthood, and relieving itself in a sort of tacit free-masonry, of which secret societies are the development; and then in sudden outbreaks perhaps of violence and blasphemy. Protestantism is a dismal evil; but in this respect Providence has overruled it for good. It has, by allowing free inquiry in science, destroyed a bugbear, and thereby saved Catholics themselves so far from the misery of hollow profession and secret infidelity.

Do not let us make real difficulties for the cause of truth, by running away from fancied ones. There is no little danger of our coming under the satire of the poet in his fable of the Needless Alarm, The sheep, to avoid the hunters and the dogs, proposed to jump into the pit. His moral runs:

Beware of desperate steps; the darkest day,
Live till tomorrow, will have passed away.[1]

So much upon the inexpedience of peremptory prohibitions on the free exercise of Reason in the subject-matter of the Sciences. Reason is really the minister of faith; but it is somewhat like some of those old, true, and really good ⟨valuable⟩ servants, who take liberties, are rude, both in act and speech, sometimes disobey and take their own course, but still are never gone from home for any long time. They are conceited, forward, perhaps patronizing; often very provoking, very unreasonable; they say things just when they should not, put in their word before fine company, damage the effect of great displays, but still they are, as we know, thoroughly trustworthy, we are used to them, and we cannot do without them. We have a bad quarrel with them now and then; there is a giving warning, and a parting; but next day somehow they are found in their old place, going about their work as usual. Andrew Fairservice when his master finds him at his work again, when he had got rid of him.[2]

Now, in arrest of the conclusion to which these representations lead, two pleas are sometimes preferred. I have been urging, that, instead of being frightened at certain reasonings which seem contrary to faith, we should take time calmly to consider how the matter stands, whether from the nature of the case there can be any contrariety, or at any rate, whether we can possibly know it all at once; — that we shall make mischief instead of curing it, unless we allow ourselves to be persuaded to cultivate the Christian virtue of patience. To this it may be answered; first, that such speculations as I have in view are

[1] William Cowper, 'The Needless Alarm', ll. 132–3; see also, *Apologia*, p. 235.
[2] In Sir Walter Scott, *Rob Roy*.

beyond all question irreconcilable with the written word; and again, even though they be not, except in appearance, yet it will be time enough to examine whether Scripture can admit them consistently with its own statements, when they are actually demonstrated. Then indeed, when we cannot deny them, it will be our duty to square Scripture by them; but meanwhile we must adopt the popular sentiment, and say that they are certainly hostile to Christianity and never can be proved. Now I will take the latter of these two objections first.

I think then I must say distinctly that I have no sympathy at all in that policy which will not look difficulties or apparent difficulties in the face, and puts off the evil day of considering them as long as it can. It is the way of politicians who live from hand to mouth, only careful that the existing state of things should last their time. It is the habit of spendthrifts who never think of the state of their affairs while they can borrow money to go on with. There are times indeed when we must get on as we can, because there is a present call for action. It is no moment to hold court martials, when an army is going to join battle. In the 16th century the Catholic controversialist was taken by surprise. Suddenly he found the whole traditionary establishment of the Christian faith, attacked on every side. It was a large, various establishment, running out into, and intertwined with, beliefs, customs, laws, institutions, possessions innumerable. It had attracted to itself and wound about itself a thousand truths, a thousand errors, a thousand opinions, good or indifferent. Thus it stood as one whole; and, while even the wisest and holiest could not at once say what was the eternal truth and what was the accretion of times and circumstances, it was almost certain that to touch any notable part of it would be in the popular judgment to destroy its essence and substance. The controversialists of the Church could not do otherwise than take things as they found them, give up what was manifestly erroneous, but defend many a point about which it was not clear whether it was really defensible or not. The text of Scripture was disputed by Protestants, the books of the Canon, the genuineness of (certain of) the Fathers' writings, (so called), the genuineness of particular passages, the genuineness of the Pope's decretals, the existence, authority, decisions of certain important Councils, the truth of the received traditions of Church History, the force or the fact of certain dogmatic definitions, or existing view of certain doctrines. It was alleged that the works of the Apostolical Fathers were spurious or interpolated; that early history confuted the notion of seven sacraments; that the Fathers and divines of fourteen centuries had settled nothing on the subject of Justification; it was said that the Pope's universal jurisdiction was the growth of centuries, not a point of Apostolic dogma; that the relics of the saints were supposititious; that the Fathers differed from each other on the doctrine of the Holy Trinity, the Holy Eucharist, and the intermediate state of souls. What was to be conceded, what could not be, was not at the moment determinable; and, under these circumstances, nothing could be conceded; for nothing had been ⟨to be⟩ sufficiently

33

examined and accurately defined. Another century might be time of peace, and allow of the accurate determination between the true and essential and the fictitious; but that the first duty was to repel the enemy.[1]

All this is sensible and intelligible; but it does not apply to our times. There is nothing to hinder us from instituting a calm inquiry into any theological or ecclesiastical subject now, and it is prudent to do so, wherever it can be done by competent persons, and not to yield a point, only when adversaries oblige us ⟨one⟩. Truth is truth; it may break upon the world only slowly, and no one may be in fault in holding errors instead of it. But, if it is known and can be known, it is the worst policy surely to hold to the error, merely because we are not challenged and shamed into abandoning it. It is not so in matters of practice and conduct. It is no fault, but a duty, for a commander to hold a place as long as ever he can, though he knows its *untenableness* till his enemies come against him; but the inquiry and controversy about truth must not be treated like a game or a party struggle. If I know for certain that St Dionysius did not write the works attributed to him, it is not just, I must not denounce those who call them spurious, merely because they are referred to as authority in Pope's Epistles. If I find that scientific inquiries are running counter to ⟨against⟩ certain theological opinions, it is not expedient to refuse to examine whether those opinions are well founded, merely because those inquiries have not attained a triumphant success ⟨reached their issue⟩. The history of Galileo is the proof of it. Are we not at a disadvantage as regards that history? and why? why, except because our theologians, instead of cautiously examining what Scripture, that is, the Written Word of God really said, thought it better to put down with a high hand the astronomical views which were opposed to its popular interpretation? The contrary course was pursued in our own day; but what is not against the faith now, was not against the faith three centuries ago; yet Galileo was forced to pronounce his opinion a heresy. It might not indeed have been prudent to have done in 1637 what was done in 1822; but, though in the former date it might have been unjustifiable⟨?⟩ to allow the free⟨?⟩ publication of his treatises with the sanction of the Church, that does not show that it was justifiable to pronounce that they were against the faith and to enforce their abjuration.

I am not certain that I might ⟨may⟩ not go further, and advocate the full liberty to teach the motion of the earth, as a philosophical truth, not only now, but even three centuries ago. The Father Commissary said it was a scandal to the whole of Italy; that is, I suppose, an offence, a shock, a perplexity. This might be, but there was a class, and even is a class, whose claims to consideration are too little regarded now, and were passed over then. I mean the educated class; to them the prohibition would be a real scandal in the true meaning of the word, an occasion of their falling. Men who have sharpened their

---

[1] Newman later noted:
March 31 1863. Somewhere the subject of *changes* should be discussed. They are ever *gradual*. If what is ever so *true* is introduced abruptly, it incurs the displeasure of the Church — as *shocking* pious people.

intellects by exercise and study anticipate the conclusions of the many by some centuries. If the tone of public opinion in 1822 called for a withdrawal of the prohibition to treat of the earth's motion, the condition of the able and educated called for it in Galileo's age; and it is as clear to me that their spiritual state ought to be consulted for, as it is difficult to say why in fact it so often is not. They are to be tenderly regarded for their own sake; they are to be respected and conciliated for the sake of their influence upon other classes. I cannot help feeling, that, in high circles, the Church is sometimes looked upon as made up of the hierarchy and the poor, and that the educated portion, men and women, are viewed as a difficulty, an incumbrance, as the seat and source of heresy; as almost aliens to the Catholic body, whom it would be a great gain, if possible, to annihilate.

For all these reasons I cannot agree with those who would have us stand by what is probably or possibly erroneous, as if it were dogma, till it is acknowledged on all hands, by the force of demonstration, to be actually such.

Now turning to the other answer which is given to those who ask for some adjustment on the part of theologians and controvertists of science and revelation on particular points on which there seems a divergence, or likely to be one, for instance, on the question of the days of creation or the interval between the deluge and the call of Abraham ⟨Christian era⟩. It is sometimes said that such speculations on the part of geologists or ethnologists are absolutely against the revealed word, (as the motion of the earth was said to be three centuries ago), and therefore to be summarily prohibited. If this be really so, it will save us all a great deal of trouble. I for certain have no intention at all of closing my ears or my heart to any declaration of Holy Church, whether conveyed by an express definition or by the clear voice of tradition in her Schools or her Bishops and faithful people. I give the assent of my innermost intellect to the voice of the Catholic Roman Church as the infallible oracle of God, with the confidence moreover that she knows the limits of Her own gifts and that she can decide imperially and sovereignly when and how far she is infallible, and where she has no commission to speak. Her declaration of a dogma, in whatever way made, is sufficient for me. I embrace and accept it by a willing and joyful act of faith. And prospectively too, I have an absolute intention of believing whatever she shall say, as well as what she has said, and what I shall learn to be dogma, as well as what I know to be such already. If then [she] shall put her anathema upon these scientific speculations, which I do not think she will, but if she shall do so, I anathematize them too. If she affirms, as I do not think she will affirm, that every thing was made and finished in a moment, though Scripture seems to say otherwise, and though science seems to prove otherwise, I affirm it too, and with an inward and sincere assent. And, as her word is to be believed, so her command is to be obeyed. I am as willing then to be silenced on doctrinal matters which are not of faith, as to be taught in matters which are. It would be nothing else than a great gain, to be rid of the anxiety which haunts a person circumstanced as I am, lest, by keeping silence on points such as that on which I have begun to speak, I should perchance be hiding my talent in a napkin. I should welcome the authority which by its decision allowed me to turn my mind to subjects more congenial to it. On the other hand it is legitimate authority alone which I have any warrant to recognize; as to the ipse dixit of individual divines, I have long essayed to divest myself of what spiritual writers call 'human respect.' I am indeed too old to be frightened, and my past has set loose my future.

And now as to what I propose to do in the following pages:- I am not directly proving any thing against Anti-Catholics, nor am I addressing my arguments to them. I am to endeavour to ascertain the position which Catholics themselves take up on a certain subject, their doctrine concerning Holy Scripture, and that by the aid of Catholic authorities and Catholic proofs, and to define that position ⟨it⟩ in that side of it, which faces the enemy. The enemy makes use of the conclusions of modern science as instruments of siege — and I am to inquire whether his new weapons of offence can reach us, or indeed can be pointed against us at all.

I am not proposing to comment on Scripture; nor am I proposing to reconcile Scripture with the conclusions of human science; so far from it, that I would rather contend that there is little to reconcile, because there is as little as possible common between them. I am to adjust rather than to reconcile; that is, I aim at showing how theology sits easy, (if I may use such an expression) in its own domain, without any fear, as time goes on, of any collision between itself and secular knowledge, as regards the statements of the written Word, provided each party will but consent to remain within its own boundaries, I shall aim at showing that no interpretation of Scripture has been formally adopted by the Church or sanctioned 'in materia fidei et morum', by the *consensus* of Fathers and Doctors, which can interfere with the demonstrations of science or history, whether existing or probably to come; as, on the other hand nothing that human inquiry ⟨science⟩ can discover is able to reach, for confirmation or for damage, those sacred truths and facts which the voice of the Church, or of her doctors and schoolmen, or of her Bishops and people in orbe terrarum, has recognized and declared to be dogma in the written word.

I wish to do my part in destroying the feverishness and nervousness which is abroad, the vague apprehensions of some coming discoveries hostile to faith, that spontaneous unwelcome rising of questionings and perplexities in the secret heart, which cut at the root of devotion, and dry up the founts of love, homage, loyalty, admiration, joy, peace, and all the other best and noblest attributes of religion. It is perfectly true that obedience is acceptable to God, and may even be heroic, when performed amid darkness, dryness, and dejection; but few people except ⟨but⟩ saints can long endure so heavy a trial; and I shall think myself most highly favoured by the God of grace and truth if He shall enable me to suggest anything useful to any one soul who is under this special visitation. If I attain this object by lawful means, I shall not stand in need of any other consolation.

(end of Introduction)[1]

February 18, 1863
After Introduction if there is to be any.
§

In all questions, whether of faith or morals, the least formal, but our most natural and immediate informant, is the popular sentiment ⟨vox populi⟩, or, to speak more exactly, the living (present sentiment) voice of bishops, clergy, and the faithful. It is by means of this informant that we know a variety of details which cannot be enumerated in the fullest catechism. It is a circumambient atmosphere of knowledge which we breathe and imbibe without any deliberate act of our own. It is attendant on us from the first dawn of reason; and when we come to years of discretion we consult and follow it as a matter of course, till we meet with special questions ⟨difficulties⟩, which from their novelty, subtlety, or moment, seem to require some formal treatment.

On the other hand the one and only sovereign and decisive authority divinely given to us in such matters is the direct decision of the Church, proceeding from the Chair of Peter or Ecumenical Councils, and recorded in written definitions.

Besides these we have a number of other informants, of varying weight and clearness; such as the teaching of the Ancient Fathers, the judgment of the

[1] In Newman's MSS. notebook, there follows 'Chapter ii Inspiration' which, as Newman himself later noted in pencil, was 'superseded, first by D, then by E'; Newman began this chapter as follows:
'Two questions present themselves for discussion, on beginning to treat of the passages in Scripture, which are considered to give us information in secular sciences; first, did the gift of *inspiration* in the sacred writers extend to whatever they might (happen to) say on the subject matter of those sciences:– and secondly has the voice of the Church, whether by formal definition, or by consent of Fathers and doctors, or of clergy ⟨Bishops⟩ and people everywhere, affixed to certain *interpretation* to any such statements as occur in Holy Scripture;— and first on the subject of Inspiration.

§1

I must begin by stating the sense in which I conceive certain terms to be used in the controversy'.
The subsequent discussion of such terms as 'Revelation' and 'Dictation' as well as §2 on 'the principal opinions which may be held concerning the Inspiration of Scripture' were either superseded or deleted. For §3 which was on the evidence which Scripture offered for its own inspiration, see below, pp. 52 ff. It was at this point also in the MSS. notebook that Newman later noted:

§1
June 23, 1861
('The Section following on the foregoing introduction is at p 127. On the Definitions of the Church. Then comes §2 viz on the idea of Inspiration as introductory to the opinions of Fathers and Divines, which is pp. 73 [i.e. the subsequent discussion] etc. etc. rewritten').
[In 1863, as already indicated, Newman referred to yet another 'commencement' to follow his introduction and this is now given here.]

Theological Schools, the history, ritual, and monuments of the Church; lastly, though first in the order of precedence, Holy Scripture.

Of these, the only informant, which at once and formally imposes upon all the faithful the interior assent of faith is the definition of the Church. The rest at the utmost only bind the conscience of particular individuals from special circumstances of their case. Thus, though there were no definition to the effect that our Lord is the Very God, still, if a man clearly saw that that fundamental truth was taught in Scripture, he would be bound, under pain of mortal sin, to believe it, as he would be bound to believe a private revelation made to him. And, if he had a conviction, from the study of early Church history, that the Apostles taught the infallibility of the see of Peter, he would be bound to believe it, in spite of ⟨though⟩ the Church's not having ⟨may not have⟩ made any definition one way or the other. And if, before the year 1854, he found he had sufficient grounds from Scripture, Antiquity, the devout sentiment of the faithful and the nature of the case, to be certain that the Immaculate Conception of the Blessed Virgin was a portion of the original Depositum, it would be absolutely incumbent on him to accept and embrace the doctrine as true, though it had not yet been promulgated in a dogmatic form. But still such promulgation as a doctrine is necessary to make it a portion of the Catholic Creed, and then belief in it is imperative, not on this or that person only, but on the whole cœtus fidelium in the orbis terrarum.

At the same time, though these other informants have not power to create an article of faith, there is nevertheless much that they can do, over and above that special obligation to believe which they accidentally impose on particular persons. They have a great negative power, when they have none other; and restrain when they do not enjoin. There is a wide difference between being bound to believe a doctrine, and being permitted to deny it; as in secular matters there is no veto upon our thoughts, when in many cases there is a definitive veto upon our actions. I may think a certain man a rogue, but, if I say it, I shall fall under the law, because I commit a breach of the peace. So, in religious matters still more, I am not at liberty to break the peace of the Church. In matters not *de fide*, if I openly and abruptly set my private judgment against the belief of the Catholic world, I shall either be fulfilling a transcendent duty, or committing a great sin. Hence it is that statements, which are not heretical, because not contradictory to dogmatic definitions, may be close upon heresy, temerarious, scandalous, offensive, and unbecoming. To oppose the consent of theologians, that is, the Schola, would be close upon heresy and temerarious. To startle and unsettle the existing convictions of the many without sufficient reason, would be scandalous. To shock wantonly the feelings of the pious and devout, is a grave offence by the very force of the terms.

And now the question before us is, in its fullest form this: what is the extent of liberty of opinion and of speech which the private Christian is permitted in his conclusions ⟨judgment⟩ about Holy Scripture; in other words, what can he hold without heresy or danger of heresy or temerity; what can he say without giving real scandal or offence, or in any way sinning against the second Table of the Law?

However, in the following inquiry, it is proposed not to do no more [sic] than to determine how far in this case the exercise of interior private judgment is not superseded by authoritative information; and as to his liberty ⟨freedom⟩ of speech, this branch of the subject will not come into consideration except so far as an anxious endeavour will be made not to offend against truth, charity, or the duty of submission to ecclesiastical authority.

In seeking an answer to my question, I propose to address myself successively to the five principal sources of religious ⟨theological⟩ teaching; first, to the definitions of the Church, and the conclusions of her divines; next, to Scripture itself, which is the subject of inquiry, to the Fathers, and to the spontaneous sentiment and action of Catholics. In taking them in this order, I begin with our most exact informants, and end with our most full. They are contrasted the one with the other, as nature is contrasted with science. The dogmatic decisions of Popes and Councils, and the judgments of the School are precise, but on that account measured and circumscribed; but the teaching of Scripture, and the Fathers, and the popular sentiment and action, are ever open, free, various, exuberant, but at the same time with little of method and definiteness. The first guard us from falling into error; the province of the latter is to draw us on to the spontaneous love of what is highest, truest, and best.

February 17, 1863   § 2 (after Introduction)

On the Dogmatic Definitions of the Church[1]

All Catholics hold the inspiration of the canonical books of Scripture. By 'canonical' is denoted ⟨meant⟩ the prerogative possessed by those books of being the rule of faith and conduct to Christians; and by 'inspiration' is denoted ⟨meant⟩ the special divine gift which makes them different from all other books, by virtue of which they are the word, not of man, but of God, and are qualified to become a canon.

Their inspiration is the work of God; their canonicity is the work of the Church; this canonicity is a very simple idea, about which there is no room for dispute; it is not so as regards inspiration, which has been understood in many different senses, which will accordingly will [sic] be the principal subject of these pages.

In inquiring into the *limits* of our liberty of opinion upon it, we naturally betake ourselves in the first place to the Definitions of the Church, as framed by Popes ex cathedrâ and Ecumenical Councils. This being so, it is remarkable that, while these Definitions clearly explain what is the canonicity of Scripture, by creating the canon, on the other hand about the inspiration of Scripture

---

[1] The title is taken from Newman's note of 23 July 1861.

they say not one word. If then what is dogma and de fide is determined by the definitions of Church, it follows that, as far as those definitions go, the inspiration of Scripture is not, in any sense of the word, de fide at all.[1]

I shall review the Papal and Synodal declarations on the subject, as they are found in Denzinger, though not even all of them are ⟨not all⟩ to be accounted de fide.[2]

1. 'Placuit ut, praeter scripturas canonicas, nihil in Ecclesiâ legatur sub nomine divinarum scripturarum. Sunt autem canonicae Scripturae, Genesis etc.' Concil. Hipp. et Carthag. A.D. 397 (Denz. 49). [186]

2. 'Qui vero libri recipiantur in Canone, brevis annexus ostendit, etc.' Innoc. Ep. (Denz. 59). [213]

3. 'Si quis dixerit vel crediderit, alterum Deum esse priscae legis, alterum Evangeliorum, Anathema sit.' Conc. Hispan. et Lusit. contr. Priscill., A.D. 447 (Denz. 121). [198]

4. Si quis dixerit vel crediderit alias scripturas, praeter quas Ecclesia Catholica recipit, in auctoritate habendas vel esse venerandas, Anathema sit. *ibid.* (Denz. 125). [202]

5. Post has omnes propheticas, evangelicas, atque Apostolicas Scripturas, quibus Ecclesia Catholica per gratiam Dei fundata est., etc. Gelasii decret. A.D. 494 (Denz. 140). [350]

6. Credo etiam Novi et Veteris Testamenti, Legis et Prophetarum et Apostolorum, unum esse auctorem, Deum et Dominum Omnipotentem. — Symb. Fid. Leon. IX A.D. [1053] (Denz. 296). [685]

7. 'Novi et Veteris Testamenti unum eundemque auctorem esse Dominum credimus.' Professio Waldens. reducum. A.D. 1210 (Denz. 367). [790]

8. Credimus etiam Novi et Veteris Testamenti, Legis ac Prophetarum et Apostolorum, unum esse auctorem Deum et Dominum Omnipotentem. Confess. M. Palaeolog., A.D. 1274 (Denz. 386). [854]

9. Unum atque eundem Deum Veteris et Novi Testamenti, hoc est, Legis ac Prophetarum atque Evangelii profitetur Auctorem; quoniam, eodem Spiritu Sancto inspirante, utriusque Testamenti Sancti locuti sunt: quorum libros suscipit et veneratur. Bull. Eugen. IV Cantate A.D. [1442] (Denz. 600). [1334]

10. Ss. Oecumenica   et Generalis Tridentina Synodus etc. . . . . proponens, ut sublatis erroribus, puritas ipsa Evangelii in Ecclesiâ conservetur, quod, promissum ante per prophetas in Scripturis sanctis, Dominus noster etc . . . . proprio ore primum promulgavit, deinde per suos Apostolos, tamquam fontem omnis et salutaris veritatis et morum disciplinae, omni creaturae praedicari jussit, perspiciensque, hanc veritatem et disciplinam contineri in libris scriptis, (et sine scripto traditionibus, quae ab ipsius

---

[1] The foregoing text, written on left-hand page 126 and on page 127, was added on 17 February 1863. After this short addition the 1861 text goes on: 'I shall review. . . .'

[2] Newman refers to the 1856 edition. The numbers of the 33rd edition (1965) are added in square brackets.

Christi ore ab Apostolis acceptae, aut ab ipsis Apostolis, Spiritu Sancto dictante, quasi per manus traditae, ad nos usque pervenerunt), orthodox-orum Patrum exempla secuta, omnes libros tam Veteris quam Novi Testamenti, cum utriusque unus Deus sit auctor, (necnon traditiones ipsas, tum ad fidem, tum ad mores pertinentes, tamquam vel ore tenus à Christo, vel à Spiritu Sancto dictatas, et continuâ successione in Ecclesiâ Catholicâ conservatas), pari pietatis affectu ac reverentia suscipit et veneratur ...[1]

Si quis autem libros ipsos integros, cum omnibus suis partibus, prout in Ecclesiâ Catholicâ legi consueverunt, et in veteri vulgatâ Latinâ editione habentur, pro sacris et canonicis non susceperit, (et traditiones praedictas sciens et prudens contempserit) Anathema sit. — Concil. Trident. Sess. iii (Denz. 666). [1501, 1504]

On these passages I remark first, as I observed just now, that they are not all of them to be considered as *de fide* definitions of doctrine. My justification in ⟨ground reason for⟩ saying so is the authority ⟨is the judgment⟩ of Tournely on this point, adduced and approved by Amort. The latter theologian thus writes:

'Notandum, inter definitiones Ecclesiae non referri, quae, in Conciliis Generalibus in Canones non relata, aut extra Canones sub anathemate ut necessario credenda, asserta sunt. Hinc quae in Concilio Tridentino in *capitulis* traduntur, vel in *Decreto* Eugenii IV ad Armenos continentur, repraesentant quidem *communem doctrinam Theologorum* tunc temporis receptam, attamen pro articulis fidei non necessario recipiuntur. Tournelius, Scriptor de novatorum erroribus minime suspectus, in suâ Theologia (de Sacramento Confirmationis, qu. I, art. 4 § Opiniones Scholae n. 4) de decreto Eugenii IV scribit: — 'Decretum illud vim definitionis seu decreti totius Concilii Florentini non habere.' etc . . . . Idem (in tract. de Sacramento Eucharist qu 4 art 6) . . . respondit '. . . illud solum tamquam de fide definitum haberi debet, quod est in Canonibus Conciliorum sub anathematis poenâ ad credendum propositum . . . non quae in Capitibus (a Tridentino) praemittuntur ad Canonum subsequentium intelligentiam et probationem.' demonstr. critic. p. 105.

Amort adds, as is reasonable, that 'ejusmodi expositiones doctrinae Catholicae, quas edunt Concilia vel Summi Pontifices, in quantum repraesentant universalem sensum Ecclesiae et Theologorum, etiamsi non contineant articulum fidei, generare tamen praesumptionem violentam de traditione universali, aut inspiratione divinâ, moderante ingenia doctorum, atque ad definitiones, suo tempore emendandas, provide disponente; ut proin ejusmodi expositionibus reluctari sine gravissimis fundamentis temerarium sit.'

---

[1] Newman later noted in pencil: 'Argue from the *parallel*, at least — that as the *traditions* only stand good for veritas and disciplina, faith and morals, so the books also.'

In the second place, I remark; that nowhere in the above definitions of doctrine is there any mention of the inspiration of the Written Word, which doctrine accordingly is not *de fide*.[1]

If it were to be found anywhere it would be in the Tridentine decree or canon and upon it Mgr. Bouvier in his Dogmatic Theology first lays down:

> 'Libri Veteris et Novi Testamenti vere fuerunt inspirati;' 'Haec propositio, non solum ad praecipuas, sed ad omnes partes Scripturarum ab auctoribus sacris exaratas extendenda est;'

and presently⟨?⟩ proceeds,

> 'Quia Sacrum Concilium ipsa voce *inspirationis* non utitur, propositio nostra, licet certissima, non est de fide Catholicâ.' [II, pp. 25 and 28]

Moreover, there *are* two Councils, one before the Council of Trent, the other after, neither binding on us de fide, both of which *by contrast do* say that the *books* are inspired. Vid Vincenzi (if he is to be believed) t   1 pp 237 and 244. Paris and Malabar.

In connection with this point, let it be observed that in the Professio of Pope Pius IV, all explicit mention of the intrinsic authority and claims of Holy Scripture are omitted. It runs:

> 'Apostolicas et ecclesiasticas traditiones, reliquasque ejusdem Ecclesiae observationes et constitutiones firmissimè admitto et amplector. Item sacram scripturam juxta eum sensum, quem tenuit et tenet Sancta Mater Ecclesia, cujus est judicare de vero sensu et interpretatione sacrarum scripturarum, admitto etc'. [Denzinger, 1863]

Moreover, in the Catechism of the Council, all that is said about Scripture is this, viz.[2] [incompleted addition.][3]
[4]There is a third remark which suggests itself on the first view of the above definitions:- that in the course of 1100 years from the African ⟨Spanish⟩ to the Tridentine Council there is so little growth of teaching and explanation in the doctrine laid down. To illustrate what I mean. The doctrine of our resurrection is confessed in all the early creeds under the formula of 'Credo carnis resurrectionem.' In the early Aquileian it is said to be *hujus* carnis resurrectio.

---

[1] Newman later noted in pencil: 'Transpose 2 and 3' and 'No where is the phrase "inspiratio scripturarum" or its equivalent found — therefore it is not de fide'.

[2] ... *non multis annis ante concilium tridentinum, synodum senonensem, etiam dictum parisiensem ... celebratam ... canone quarto ... decreverunt Scripturae auctores divinitus inspiratos esse* ... Aloysius Vincenzi, *Sessio Quarta Concilii Tridentini vindicata*, I, Rome 1842, p. 237. On p. 244 Vincenzi quoted Chapter XIV of the Diocesan Synod of St Thomas's Christians at Malabar in 1599: *Unum similiter, eundemque Deum auctorem fuisse veteris et novi testamenti, idest Prophetarum et Evangelii ; nam testamenti utriusque scriptores afflati Spiritu Sancto scripserunt. Itaque recipit Ecclesia omnes libros Canonicos testamenti utriusque, infallibilem in se veritatem continentes, atque a Spiritu sancto dictatos ...*

[3] Newman left a space for the quotation: *Omnis autem doctrinae ratio, quae fidelibus tradenda sit, verbo Dei continetur, quod in scripturam traditionesque distributum est.* Preface to *The Catechism of the Council of Trent*.

[4] Newman again noted in pencil: 'transpose 2 and 3.'

It is defined in the Council against Origen, that the caro or corpus will not be etherial or spherical, and therefore cease to be really a body (Denz. 196 [407]), but, instead of being quaelibet alia caro, will be *ista, quâ vivimus, consistimus et movemur*; (Denz. 234 [540]) In Pope Leo IX's creed, 'credo veram resurrectionem *ejusdem* carnis *quam nunc gero*.' (Denz. 295 [684]). In the fourth Lateran 'propriis resurgent corporibus *quae nunc gestant*,' (Denz. 356 [801]) 'hujus carnis, *quam gestamus*, et non altioris, resurrectionem,' (Denz. 373 [797]) 'veram resurrectionem *hujus carnis quam nunc gestamus*.' (Denz. 386 [854]). Now it is plain that in this dogma there has been no advance whatever; that nothing whatever is revealed about it, but the fact that this body of ours is to rise again. And as much as this was known from the beginning.

On the other hand there are doctrines about which it is impossible that the Church should say every thing at once, because there is so much to say about them out of the apostolic depositum with which she is intrusted. Such is the doctrine of the Holy Trinity and the Incarnation, such the doctrine of grace, separate portions of which receive their perfect expression only gradually in the course of many centuries.

Now the doctrine of the authority of Scripture ⟨inspiration⟩ is like the former of these; various dogmatic documents mention it, as we have seen, but with a cautious repetition of what had been said before. The Spanish Council of A.D. 447 says that Scripture is to be counted as authority and to be venerated. Accordingly Pope Eugenius and the Council of Trent say that the Church 'suscipit et veneratur libros utriusque Testamenti.' In like manner the Council of Trent says that one God is author of both Testaments; and before it Pope Eugenius had spoken of 'one and the same God as the author of Old and New Testaments;' and before him the Creed of A.D. 1274 ⟨why M. Palaeologus?⟩ of 'The Almighty God and Lord as the one author of New and Old Testaments;' and further back, the Creed imposed on the Waldenses, of 'the Lord, as one and the same author of New and Old Testament;' and so too the Creed of Leo IX ⟨against whom?⟩; and in the fifth century the Spanish Council denounced the tenet that 'there was one God of the Old Law and another of the Gospels.'[1]

This last head of remark leads us on to the consideration of the definitions themselves, of which the phrase ⟨expression⟩, to which I have been calling attention, 'One God the author of both Testaments' is the expression. I say that these definitions, taken all together, contain hardly more than this proposition. They call indeed the Scriptures divine, sacred, venerable, authoritative, and even the Church's foundation, but the declaration which on the one hand is most definite and particular, and which is so frequent as to be the feature of the whole is that God is the Author of both Testaments. Here then

---

[1] Newman later noted: 'This remark will be found to have still greater force when we come to the consideration of the Theological Schools, — when, it will be found that, so far from there being a progress in the doctrine as time has gone on there is now far greater uncertainty and vagueness on the subject of inspiration than in the earlier centuries of Christianity.'

at first sight it is plain, that, whatever is meant by that proposition, it is relative rather than absolute; it does not so much predicate anything positive about the two Testaments, as declare that God is the author of the Old *as well as* the New, not only of the New but of the Old also. The stress is not so much upon the word *auctor* as on the word *utriusque*. Or again it is a negative proposition quite as much as a positive one, as is expressed in the Spanish Canon when first the doctrine is enunciated. 'Si quis dixerit vel crediderit, *alterum* Deum esse priscae legis, *alterum* Evangeliorum, Anathema sit.' And so again Pope Eugenius, in the Decretum pro Jacobitis, (Cantate) immediately after his declaration of the inspiration of the Saints of both Testaments, adds: 'Praeter-ea Manichaeorum anathematizat insaniam, qui duo prima principia posuerunt, unum visibilium, aliud invisibilium; et alium Novi Testamenti Deum, alium Veteris esse Deum dixerunt.' [Denzinger, 1336] ⟨query Leo IX and of 1274 against the Paulianists?⟩

That this is no subtle distinction will be plain in pursuing the inquiry. It will be observed that the canon last quoted is levelled at the Priscillianists, heretics of a Gnostic or Manichean origin, who considered that the Old Testament, as the material⟨?⟩ universe, was the work⟨?⟩ of the Evil Principle. The Waldenses too in the Middle Ages professed the same⟨?⟩ doctrine, and they too, as was natural, were made, on their reconciliation to the Church, to confess that the author of both Testaments was one and the same God. The phrase then 'auctor utriusque Testamenti' does not mean that God inspired the whole Bible, but that 'the Mosaic Covenant as well as the Christian has come from the One God.'

That this phrase in the Spanish Canon, adopted by subsequent Council, really means this, will be clearer still by going yet further back, and referring to the works of St Irenaeus in which it first occurs.

St Irenaeus is the earliest writer who treats of the authority of the Holy Scriptures, both in themselves and relatively to Tradition, and he is led to do so by the heresies against which he writes. As to the Scriptures, considered in themselves, he appeals to them as perfect, spiritual, and divine; but, as will also be found presently⟨?⟩ in closely examining the above dogmatic definitions on the subject, he never confuses them with the Testaments, Covenants, or Dispensations. By the Scriptures he means the sacred books, written *under* the two Covenants; of these he never calls God the Author of the Scriptures, but the God of both Covenants or Dispensations. The Old Testament or Covenant he sometimes calls the Law or the *Lawgiver*; or the Law and the Prophets, ⟨where?⟩ as our Lord says 'the Law and the Prophets' were until John, meaning the Dispensation or Testament of the Law and the Prophets; and the New Testament he sometimes ⟨where?⟩ called the Gospel, or the Apostles and Evangelists. These latter, Prophets, Apostles, Evangelists, he speaks of ⟨are said⟩ ⟨where?⟩ to be inspired; he does not so speak⟨?⟩ of the books. It is obvious how such a discrimination in the use of words coincides with phrases used in the above dogmatic declarations of Popes and Councils,

44

in which we read of the Scriptures as divine and venerable, of the 'Old Law and the Gospels,' 'the Old and New Testament, Law, Prophets, and Apostles,' 'the Old and New Testament, that is, Law, Prophets and Gospel,' and of the one God as their author.

But to return to St Irenaeus. In one place he speaks of *four* Testaments, those of Adam, of Noe, of Moses, and of Christ, [*Adversus Haereses III*, xi, 8] p. 191, where the word can mean nothing but Dispensations. Presently he speaks of two, the Old and the New; and says, 'Omnes, qui sunt malae sententiae, moti ab eâ *legislatione* qua secundum Moysen, dissimilem eam et contrariam *Evangelii* doctrinae arbitrantes, jam non sunt conversi, uti differentiae *utriusque Testamenti* inquirerent causas.' [op. cit. III, xii, 12] p. 198. Thus utrumque Testamentum is equivalent to the Lawgiving and the Good tidings. He goes on to speak ⟨where?⟩ of those heretical speculators practising in consequence upon the Scriptures which are the record of those two Testaments. He ends by saying, 'Haec omnia contulit eis Scripturarum et Dispositionis (i.e. οἰκονομίας, Dispensationis) Dei ignorantia.' In another place: 'Nec alterum (that is, auctorem) quidem vetera, alterum vero proferentem nova docuit; sed unum et eundem . . . Ea, quae de thesauro proferuntur nova et vetera, sine contradictione duo *Testamenta* dicit; vetus quidem, quod ante fuerat, *legislatio*; novum autem, qua secundum *Evangelium* est *conversatio* . . .' 'Heremias ait, Ecce disponam testamentum novum, etc. Utraque autem Testamenta unus et idem paterfamilias produxit, Verbum Dei, Dominus noster Jesus Christus, qui et Abrahae et Moysi collocutus est, et nobis in novitate restituit libertatem, et multiplicavit eam, quae in ipso est, *gratiam*.' [op. cit. IV, ix, 1] p. 237.

It is abundantly clear then that the Church has not declared Almighty God 'author of all the Scriptures,' as if He had written them, dictated them, or inspired them, but 'Author of the two Dispensations,' the Law and the Gospel, the instruments and ministers of which, Prophets and Apostles, were inspired. Hence the Tridentine Decree says, 'omnes libros tum Veteris tum Novi Testamenti, cùm utriusque (i.e. Testamenti, not "omnium" i.e. librorum) unus Deus sit auctor'. But (for the purpose both of preaching and of writing), this will become more evident still on examining the Tridentine Decree in extenso in connexion with the Bull of Pope Eugenius.

The Pope says: 'Eodem Spiritu Sancto inspirante, utriusque Testamenti sancti *locuti* sunt;' not simply wrote, but spoke, as referring primarily to oral tradition. Now in the decree of Trent, this 'speaking under divine Inspiration' is especially interpreted of 'tradition': 'contineri in libris scriptis, et *sine* scripto *traditionibus*, quae (which traditions, not qui libri) ipsius Christi ore ab Apostolis acceptae, aut, ipsis Apostolis, *Spiritu Sancto dictante*, quasi per manus traditae, ad nos usque pervenerunt.'

And so again, pointedly: '*traditiones* ipsas, tum ad fidem tum ad mores pertinentes, tamquam vel ore tenus à Christo, vel à *Spiritu Sancto dictatas*, et continuâ successione in Ecclesiâ Catholicâ conservatas.'

Thus, twice are traditions said to be dictated to the Apostles by the Holy Spirit. The Holy Scriptures are twice spoken of also, twice distinguished from Tradition, and twice treated of with an utter silence about their inspiration, which is more emphatic of course in consequence of the contrast.

Another contrast, which is found in these great documents of faith, and comes to the same thing, is that between the writers and the books; not the books, but the writers are said to be inspired. Eugenius says: 'Eodem Spiritu inspirante, utriusque Testamenti *Sancti* locuti sunt, *quorum* libros suscipit et veneratur.' And in like manner at Trent: it is said, ('in libris scriptis, *et*) the unwritten traditions, quae . . . Spiritu Sancto dictante . . . per manus traditae, etc;' and (omnes libros etc., *nec non*) 'traditiones ipsas, à Spiritu Sancto dictatas'), it is nowhere said, 'libri à Spiritu Sancto dictati,' or 'libri, qui, Spiritu Sancto dictante, scripti sunt.' What *is* said of Holy Scripture is this: that it is written by those who *were* inspired; and next, that it *contains in* it (i.e. conjointly with Tradition) that salutaris veritas and morum disciplina (matters of faith and morals), of which the inspired Apostles were the fons. It will be observed also that the only teaching which is spoken of as committed to the Apostles, and for which they are said to have been inspired, is this matter of faith and morals, salutaris veritas et morum disciplina. Nothing is said of any other kind of knowledge as being the point of the gift. And this remark is corroborated by the decree which follows about the *interpretation* of Scripture, in which faith and morals are specially singled out as the matter, concerning which the Holy Fathers are the authoritative interpreters. 'Nemo, suae prudentiae innixus, *in rebus fidei et morum*, ad aedificationem *doctrinae Christianae* pertinentium, Sacram Scripturam ad suos sensus contorquens, contra eum sensum, quem tenuit et tenet Sancta Mater Ecclesia, cujus est judicare de vero sensu et interpretatione Scripturarum sanctarum, aut etiam contra unanimem consensum Patrum, ipsam Scripturam sanctam interpretari audeat, etc.' (Denz. 668 [1507]).

Such on the whole then is the teaching of Pope and Councils (the Catholic Church) concerning ⟨on the subject of⟩ the Holy Scriptures, as conveyed to us by the authoritative declarations of Popes and Councils. She teaches us by these supreme and sovereign informants that the Scriptures are sacred, authoritative, divine, the object of veneration, one of her foundations, the writing of inspired men *in* matters of faith and morals, and possessed of a fellow (parity of) claim upon our devotion and veneration with that which the traditions dictated by the Holy Ghost possess. No declaration of hers teaches us more than that the Scriptures are indirectly inspired as being the writing of inspired men; still less or again that every word of Scripture is inspired; or again ⟨and⟩ much less still, that any part is inspired except with a view to religious ⟨revealed⟩ truth and moral discipline. She does not prohibit us by any formal decree from holding that they are inspired; and we all do hold them to be so; but she does not oblige us to do so.

§ 5

On the available force of the definitions of the Church
on the inspiration ⟨authority⟩ of Holy Scripture.[1]

It may be objected, in answer to the mode of treating the definitions of
Holy Church, as adopted in the foregoing section, that it is a cold and grudging
faith which accepts nothing more than the letter of a dogmatic statement, and
subjects itself to the word of authority as little as ever it can. This is not the
temper of loving docility, of loyal devotion, of generous confidence, but of
distance and suspicion. Not to speak of the want of gratitude for so precious a
gift as the Bible, which is shown in measuring its divinity and in wishing to
think little of it, it is the sin of servility, which will not hear God's voice in
His Church, more than it cannot possibly help hearing it. Scripture itself
surely teaches us, that it is more pleasing to God if we ⟨for us to⟩ believe more
than to believe less. This is what may be said, and I observe upon it thus:-

As to accepting the definitions of the Church in their true and full meaning, I trust that nothing from me would ever tend to countenance any other
line of conduct towards them; by such acceptance I understand the honest
inquiry what the Church meant to propound in them, and the resolution
⟨termination⟩ of it in ⟨by⟩ a faithful appeal to the testimony of the Fathers
and divines upon them. But I do not consider it a throwing oneself into the
sense of a dogma to add to its definition something over and above it and
independent of it. When Nestorius professed the Article in the Creed that the
Son of God was made man, but refused to believe that strictly speaking He
was that man in whom the Incarnation resulted, he refused to throw himself
into the sense of the Church; but, had he refused to acknowledge that every
portion of the blood shed in the Passion was before His resurrection in
hypostatic union with the Word of God, he would have been refusing a doctrine which, whether true or not, was not intended by the Church in the 'Et
homo factus est,' and therefore would not have been evading her meaning.
And so again, in like manner, if, because we obtain ⟨gain⟩ through Christ a
new garment of justice to replace that which we lost in Adam (Conc. Trid. de
Justif. 7, vide Denz. 681 [1528]), I were to consider it only throwing myself
into the Tridentine doctrine to argue that, since Adam had the gift of immor-
tality before his fall, so do we receive it in baptism, and accordingly that no
one can die who is in the grace of God, that is, that no one is in matter of fact
saved because all do die, and to pronounce that this deduction of mine was to
be received as obligatory on ⟨by⟩ all Catholics de fide, I should be very
presumptuous as well as extravagant, and, instead of throwing myself in the
sense of the Church, should in matter of fact be throwing myself out of her
pale. And in like matter again, if I argue, from the Council's saying that

---

[1] The original title of this section was 'Opinions of Holy Fathers and Theologians of the
School on the inspiration ⟨authority⟩ of Holy Scripture'. It was probably changed at the
time Newman noted in pencil: 'Surely this section should be part of the Introduction February
17/63'; the number of the section was also superseded.

Scripture is sacred, divine, a foundation of the Church, the work of inspired men, that therefore it is, not only free from errors in historical details, but from errors of grammar and imperfection of language, and therefore that the earth, as Scripture says, *stat*, that is, never can move through space, I am saying that which must be judged on its own merits, and not as contained in the Synodal ⟨Catholic⟩ declarations about Scripture. It is not refusal of the teaching of the Church to remain in suspense about the truth of the inspiration of Scriptures, and of what inspiration means.

But this is not all that has to be said in answer to this objection. The definitions of the Church are not only a guide, but a support to the Catholic; they not only direct him into ⟨towards⟩ truth, but protect him from error; and educated persons require the latter benefit still more than the former, especially if they are laymen. Accordingly we shall find, that, if it be unkind to oneself to narrow a definition of faith, it is ⟨a presumption presumptuous⟩ unkind to others to expand it. I must explain what I think very important to bear in mind.

Observe how the case stands between Reason and Revelation; Reason is what is called 'in possession.' It can form its opinion on any question whatever which comes before it, and it has a right to do so except so far as Revelation has superseded its exercises by the certainty of a divine declaration. And where those declarations are proposed for its acceptance, it may not know, if so be, the evidence of their being portions of the divine revelation, it may be in a state of legitimate doubt whether they are portions of it or not, whether they all belong to it or which of them belong to it. It may be thrown upon the necessity of judging of the probability of their belonging to it by their intrinsic credibility; and thus, if left to itself, it may be in the way to reject by an act of private judgment what really comes from God. And moreover, it may happen that one or other of these portions of the divine revelation may be so strange to the imagination, so foreign to experience, so utterly remote from the reach ⟨investigations⟩ or deductions of reason, that the inquirer, if left to himself, would absolutely reject it as incredible, and that without any intention of rejecting the Word of God, if he knew for certain that this doctrine were a portion of it. Under these circumstances the expression of his state of mind would be this, 'I will believe it, if it be revealed — I will believe it so far forth as it is revealed. Otherwise, I cannot believe it at all.' In thus speaking he submits himself to the judgment of the Church. He believes the doctrine, if the Church has defined it — and so far forth as she has defined it — and he professes that he is ready to believe it, whenever the Church has defined. Or again he believes it, if it really has come down to us from Apostolic tradition, and whenever it shall be made clear to him that it belongs to Apostolic tradition. He believes it, if there is a *consensus* of Fathers and theologians in enunciating it, but otherwise he will not, he cannot believe it. If he is to accept it in spite of his imagination, without his experience, and against the anticipations of his reason, it must be as faith; it can be in no other way.

Such a doctrine is that our Saviour is God; such that His death has atoned for our sins; such that our race fell in Adam; such that there is everlasting punishment; such that there is everlasting life; such that the body will rise again; such is the divine predestination. One and the same doctrine is not a difficulty to all; one man feels this doctrine to be hard, another that. Some persons, many persons in this day, are greatly troubled at those portions of the Old Testament which appear to interfere with the discoveries of physical science. He will not take upon himself to say that they are absolutely proved, but they are so likely (verisimilia) on the whole, so probable from adducible facts and reasonings, they so hang together, they promise so much more of proof in their behalf in prospect, that he has grave misgivings lest he should be obliged to give up those impressions derived from the sacred text which hitherto he has cordially and unsuspiciously accepted. What is to hinder him from wiping away some of those impressions from his mind? He is answered that Scripture is the Word of God? he replies, in what sense? is it *all* Scripture? Who says so? Nothing has a claim to subject reason but faith. Till he comes under the shadow of God's Word and Wisdom he must guide himself by his own; and it may happen that his own so overpowers him with a sense of the incontrovertibility of its deductions, that nothing can subdue it but his conviction of possessing a more trustworthy informant; — nothing can make him, or has a claim to make him, put aside his own judgment, but the luminous assurance that God has spoken contrariwise. In such awful conflicts, when they occur, between the internal and the external voice, he has a plain right, and duty, to demand whether God has spoken, and what he has said, and to look very sharply that he gets a really good and distinct answer to his question. What his reason has accepted is, I do not say so true, (for that would be closing the question altogether, for truth cannot contradict truth) but so specious ⟨plausible⟩, so like truth, that he will continue to accept it, till some more satisfactory information says that it is not true. Such would be the voice of the Omniscient God. His voice, ruling the point in question the other way, is the most absolute of demonstrations. Has it spoken in the particular case before us? if not, I will remain where I am. Has God said that the sun goes round the earth? if not, I will believe that the earth goes round the sun. Scripture, you tell me, says 'Terra autem stat;' and 'stat' means has no motion in space. This is what you say; but has God said 'the earth has no motion in space?' Are those words 'Terra stat' in any sense the direct words of God? or are they the words of Ecclesiastes? And, if they are immediately His Words, is this the meaning of them? I will yield to express Revelation, because God knows better than I. If God has said it, I will bow my own reason, and distrust, discard my own reasonings; but I will bow to nothing else; I will not submit in this matter to the greatest of theologians, to the highest of Saints, because they knew nothing at all about physics; I will yield to nothing but God speaking through His Church, to nothing but a definition de fide or to its equivalent. Has the Church ever said, 'God says by me, God has said in the Written

Word, that the earth is fixed in space and moves not?' — Such is my case; and what is ungrateful, jealous, disloyal in such a careful questioning? What that is not on the contrary generous, straightforward, and rational in exercising it?

This is why it is so necessary to inquire what the Church distinctly teaches, in the name of God, about the authority of the Scriptures. This is why I make much of the fact that she has nowhere in her definitions declared that they are inspired. Mgr Bouvier declares that, though she has not done so, yet their inspiration is 'most certain.' Well, but why is it certain? On the answer to this question it depends whether I am bound to believe it or no. It is a human certainty; unless it be founded on the infallible word of God, who can neither deceive, nor be deceived. I as well as that revered theologian say that it is a most certain truth; but till this point is answered, I will not at once put it on a level with divinely declared truths, I will not impose it on the consciences of others. How can I, when I cannot give them the support and the protection of the Adorable enunciation of the Most High to enable them to subdue the risings of their own intellect? I can only tell them that they ought to be very certain of their scientific conclusions, if they issue in a contradiction of the express declarations of documents written by inspired men; but if they still persist and will maintain that it is as clear to them as day that the earth goes round the sun, I can but say to them, 'Perhaps Scripture does not say the contrary,' — or, if that will not do, 'perhaps Scripture is not inspired in matters physical.' And then if they say, that the Father Commissary thought the contrary in the case of Galileo, I answer that individual theologians are not the Church, and that the Church, whether represented by Pope or Council, has determined nothing about the inspiration of the Scripture text at all.

Now to apply what has been said to questions of this day. 'People come and tell me that the book of Genesis is made up of various documents; am I called on *de fide* to believe that it is all written by one author, and him Moses?' No: — 'then I need not fret myself about the chance of some collision, as time goes on, on this matter between criticism and faith'.

'The book of Psalms clearly seems to me the work of various authors; am I bound under an anathema to believe that it is all written by David?' Certainly not: — 'then I need not fear to open my mind to such principles of investigation and sources of information as prove or assume that they are written in successive centuries'.[1]

'I have difficulty in believing that the book of Ecclesiastes is written by Solomon: am I bound to do so?' By no means.[2]

'Am I bound to believe any single word of the book of Esther dictated from above?' there is nothing at all to bind you so that *you hold from thy heart* that it is sacred and canonical.

[1] Newman later referred to Pallavicino.
[2] Newman later noted: 'Carthage and Innocent say they are, Canus says "not de fide". Vid Canus on this point about the 5 books'.

'The verse about the enrolments in the presidency of Cyrenius in Luke ii is difficult to reconcile with the facts of history; am I bound to maintain its chronological exactness?' You are bound to do so, when a definition of the Church is adduced from which that exactness legitimately follows.

'I cannot help doubting the genuineness of the text of the Three Heavenly Witnesses; must I suppress these doubts?' You must think many times before you allow yourself to doubt; but if you ask me whether the Church has definitely pronounced or implied the genuineness of that verse, I am bound to tell you that she has not done so.[1]

'I cannot believe that there were only fourteen generations from David to the captivity ⟨deportation of the people to⟩ (transmigration to Babylon), I believe there were four besides, though St. Matthew says, "From David to the transmigration of Babylon are fourteen generations;"' You need not believe it, but you should keep yourself in that state of mind, as to be ready to believe it to be true, should the Church ever determine, as a dogmatic fact, that there were not eighteen generations, but only fourteen.

I conclude from all that has been said, that, by a grudging and suspicious faith is meant, not the refusing to take for dogma what is not in the determinations of the Church, but to be ready to accept as dogma whatever more the Church in time to come may determine than she has determined. In other words, faith in the Church, in order not to be cold and niggardly, must be *implicit*. I have remarks on this subject in my Anglican Difficulties, Lecture xi;[2] and my Essay on Development is founded on the same truth.[3]

---

[1] Newman again referred to Pallavicino.

[2] See e.g. *Certain Difficulties felt by Anglicans in Catholic Teaching*, London 1901, vol.I, pp. 350–1; *An Essay on the Development of Christian Doctrine*, London 1906, pp. 326–7.

[3] In Newman's MSS. notebook, §6 'On the teaching of the schools concerning the Inspiration of Scripture' began as follows:

'I said just now that real acceptance of the definitions of the Church was an acceptance of them in their full meaning, and that this meaning was that which a consensus of Fathers and divines gave to them. The question follows, whether allowing that the inspiration of Scripture has ⟨is⟩ not been declared by Popes or Council, nevertheless it is not a dogma of faith from the concurrent belief in it by Fathers and divines, and in consequence of the fact of an apostolical tradition upon the point, which that concurrence implies. Bouvier says that the inspiration is certissimum; Canus lays down that "Sancti simul omnes in fidei dogmati errare non possunt"; and that "concordia omnium theologorum schola, de fide aut moribus, sententiam contradicem, si haeresis non est, at haeresi proximum". This certainty then, which as Bouvier says belongs to the doctrine of the inspiration of Scripture, does it arise from such a concurrence of as Canus speaks of Fathers and theologians?' The rest of this section was superseded or deleted.

§7 'The teaching of the Holy Fathers concerning the inspiration of Scripture' consists of one page which reads: 'Doubtless the teaching of the Fathers concerning the inspiration of Scripture is much higher, as it may be called, than the modern teaching; but this will seem to be the case far more at first sight than when we examine the circumstances under which they do so. It is accounted for by this simple circumstance, that the Canon of Scripture was not the same to them as it is to us. Since the age of most of them the deuterocanonical books have been received by the Church; and it will be found, as is natural, that, in consequence of ⟨according as⟩ the number of sacred books has increased, the idea of inspiration has been lowered. It stands to reason that the divine operation necessarily implied in prophecies ⟨a prophecy⟩ such as the book Isaias is not implied in the additional chapters of the book of Daniel'. See below pp. 82, 88, 94–96.

§ 3

[The Biblical Evidence[1]]

From what has already been incidentally said, we may gather[2] that little has been defined by the Church or handed down by tradition on the subject of Inspiration. Inspiration being granted as a fact, it would still appear ⟨still we are left⟩ very much to ourselves to determine its nature, mode and influence in the canonical books, and it is upon the answers to these questions that its relation to human science must depend. However, I must not lightly assume that so little has been told us on the subject; accordingly, I shall investigate successively what light is thrown upon it by Scripture, the decisions of the Church, and the teaching of Theologians; and after bringing this examination to an end, I shall state and defend my own view of the matter.[3]

And first on the testimony given by Scripture concerning its own inspiration.

It stands to reason vide Malou t 2 p 26 that the Bible, considered as one volume or whole, cannot recognize itself, for its books were collected into the sacred Canon at various times, down to the fourth century of our era. Till then, it did not exist as one, and therefore it predicates nothing of itself, and inclusively, not its inspiration. Yet, true as this is, still it so happens that more can be gathered in proof of its inspiration from its own pages, than from the definitions of the Church and the consent of theologians. Its testimony about itself, as far as it goes, is both clear and consistent; it is as follows.

A revelation in its very idea involves the necessity of organs through which it is made. These organs or instruments under the Old Covenant, were called prophets; under the New, Evangelists and Apostles; and, from the fact of their being organs, their instrumentality consists into their enunciating distinctly, and purely, without error, and professing to enunciate, the truths of the revelation. This they cannot do except by means of ⟨from⟩ a divine gift, and this gift is that of divine dictation or inspiration.

This view of the subject, which arises out of the nature of the case, is fully exemplified in the sacred writings. Under both Covenants the gift of inspiration was the qualification of the organ of the revelation. When Moses pleaded his want of eloquence, Almighty God said Exod 4 'Who made man's mouth? or who made the dumb and the deaf, the seeing and the blind? Ego ero in ore tuo, doceboque te quid loquaris.' Then, allowing Aaron to be his spokesman ⟨assistant⟩. He says 'Ipse loquetur pro te ad populum, et erit os tuum; tu autem eris ei in his quae ad Deum pertinent.' Here too we see in what matters his inspiration consisted; 'in his quae ad Deum pertinent,' theological truth.

---

[1] This is §3 in Newman's MSS. notebook, see below, p. 64.
Fr. Seynaeve entitled this section 'On the Scripture Argument' from Newman's note of 23 July 1861.
[2] Originally the first sentence read: 'It is plain, from what has already been said incidentally, that has been sufficiently to suggest to us.'
[3] Compare this with Newman's later plan on p. 39.

In like manner of Josue: Tolle Josue filium Nun, virum in quo est Spiritus, et pone manum tuam super eum. Num. 27.

Before these instances, the same gift of inspiration was witnessed to by Pharaoh in the case of Joseph: Num invenire poterimus talem virum, qui Spiritu Dei plenus est. Gen. 41.

And so in the case of Samuel. His first words are his answer to Almighty God, Loquere Domine quia audit servus tuus; 1 Kings 3 and then we are told, Dominus erat cum eo, et non cecidit ex omnibus ejus in terram. And it was known to all Israel that he was fidelis propheta Domini.

As to the Prophets of future events, St Peter does but declare generally, what without his saying it, is a necessary truth. Non voluntate humanâ allata est aliquando prophetia; sed, Spiritu Sancto inspirati, locuti sunt sancti Dei homines. 2 Pet. 1.

What the Prince of the Apostles ascribed to the Prophets, that the first ⟨most eminent⟩ of the Prophets predicted of the Apostles and their successors. Isai. 59 fin.

Hoc foedus meum cum eis, dicit Dominus; Spiritus meus, qui est in te, et verba mea, quae posui in ore tuo, non recedant de ore tuo, et de ore seminis tui, et de ore seminis seminis tui, dicit Dominus, amodo et usque in sempiternum.

Thus the gift was promised in continuance from the Old Covenant to the New, and in the history of the New Covenant we read of its bestowal.

First our Lord says, 'When they shall deliver you up, take no thought how or what to speak; for it shall be given you in that hour what to speak. For it is not you that speak, but the Spirit of your Father that [speaks]. Non enim vobis estis qui loquimini, sed Spiritus Patris vestri qui loquitur in vobis' Matt. 10. 'Spiritus Sanctus docebit vos in ipsâ horâ quid oportet vos dicere.' Luke 12. And again, 'Ego dabo vobis os et sapientiam.' Luke 21. Again, 'Paraclitus, Spiritus Sanctus, quem mittet Pater in nomine meo, ille vos docebit omnia.' John 14. 'Cum venerit ille Spiritus veritatis, docebit vos omnem veritatem.' [John 16: 13.] Further, when our Lord was departing, He told them not to depart from Jerusalem, but 'exspectarent promissionem Patris, quia baptiza-bimini Spiritu Sancto.' Acts 1. This, we know, was fulfilled on the day of Pentecost, and forthwith first St Peter spoke 'repletus Spiritu Sancto,' Acts 4, and St Stephen both before his ordination is said to be 'plenus Spiritu Sancto et sapientiâ,' and after his speech which issued in his martyrdom again to be 'plenus Spiritu Sancto.'

So much as to the inspiration of the instruments of the Revelation; next, that these men, so endowed, wrote great part of the Bible is certain, and there is no reason to be given why, if they were inspired in speaking, they should not be inspired in writing; and every reason to be sure that they were, if they profess to write as if ex cathedrâ and on matters of the Revelation. Such writing, beyond all doubt, must be accounted the Evangelical History (as it may be called) contained in the books of Genesis, Exodus, and Numbers; the Decalogue and Jewish ritual; the recapitulation of the Law, and the instructions and exhortations, delivered by Moses in Deuteronomy; the Psalter; more or less the Proverbs; the Prophets; except Jonas and part of Daniel; the four Evangelists; St Paul's Epistles except Philemon; those of the other Apostles; and the Apocalypse.

Further these writers, in the course of their writings, appeal to their mission and endowments, and profess to be speaking the words of the Most High. 'Thus saith the Lord' is the ordinary formula by which they assert their dogmatic authority, in the Old Testament. In like manner in the New Testament, (we read in Acts xxi 'Thus saith the Holy Ghost'). St Paul says, 'I think that I also have the Spirit of God.' 1 Cor. 7. Again, 'Nobis revelavit Deus per Spiritum suum.' 1 Cor. 2 'Deus illuxit in cordibus nostris, ad illuminationem scientiae charitatis Dei etc' 2 Cor. 4. 'Neque ab homine accepi' my gospel (Evangelium) 'neque didici sed per revelationem Jesu Christi' Gal. 1; and this is his ground for having said, 'Licit *nos*, aut Angelus,' preach to you any other gospel, 'anathema sit.' He gives thanks that his converts receive his preaching 'non ut verbum hominum, sed, sicut est vera, Verbum Dei;' 1 Thess. 2, and says that 'qui hoc spernit, non hominem spernit, sed Deum, qui etiam dedit Spiritum Sanctum in nobis.' 1 Thess. 4. Elsewhere 'Spiritus manifeste dicit, etc.' 1 Tim. 4. It is then impossible to doubt that St Paul declares deliberately and unequivocally the inspiration of what he has written. To the same purpose St Peter speaks of St Paul writing his Epistles 'secundum datam sibi sapientiam.' It is observable that in St Peter's words, quoted above in behalf of the inspiration of the Prophets, he not only speaks of them, but of their writings: 'omnis prophetia *Scripturae* propriâ interpretatione non fit', is his introduction to his testimony to the inspiration of the Prophets.

Though then the Bible as a whole cannot speak of itself and though the inspiration of the writers does not involve the inspiration of all they said, or of the books in which their speeches or writings are embodied, large portions speak distinctly of their own inspiration. The claims ⟨texts⟩ already quoted or referred to cover a great deal of ground. But this is not all; books, which are not on *the face* of them written by inspired men, still contain portions which profess to be inspired. Josue, as we have seen, had the Holy Spirit given to him, in order to succeed Moses; and it is said that even 'Eleazar the priest' Num. 27, before? or through Josue 'consulit Dominum.' Again the last three chapters of the book called after him, consist of his speeches. Other parts, as the whole of the first chapter is nothing else professedly than a divine message. Other passages are prefaced by 'Dixit Dominus.' Judges in like manner contains various Angelic communications, and the whole of the 5th chapter is the canticle of the Prophetess Debbora.

Moreover to all the books of the Jewish canon St Paul must be considered to bear witness, when, after saying that St Timothy from his infancy had 'known the Holy Scriptures,' he adds 'all Scripture, omnis scriptura, divinitus, inspirata, utilis est ad docendum etc.' 2 Tim. 3.

This testimony of St Paul is as large as the Apostle could give in his day, because the Jewish canon was the only canon formed; but he and others of the sacred writers of the New Testament supply a multitude of testimonies in detail to the different books of which that canon is composed. The fact of their appealing to them, and still further, their mode of appealing, is in most cases an evidence of the authority of those books in a case where authority cannot be at all without inspiration. They appeal to them under such formulas as 'It is written' 'Scripture saith' ⟨'The Holy Ghost says by David, etc.⟩ which in themselves imply the authority of the documents to which the appeal is made, and still more so, when we find that such phrases were ⟨are⟩ the very forms in use among the Rabbins themselves. Whatever pre-eminent authority the Jewish commentators? gave to their own Scripture, such the writers of the New Testament give to their also. (vide Davidson, Hermeneutics, p. 449).

And then as to the number of quotations thus made in the New Testament from the Old; these are no fewer than from 253 to 254 or 255 (Davidson); the books quoted being: Genesis, Exodus, Leviticus, Numbers, Deuteronomy, 1 Kings, 2 and 3 Kings, the Psalter, Proverbs, Job, Isaias, Michaeas, Osee, Jeremias, Malachias, Zacharias, Joel, Amos, Habacuc, Haggaeus, Daniel, that is, all the books except Josue, Judges, Ruth, 4 Kings, Paralipomenon, Esdras, Esther, Ecclesiastes, Canticles, Ezechiel, Abdias, Jonas, Nahum and Sophonias; or [14] out of the 22 books of the Jewish Canon. Besides this, there are various? allusions to other books, as to Jonas; not to say that the Apocalypse is based on an accurate knowledge of Isaias, Ezechiel, and Daniel. Perhaps too there is an allusion to Ecclesiastes xi in John iii, 8.[1]

It is remarkable moreover, that, though the Deutero-canonical books (is this right term?) of the Old Testament are not expressly referred to as authorities in the New, various allusions to them occur there, investing them with a religious character. Such may be even the passage intended by St James, which he calls 'the Scripture,' and which cannot clearly be referred to any extant writing, but which has been considered (by Witstein) to refer to Wisdom vi, 11. 23 (Greek. 12.15 Vulgate) St. Paul in Hebrews recognizes a passage of Wisdom and explains it of Enoch. Hebr. xi. 5 with Wisdom iv, 10. 2 Pet. ii with Wisdom x. 6. The epithet 'just' given to Lot by St Peter, unsupported by any notice in the books of the Jewish Canon, is apparently taken from the book of Wisdom. The passage in Romans i on the subject of natural religion, of the lapse into idolatry and corruptions in morals, together with the very structure of the sentences treating it, seems borrowed from Wisdom xiii and xiv. The language about the potter in Romans ix, is taken from Eccles. xxxiii, 13, 14; and a somewhat parallel passage in 2 Timothy from Wisdom

---

[1] Newman later also noted in pencil:
'Ecclesiastes in John 3. 8?
with allusions to Jonas 4 Kings Numbers.'

xv, 7. Our Lord, in His parable of the man with much goods, seems to be using Ecclesiasticus xi. 18, 19; and in that of the importunate widow He follows Ecclus. xxxv. 15–19 clause by clause; St Paul in Rom. xii. 15 seems to refer to Ecclus. vii. 34, and in 2 Cor. vi. 14, to Ecclus. xiii, 17; St Paul's 'sacrificing to devils and not to God' 1 Cor. x. 20 seems taken from Baruch iv. 7. Esther says, 'Give me an eloquent speech in my mouth before the *Lion*' meaning the Persian King, while St Paul speaks of being 'delivered out of the mouth of the lion.'

These instances suggest to us a broader and remarkable fact that a further remark is true ⟨what may be said on the whole,⟩ and which forms in itself, independent of all professions of the sacred writers, a noticeable internal proof, or at least confirmation of such evidence as I have been offering from their express words, of the inspiration of the Bible. That there is that minute connexion between nearly the whole of Scripture, part by part, that, though it be not one book, it bears strong evidence of its coming from one origin; and if that origin be supernatural, that is, inspiration, in our case, it is probably such in all. And this remark might be followed out in detail quite ⟨most⟩ marvellously as regards, for instance, our Lord's teaching and St James' with St Paul's, and next, without assuming any part to be supernatural, this harmony of teaching in itself creating ⟨giving⟩ a strong reason for saying that one Spirit, and therefore one supernatural Spirit is the animating principle of the whole.

There is another obvious reflection to be kept in view and it is of the first importance. If the sacred authors were not inspired, and yet [claimed] so pointedly that they themselves and each other were, what are we to think of them? For what are they trustworthy witnesses if they can be mistaken in this cardinal point? How can we believe anything they have said on the ground of their saying it, if they are incorrect here? What truth of religion can we believe on their authority, if sic? Thus there is no middle ground between believing they come from God [and] discarding them altogether as religious teachers.

This then is the sort of evidence which Scripture offers to us for its own inspiration.

III Ecclesiastical Teaching and Biblical Inspiration, 1863

March 7, 1863

On The Idea and Prima Facie Aspect
of the Inspiration of Scripture[1]

§ 1

By Inspiration is meant literally a 'breathing into'; thus involving in its notion, a breath, an agent ⟨a source⟩ from whom the breath ⟨which it⟩ comes, and (a recipient ⟨subject⟩ into which it passes.) Such is its active sense; but it may also be taken passively for the state or habit of its recipient after the action has taken place.

The appropriateness of the word in theology arises from the circumstance that the word 'spirit' or breath is used in Scripture both for the Supreme Being and for His gifts. Divine Inspiration in its active sense is Almighty God's ⟨the Creator's⟩ communication to the creature of Himself, Altissimi donum Dei, viz., the Third Person of the Blessed Trinity, or again of certain powers or qualities, intimately His, and beyond nature; In its passive sense, it denotes the state of the creature consequent upon that communication.

Thus, when God 'formed man out of the mud of the earth,' 'inspiravit in faciem ejus spiraculum vitae,' and 'man became a living soul.' This was an inspiration, and was being a gift over and above the creation of the animal frame. Again, in one of the visions of Ezechiel, the Prophet is directed to pray over the multitude of corpses which lay upon the face of the plain in these words, 'Veni, Spiritus, et insuffla super interfectos istos, that they may revive.' Here is a second inspiration of life; exercised on a corpse. Again; 'Thou shalt send forth Thy Spirit, and they shall be created; and Thou shalt renew the face of the earth.' Here too inspiration is the communication of a quality, viz., restoration, or refreshment to a subject already existing. In this instance, it is true, creation is also mentioned; 'et creabuntur;' but ⟨by the power which is spoken of as exerted need not be meant anything else but the concursus, of which divines speak, with which the Almighty, in His work of creation, aids the nascent creature in order to its being duly brought into being. And, if it need mean nothing else, there is no reason for putting a sense on the word 'inspiration' inconsistent with its etymology?⟩[2] this is not really the case, as will be seen by referring to the preceding verse. The word creation means

---

[1] Newman wrote this whole section in a distinct notebook from C; Father Seynaeve referred to it as Document H, see pp. 55*–6*.
[2] The words in angle brackets were crossed out.

merely formation of the existing material ⟨dust⟩ into a living being, in opposition to the preceding verse. 'Thou shalt take away their breath, and they shall return to the dust.'

Such being the general meaning of the theological term, it designates, when applied to men ⟨mankind⟩, those favoured persons whose minds God has visited with a peculiar presence or grace, which remains within them, giving them powers or characteristics which they had not before. They speak, they act under its influence; and their deeds and words, in the province and for the object of their inspiration have a claim upon the veneration and acceptance of their fellows, as being more than human, as being referable to a divine origin.

What that province is and that object of the inspiration of the Prophets and Apostles, is very determinate. It is religious truth. Moses, Isaias, St Peter, St John, St Paul, and their fellows have in their respective times been introduced into special direct intercourse with Almighty God, and have been favoured with supernatural knowledge. This has been their privilege, but that privilege has been, not for their own sake merely, but for the sake of all mankind. They have been chosen as the instruments of the Lord of all, in dispelling the ignorance in which the race of Adam lies so far as is necessary for their fulfilling adequately the ends of their creation. They have been raised to the dignity of divine messengers and representatives, and commanded to communicate to others what has been communicated to them. First, they have been recipients ⟨received⟩ [of] the revelation; next they have been organs of it.

Having received then, and having to transmit, their first duty is fidelity to Him who has put them in trust. Thus St Paul says, 'As we were approved of God that the Gospel should be committed to us, even so we speak, not as pleasing men, but God who proveth our hearts.' 1 Thess. ii. And St Peter and St John 'We cannot but speak the things which we have seen and heard'. Acts iv.

But since ⟨if⟩ their natural powers were not equal to the attainment of the knowledge revealed to the Prophets and Apostles, why should they be any more equal to their transmission? There was needed then some provision, and some guarantee, that they should be able to report the supernatural message adequately. Their memory, and intellect, and language needed to be as exact as their hearts were faithful; so that they might deliver, without addition or diminution, just what they had received. They needed to be made infallible. This gift, being supplemental to the act of revelation itself, is what is meant by the *inspiration* of the Apostles and Prophets, of the sacred writers, of Holy Scripture.

Moses asked and obtained this supplemental gift, when, on God's appearance to him in the burning bush, after first shrinking back in dismay from a deep feeling of his need of it. 'The Lord said, Come, I will send thee to Pharao, that thou mayst bring forth my [people?] out of Egypt. And Moses said ... I beseech Thee, Lord, I am not eloquent; and, since Thou hast spoken to Thy servant, I have more impediment and slowness of tongue ... The Lord said to him, Go, and I will be in thy mouth, and I will teach thee what thou shalt speak.' St Paul, in like manner, when speaking of the preaching of the Gospel, exclaims, 'Who is sufficient for these things?' He continues 'not that we are sufficient to think anything of ourselves, as of ourselves, but our sufficiency is of God, who hath made us sufficient for the ministry of the New Testament.' This sufficiency, which is in fact infallibility, is the end and the effect of inspiration.

And, since the end contemplated in inspiration is the correct enunciation of what has been revealed, therefore with an appropriateness over and above the more obvious meaning of the phrase, the Holy Ghost is called 'the Spirit of Truth;' for He not only reveals what is eternally true, but secures a true, that is, a faithfully exact, report of it from [the] mouths ⟨by the hands⟩ of the Apostles. 'The Paraclete, the Holy Ghost, will teach you all things, and *bring all things to your mind* whatsoever I shall have said to you ... When the Paraclete cometh, the Spirit of Truth, He shall give *testimony* of Me.' And this would seem to be implied in the words, 'When He, the Spirit of Truth, is come, He will teach you all truth; for He shall not speak of Himself, but what things soever He shall *hear*, He shall speak.' He is not only the source, but He is the safeguard of the revelation.

Let us then consider Inspiration to be that spiritual endowment, whereby the recipients of a revelation are enabled, to be adequate ⟨sufficient⟩ organs of the matters revealed, and that, whether by word or by deed. Here, however, we are only concerned with the gift, as regards their words, and, of their words, only their written words, not their vocal.

§ 2

If I have been giving a correct account of inspiration, there is no difficulty in understanding what is meant by saying that a Prophet or Apostle is inspired. It means that an illumination from the source of knowledge is imparted to him and possesses him, and enables him to speak on religious subjects with an extent ⟨a fulness⟩, an exactness, and a certainty which is impossible to unassisted human nature. This is intelligible; but it is not so obvious what is meant by predicating inspiration of a writing. What is meant by saying that words and letters, written with a pen, inscribed upon wax, or printed by types, have in them a secret divine gift, and are different from other words, spoken by whomsoever?

An inspired Prophet exists before his inspiration; he is a man as other men; he has a human mind, human thoughts, human knowledge. Inspiration does not create, does not destroy his human nature; it adds to it. It raises him in religious thought and knowledge above himself. He is breathed into and filled with a power greater than what nature has given him; but nature is still there.

And inspiration might leave him again, and then he would be what he was before he was inspired. The notion denoted by the metaphorical expression is exactly satisfied ⟨fulfilled⟩. But the words of inspired men do not exist before they are written, that is, before their inspiration; what then is it which it is breathed into? and when they actually are written ⟨brought into writing⟩, what is that breath, that supernatural gift, which makes them more than themselves? And how could inspiration leave them? for what and when would they be, were they reduced to the state in which they were before inspiration came upon them?

This is the point to which we must now direct our attention.[1]

1. Does the inspiration of the words of Holy Scripture mean that those words are actually *dictated* by Almighty God? This is the highest view which can be taken of their sacred character; and it has been taken. (At the moment I will neither assent to it, nor deny it). But first, in proportion as it raises the sacredness of Scripture, so on the other hand it lowers the dignity of the inspired writer, who becomes a mere instrument or organ, etc. etc. I will only say that it [dictation] represents an idea very different from any which the term ⟨word⟩ 'inspiration' is capable of bearing ⟨receiving⟩ in the proper meaning of the word. Dictation differs from inspiration in kind; one of these can never be the other. In everyday matters of the world, we tell of a man's dictating a letter; in that case he does everything but use his own hand. On the contrary, we speak of a journal, or review, being written under the inspirations of the ministry ⟨government⟩ or some political party; by this we mean that as far as the purposes of government or of the particular party are concerned, the spirit breathed into it, the spirit it breathes, is conservative, or liberal, or progressive, or the like as the case may be. Portions of such a journal ⟨the publication⟩ indeed may actually be dictated by the persons whose organ it is; but, looking at it as a whole, as an existing publication which, without ceasing to give the general news of the world, law intelligence, commercial intelligence and whatever a newspaper contains, is, over and above all this, the channel

---

[1] Newman later noted: I do not deny it is a difficult one. The easiest solution would be to say that the word inspiration is applied to Scripture by a metonymy, as being the writing of inspired men, but this would be repugnant to the common feeling of Catholics as well as to the letter of Scripture itself. March 22 1863. This resolution of the question (that it is a metonymy) I should adopt, it would avoid a host of difficulties — did I not find the popular feeling and the sentiment of divines opposed to it. As to St Paul's declaration about 'divinely inspired Scripture,' I do not see that it interferes with the view I speak of; for, as theologians interpret his doctrine that concupiscence is sin to mean the cause or consequence of sin, so by a parallel figure he may be taken to mean that Scripture is not inspired, but the effect of inspiration, i.e. in inspired men. Nay, considering St Augustine? speaks on the same subject (concupiscence) as strongly as St Paul yet is not taken to the letter by theologians, so in like manner theologians themselves may be taken to speak with a natural figure when they say that Scripture is inspired. However, I shall not insist on this point, and since Mgr Bouvier in his dogmatic course says that the inspiration of Scripture 'licet non de fide, certissima est,' I ⟨we⟩ will here take his words as enunciating a theological truth.

Newman also noted at this point:

N.B. State these four as *explanations, all* of which I receive, but especially the fourth. March 16, 1863 [and later still] N.B. Should not I notice the distinction between res et sententiae and verbal inspiration? though I confess I cannot understand the former *except as giving up* the inspiration in every minute part. March 22, 1863.

⟨informant⟩ and advocate of Whig measures or Tory measures, we should say that it was under the inspiration of this or that political party. I am using this illustration, not as a sufficient description of what inspiration is, but in order to mark the difference between dictation and inspiration.

2. Next, shall we, instead of confusing two ideas which are simply distinct from each other, consider that, when Scripture is said to be inspired, the intrinsic gift which is denoted as supernaturally imparted, is that it is absolutely and in all matters the Truth? This is a view which also has been maintained by great authorities, and it is the lowest view of inspiration, as dictation is the highest. That inspiration is given in order that Scripture may be true, is undoubted, and I have already stated it; but ⟨or⟩ truth is the end ⟨object⟩ of inspiration, it is the effect of the gift, but not that in which the gift consists. The question is, what is meant by the *inspiration* of Scripture; but it may be every word true, yet only in portions inspired. The theological writings of St Gregory Nazianzen are said to be free in all parts from any error; yet they are not inspired. As dictation expresses one idea and inspiration another; so it is one thing to be inspired, and another thing to be true. If it be said that considering on the one hand the profundity and on the other hand the variety of the matters contained in Scripture to be absolutely exact is a supernatural gift; this is certain; but that exactness ⟨it⟩ requires a supernatural gift in the writers; it is not synonymous with some such gift in the writing itself. As then dictation is more than inspiration, so it would seem that exactitude is less.

3. But this may be said: — the inspiration of Scripture consists in its quasi-sacramental power. It has a force, an influence, and an operation, which is simply supernatural. This gift is described in the words of the Prophet: — 'As the rain and snow come down from heaven, and give seed to the sower, and bread to the eater, so shall My word be, which shall go forth from my mouth; it shall not return to Me void; but it shall do whatsoever I please, and shall prosper in the things for which I sent it.' If such be the gift of inspiration, inherent in Scripture, it implies ⟨follows⟩ that Scripture language can do what no other words can do, though the sense of those other words be the same. A blessing and a success will go with the use of the sacred text, which will not follow from any mere words of man. The announcement 'the Word was made flesh,' or, 'By grace you are saved through faith,' will have a power to affect the heart and change the life, which the same truth spoken in the words of St Athanasius or St Augustine will not have. Our Lord's prayer will kindle our affections and help us in devotion, as no other prayer can. The Psalter will create a union in ⟨united⟩ worship, more spiritual, more sublime, more affectionate, than any hymns which St Ambrose or St Thomas has left as legacies to Holy Church. As the form in baptism sanctifies the water and impregnates it with grace, as the Eucharistic words effect a transubstantiation, so all the words of canonical Scripture will ⟨may⟩ in their degree possess a sanctifying, a transforming power in the soul; by virtue of that Spirit which

dwells in them; and thus in a large sense will be fulfilled our Lord's saying, 'The words that I have spoken to you, are spirit and life.'

I do not in any way question the correctness of this representation either. Scripture certainly has in it a power, and carries with it a blessing, which no writing but the Word of God can show. Still other writings and other preachings and discourses have and had a like influence in their degree. Are we to say then that these have a portion of inspiration also? Is it a question of more or less inspiration between St Paul and St Vincent Ferrer? Again, have not some uninspired sermons or writings had more powerful effects than certain portions of Scripture? If the power of touching the heart, converting the sinful, consoling the troubled or instructing the devout are to be the criterion of inspiration, has not the Imitation of Christ more claims to be considered an inspired work than the Book of Esther or the second book of Maccabees?

For these reasons I cannot acquiesce in the doctrine that the inspiration of Scripture consists in the special force of the letter, as applied to the soul, though I do not doubt that a special force really exists.

4. Perhaps it will be said that by the supernatural breath which dwells in the text of Scripture is meant its ⟨the⟩ divine meaning, (of the letter). This perhaps is the most satisfactory account of it; (but it is *not*? clear enough to stand instead of a definition). Verbal inspiration will then ⟨mean the⟩ be considered to lie in heavenly doctrine, instruction ⟨teaching⟩, warning, or consolation, such as man could not give, which is conveyed to us through the words of Moses or Jeremias, Paul, or John.

Two questions have to be answered here; first, what is the inspired sense of Scripture, and next how it is to be ascertained. As to the former, here, however, the first question which occurs is, ⟨it is obvious to remark, that⟩ the text has more than one sense; which of these is given by inspiration? The double sense of Scripture is frequent in prophecy; and, in devotional works, every part of Scripture yields, not two only, but an indefinite number of spiritual and mystical meanings. Are all these inspired senses? That they have been all foreseen by the Divine Author of inspiration, and that they are allowable and edifying, as being drawn from ⟨ascribed to⟩ the sacred text by His own dear children, who are inhabited by the same spirit which is present in it, this is certain; but are they His sense? if they are the sense of inspiration, they are of authority; and this no one would say of such devotional applications of the text of Scripture as I have in mind. When Scripture is emphatically called 'the Word of God,' it is considered surely in that sense in which God spoke it. Every sentence of Scripture is His Word, viewed in that divine sense; for though a portion of it is in its first instance ⟨origin⟩ the word of man, as the speeches introduced into the historical and other portions, yet He has, as it were, spoken the whole of it over again and made it His even in those human parts by the new sense or drift which He has put into them. This is the inspired sense; and it is the presence of this divine authoritative voice in Scripture, as it is in no other writings, which constitutes its inspiration.

As to the second question, who is to ascertain the sense of Scripture, the answer to a Catholic is easy. (However, this view is not without its difficulties). Who is to declare *what* Almighty God has spoken through ⟨in⟩ the letter of Scripture? Every Catholic will answer, that the Church is its divinely appointed, ⟨the authoritative⟩ interpreter in that divine authoritative sense. There cannot be a more important and necessary truth; but it seems to follow from it that we only know in part and probably what the divine sense is. The Church has never taken on herself an authoritative comment in extenso. She has in the long course of controversies shed light upon particular passages, and fixed and ratified the meaning of particular texts. Again, she has forbidden certain interpretations, and specially such as run counter to the unanimous consent of the Fathers. But as to the Scriptures in their length and breadth, that meaning which is inspired has never yet been determined, and still remains in the bosom of the Church. The comments of great doctors, though vested with great 'authority,' are still human; they are not the voice of the Infallible God. The adaptations of mystical writings are most important for the purposes of meditation and devotion; but they are no guide to the exegetical theologian.

If this be the true view of what is meant by ⟨the meaning of⟩ the inspiration of Scripture, the phrase means that there is in every word and clause ⟨part of it⟩ a sense, or senses, which is divine, in consequence of which it is the Word of God, and claims our absolute homage and our profound faith. At the same time this sense is in great measure still latent in the letter, and at most only probably known, so as not to claim our implicit acceptance in the unconditional way with which we embrace the dogmas of the Catholic Church.

5.[1] To some persons (if to any one) this account of the *formal cause* of the inspiration of Scripture seem refined;- I do not suppose them to dispute the fact ⟨not as if it were not true⟩ that the Church determines the sense of Scripture; but, this being granted, still is it correct to consider that the presence of this latent, partially developed divine sense is that which constitutes its inspiration. If this objection is valid, then I should be led to maintain ⟨(then I would have him determine)⟩ that Scripture is said to be inspired, simply because it is the writing of inspired men. In this case inspiration is predicated of Scripture by a metonymy, the phrase 'inspired Scripture' not being parallel to that of 'inspired writers,' and the *form* of its inspiration, not being an internal form, but external, as charity is the form, but an external form, of justifying faith.

March 14, 1863.

---

[1] Newman lated noted:
Omit 5. March 16 1863.

§ 3

It follows to compare and adjust the sense in which a sacred writer is to be considered inspired, and that in which a book of Scripture.

When we say that a Prophet or an Apostle was inspired, we do not thereby [mean] to claim inspiration for everything that he said or did. To Moses it was said, 'I will be in thy mouth;' yet in one occasion 'they embittered ⟨exasperated⟩ his spirit' and 'distinxit? labiis suis.' It was promised ⟨pronounced⟩ to the Apostles, 'I will give you a mouth and wisdom' Luke 21; but this does not oblige us to think that Paul and Barnabas, in the quarrel which led to their parting asunder, used the words of inspiration, or that the words of both Peter and Paul were full of the Holy Ghost, when there was the difference between them at Antioch. And in like manner as their inspiration did not extend to all occasions, so neither did it embrace all subjects; had St Paul been led, as St Thomas Aquinas was, to speak incidentally of the motions of the heavenly bodies, we have no reason to suppose that he would have spoken of them according to the Copernican philosophy, nor is there any reason to suppose that by any infused knowledge ⟨or that⟩ he would have been able [to have] discoursed of the animal kingdom as well as Aristotle. Admitting then that the Prophets, Evangelists, and Apostles were inspired, it was not in all that they said and wrote ⟨their words⟩ that they were under the influence of their inspiration, but in those which treated of certain subjects and in a certain manner. It is therefore of consequence to ascertain whether the Scriptures, though the writings of inspired men, have been written directly under the influence of their inspiration, i.e. whether they precisely are inspired.

What then that matter and manner must be is best illustrated and proved by the books of Scripture themselves, which for the most part carry their own evidence with them so far as this, that they are written just as (in that way in which) they would have been written, were they written, by inspired men when under the influence of inspiration.[1] As to the matter of writings so inspired, we should be sure ⟨(have a right to expect)⟩ that it would be on the subjects revealed to them; and as to the manner, we should have a right to be in some such way as is expressed ⟨implied⟩ in the term *ex cathedrâ*.

As to the latter condition, the very fact of writing in a measure implied it; and here what is written has an advantage in point of authority over what is spoken. Vocal words are the medium of easy and familiar intercourse, as well as of what [is] of moment and solemn; but the mere fact of writing, and much more when it is attended by an effort, as it is especially was in the Apostles' days, when the materials of writing were not easy, and when it had to be sent safely to others, and that perhaps at a great distance, and again, when, as in

---

[1] Newman later noted:
which is the evidence of inspiration? and has the Scripture got it?

St Paul's case, an amanuensis was employed, and still more if we find copies were taken ⟨made⟩ of the writing, all imply a formal act.

This applies more or less to the whole of Scripture, but there are definite proofs of its ex cathedrâ nature, which cannot be mistaken. Such is the phrase 'Thus saith the Lord,' so frequent in the Prophets. Such again in St Luke's exordium, in which he professes to be undertaken [undertaking] an account of our Lord's life which may be trusted and received in addition to stories which were not of authority. Such again a certain solemnity of introduction, as in the first words of Genesis, of St John's Gospel, of his first Epistle, and the Epistle to the Hebrews; and I may add the apostolic salutation at the beginning of the other Epistles. Such especially the claim of inspiration, as when St Paul says that he has the Spirit of God, a claim which cannot be kept from embracing the particular epistle on which he was engaged when he said it.

Then as to matter, here too Scripture fulfils the condition which is necessary for a writing in an inspired person having a claim on being considered inspired. For first all dogmatic subjects are exactly ⟨necessarily⟩ those for which the gift of inspiration was given. Next everything of a prophetic character is such as not only becomes, but requires the presence ⟨exercise⟩ of inspiration. And thirdly everything of the nature of ecclesiastical law and rituals, and ethical ⟨moral⟩ teaching, proceeding from inspired persons, must be considered of an inspired character. And further, an authoritative account of the life and actions and sayings of our Lord and Saviour, in whom the whole revelation centres, is naturally the sort of writing for which divine inspiration would be given. Again, any ex professo account of great works and acts of God, though in nature, and still more all accounts of His miraculous operations, and, considering that His revelation is especially of an historical character, that disclosures have been made at diverse times and in diverse manners, and that prophecy has so often taken the form of types, that is an historical form, for these reasons the current of sacred history presents a subject on which, if inspired persons wrote, they would write under the influence of their inspiration. And lastly in the prayers, devotions, praises, of inspired persons, they scarcely can be supposed to be left to themselves, or to write them with the mere authority of holy but uninspired men.

From all this it appears that even at first sight and from the surface of Scripture, we should have reason to conclude, that, if the Prophets, Evangelists and Apostles were favoured with the gift of divine inspiration, and if they wrote the books of Scripture attributed to them, then there is a clear primâ facie reason for saying that those books are inspired.

And as to the former of these two conditions, from what has been said above, it would seem that the personal inspiration of the sacred writers is naturally supplemental to their miraculous mission; if then they were miraculously called and instructed in divine matters [and] sent to preach to others, their inspiration is included in that supernatural economy.

The probability of their being the authors of the books which bear their name is not so direct, for nothing is more natural or more common than to ascribe to great names works which do not belong to them, as is exemplified by the inaccuracies which have abounded in determining the writings of the Fathers. To meet this difficulty, however, it must be observed as regards the Old Testament, that the Prophets were from an early time an *institution* in the Hebrew state; they were a public body to whom the gift of inspiration was formally assigned in the religious system; so that, even granting that this or that book be ascribed erroneously to a particular author, yet the fact of its being placed in the sacred catalogue, makes it natural to refer it to this or that source ⟨member⟩ of that Prophetical College by whom the gift of Prophecy would [sic] conveyed in solidum? As to the New Testament certainly I do not see what ground we have except one of fact, if fact can be shown, to say that the gift of inspiration was confined to this or that circle of our Lord's first followers. It was not confined to the Apostolic College, for two Evangelists were external to it; nor to the seventy disciples of our Lord, because the Epistle to the Hebrews has been ascribed by some of the Fathers to St Clement, St Barnabas? or to Apollos, without their meaning thereby to say that the author was not inspired in writing it. Moreover, modern divines have sometimes recognized in the writings of other disciples of the Apostles the capability of being exalted, should the Church be so guided, to the dignity of canonical books. (Vid. below). Now the disciples of the Apostles, 'Apostolical men', as they are sometimes called, lived down to at least the year 167, for in that year St Polycarp, the disciple of St John, was martyred. Here, then, as in the case of the Old Testament, we may consider without any violence ⟨harshness⟩, that, however much later than the Apostles we were ⟨should feel ourselves⟩ obliged to place certain books of the New Testament, nevertheless we may presume the existence of an inspired College or order of men, to whose authorship those books, from the fact of their afterwards being recognized as canonical, may reasonably be referred.

Taking for granted then [that] the Scriptures were the work of inspired men, writing under inspiration, what was it that we are to suppose in consequence that this gift did for their minds and their pens as they wrote. I suppose the direct answer to this question is, that the gift answered their needs, was equal to their wants, whatever in each particular case it might be; if illumination as to doctrine was wanted, it was the gift of illumination; if prudence in selecting or rejecting matter, it was prudence; if the power of prophesying, it was foreknowledge; if the knowledge of facts, historical accuracy; if faculty of expression, the use of language. First, it illuminated them generally, vivified their memory, and raised their minds in knowledge and comprehension above the very subject-matter which was to be the substance of their writing; so that they might be said to master it, in such a sense that they could have said much more upon it than they were led to say, saw its connection with other subjects, and were in consequence fit recipients of the further gift of (supernatural?) prudence; by which they selected the points to be treated, or incidents to be mentioned, and used the exact words suitably to express their meaning, in order to subserve the great ends which were (enable) to put before them as the scope of their writing at all. This is analogous to the grant of grace in ordinary cases and for ordinary purposes; and, if we may fairly be guided, as I think we may, by analogy in a matter of this kind, then it will be as impossible to reduce the aid given to a definition, as it is impossible to state what is given to the soul by grace by some account which will apply to all cases where it is given. As grace is given to all men, sufficient for their salvation, but in various measures now and here, according to what is in every case required for that end, and acts sometimes as a suggestion, sometimes as a warning, sometimes as a guidance, sometimes as a shield ⟨safeguard⟩, and sometimes as an elevation or fervour of spirit, a softening of the heart, or a strengthening of the will, so too inspiration is no one operation, but is a miraculous action of God upon the soul, efficacious for the end for which it is given, viz., for the accomplishment of works which shall be equal to those ends for which the revelation was made. But on this point, and some others which we have incidentally mentioned, there will be an opportunity of saying more in the next chapter.

On the application of the foregoing account of Inspiration to Scripture as we find it ⟨the actual state of the case⟩.

§ 1

Were the writings to which the prerogative of inspiration is assigned as simple as the idea of inspiration itself, even then this gift would not be without its difficulties, for there are difficulties, as we have seen, in ascribing inspiration to written words ⟨a writing⟩ at all, but still not many words would be necessary for its explanation. Whether by an inspired work ⟨writing⟩ were meant a text dictated from above, or an absolutely accurate ⟨true⟩ statement ⟨account⟩ of revealed doctrines and facts, whether it be a writing ⟨proclamation⟩ blest and instinct with a supernatural virtue, or the oracle and vehicle of a latent, profound, and indeterminate divine sense, in any of the meanings [which] can be predicated intelligibly of a Psalm, of a Prophecy, and of an Epistle; but the greater part of the Bible is not so simple a structure, [not even those three forms of writing just mentioned when viewed in their connexion with the other sacred books. Out of the books of which Scripture is composed, 23 are historical; 7 more partially so; (Ex. Lev. Deut. Job. Isa. Jer. Dan) and the history is substantially human history, relating to things not supernatural. Another portion, running through ⟨contained⟩][1] but not many portions of Scripture are thus simply devotional, predictive, or didactic, not even those which are formally or substantially such. Even the separate books of Scripture

---

[1] The paragraph in brackets was deleted.

are of very composite structure, and, when it is said that every part of them is inspired, a number of questions arise which require very careful consideration. This complex character of Scripture may be considered in three points of view — first, as to its text, next as to its matter, and thirdly as to its meaning.

And first, as to its text.

June 25, 1861[1]   [E]

These being some of the various senses, which may be given to the word Inspiration and its kindred terms in relation to Holy Scripture, the question follows, which of them is to be accepted, in the absence of any dogmatic definition on the subject, as adequate to ⟨the fulfilment of⟩ the idea which is conveyed in the words sacri, divini, and canonici, which do belong to the books of Scripture de fide.

The difficulty of answering it is threefold: — 1. because we have to find a definition of the word compatible with its grammatical import, and consistent with itself. 2. because of the great variety of opinions on the subject which have been entertained by theologians, and 3. because of the necessity of finding one sense which is applicable to all the parts of a collection of writings so multiform as the Bible.

It will not require many words to give ourselves an insight into this difficulty. Let us start with the idea of Revelation itself. The res revelata is, in other words, the Verbum Dei, which is spoken of by the Council of Trent under the two aspects of oral and written, or Tradition and Scripture, according to the channel through which it comes to us, the transmitted words or the transcribed books ⟨volumes⟩ of Prophets and Apostles. And this Verbum Dei, according to the Council, is not only from our Lord, or mediately through Prophets and Apostles but in part immediately from Himself.

From this it would seem to follow, that Scripture, the Verbum scriptum, (or rather transcriptum), is said to be inspired because its writers were inspired, and that by the inspiration of Scripture was really meant the quality or property of being the work of inspired men.

But on the contrary it may be urged, that the Verbum Dei ore traditum, (or rather ore transmissum,) though coming from inspired men, is not said to be inspired, whether viewed simply as traditum, or as defined by the Church. If the inspiration be [a] gift attaching to the Verbum scriptum and not to the Verbum traditum, it must be something more than the quality of being the work of inspired men.

But then, it may be rejoined on the other hand, that the Verbum scriptum in its very idea is a personal work or offspring of the inspired mind, whereas the Verbum traditum is only ultimately referable to its author; that the one comes from him immediately, the other mediately; the Verbum transmissum is but the substance of what he said, but the Verbum transcriptum is the very

[1] See also §2 June 27, 1861.

letter of what he wrote. Accordingly Scripture may be said to partake of his personal gift, or may be called (improperly) inspired, while Tradition cannot.[1]

Here then are two distinct views which may be taken of inspiration, one that it really attaches as a property to the sacred text, and to every word and letter to it; the other that it really attaches to the sacred writers, and is only by a figure of speech, however significant and appropriate, predicated of the writings. According to the former, (teaching), the words are literally the words of the Holy Ghost, with the mere and bare instrumentality of the writer, and in every aspect and in their fullest meaning divine, perfect, and eternally true. According to the latter, the writers, being by inspiration fully instructed in the Verbum Dei, revelatum, prompted ⟨excited⟩ to write, and superintended while writing, wrote books, which (nevertheless) were personally their writing, and which therefore in themselves do but really possess the necessary consequence of that inspiration, viz., the gift of being absolutely free from error. The former may be called the doctrine of dictation, the latter of inerrancy.[2]

The former of these is simple and complete, scarcely allows of further question, and is incapable of subdivision; it is otherwise with the latter. As it introduces into the process of writing the sacred books the idea of a human element, it involves the question of the degree of that element, and the extent and nature of its operation:- such as ⟨in other words⟩, whether Scripture *is* or *contains* the Verbum Dei, when its writers, being men, ever wrote as men, whether it is in one aspect inspired, and in another not. Accordingly, it may be asked, whether the inspiration extends to *matters of history* recorded by the sacred writers, so far forth as they were not gained by revelation, but from the senses or through ⟨by⟩ testimony. It may be asked whether the superintendence *guided* or *guarded* them, suggesting what was divine, or protecting and controlling what was human; in a word, whether it was a positive or negative *assistentia*. It may be asked whether the inerrancy of ⟨absence of error in⟩ Scripture is absolute and entire, and therefore in human science, physics, antiquities, politics, and in the minute details of fact and in chronology, or in dogmas of faith, morals, and essential facts. Those questions lead to others; and the answers to them all, affirmative or negative, may be variously combined, to form a whole theory, both with each other, and with the doctrine of dictation. From which it will follow that a great variety of teaching is both conceivable, and admissible on the subject of the divine inspiration of Holy Scripture.

---

[1] Newman made a reference in pencil to Billuart, Bannes, and Rabaudy which is difficult to decipher. See below.

[2] A note, not deleted, in draft 'D' refers to

'Potter p 128' who 'speaks of the Jews, as holding four modes of revelation. 1. by visions (waking), 2. by dreams, 3. by voice, 4. by inspiration — The last, which is the "inferior", was proper to Hagiographi, viz. Psalms etc. Beyond all these was face to face, Moses'. The writers' freedom from error referred to 'either 1. what matters they would not have known or remembered, a sort of *revelation* or *suggestion*, 2. *guidance* or *direction*. Thus verbal inspiration is not necessary and at most seldom. But *all* has *divine authority*'.

And this has been the fact; and, before tracing some of the main features of it, I will set down, not before alluding ⟨in reference⟩ to the history of the doctrine, but as illustrating the capabilities of the controversy some of the enunciations of divines corresponding to some of the various points on which I have been touching.

[There follows the deleted rough draft of § 2 and § 3 dated 27 June, 1861].

[Another draft with a rather significant variation (see, *Inspiration of Scripture*, p. 19, n). reads as follows:]

June 25, 1861

Let us start with the idea of Revelation itself. The res revelata is, in other words, the Verbum Dei; and this Verbum Revelatum is spoken of by the Council of Trent under the two aspects, of oral and written, or Tradition and Scripture, according to the channel through which it comes to us, the transmitted preaching and the transcribed writing of Prophets and Apostles. And this Verbum Dei Revelatum, according to the Council, not only proceeds from our Lord mediately, by means of Prophets and Apostles, but in part immediately from Himself.

From this it would seem to follow, that Scripture is not so much itself inspired, but rather said to be inspired, and that, because its authors were inspired; and that by the Inspiration of Scripture is really meant the quality or property of being the work of inspired men.

But no; for it may be urged that the Verbum Dei ore traditum, though it comes from inspired men, still is never considered inspired, whether it be viewed simply as traditum, or as defined by the Church. If the inspiration be a gift attaching to the Verbum Scriptum, and not to the Verbum Traditum, it must be something [other] than that quality which attaches to the Verbum traditum, viz: that of being the work of inspired men.

But yes; for it may be rejoined, that the Verbum Scriptum in its very idea is a personal work or offspring of the inspired mind, whereas the Verbum traditum is only ultimately referable to its inspired author; that the one comes from him immediately, the other mediately; that the verbum transmissum is but the substance of what he said, but that the verbum transcriptum is his in the very letter. Accordingly, Scripture may be said to partake of an Apostle's personal gift, or may be called (improperly) inspired, while Tradition cannot. (This is in fact Billuart's reply to the question of the difference between Scripture and a dogmatic canon. Bannes in Rabaudy p 476, says that the notary who draws the rough draft of a decree of Council does not write *instigante Spiritu Sancto*).

Here then are two distinct views, which may be taken of Inspiration:- the one, that it really attaches as a property to the sacred text, and to every word and letter in it; the other that it really attaches to the sacred writers and to them alone, and that only by a figure of speech, however significant and appropriate, is it predicated of the writings. According to the former, the words are literally the words of the Holy Ghost, with the mere and bare instrumentality of the writer, and are, in every aspect and in their fullest meaning divine, perfect, and eternally true. According to the latter, the writers, being by inspiration fully instructed in the Verbum Dei Revelatum, being prompted to write, and superintended while writing, wrote books, which, as being immediately their personal work, are gifted, not with inspiration, but with the necessary consequence of the inspiration of their writers, viz: with the privilege of being absolutely free from formal error. The former may be called the doctrine of dictation; the latter of inerrancy.

Each of these antagonist views admit of subdivision. Under the former the question may be raised, whether the words of Scripture are directly from above, or whether they are only used to convey a divine sense (verbal); or whether every part is made divine in such sense that nothing is inserted without a divine recognition (plenary) or without subserving some divine end.

[Note in pencil:]

'plenary admits of whole passages being historically human (e.g. speeches of Job's friends) though turned to good purpose, or again the *selection* of matter, but verbal implies the patristic view of scripture being full of mysteries, the double sense, etc.'.

IV The Inspiration of Scripture, 1861

July 6 and 7, 1861.[1]   E

No doubt, I think, can be raised as to the fact, that, in all ages of the Church, from the earliest to the present, it has been the universal belief of Catholics that Holy Scripture is divinely inspired. It has been the belief of Fathers, the belief of the schools, the belief of clergy and people. When, however, this being assumed as indisputable, we proceed to inquire definitely what is meant by the inspiration of this or that particular book of Scripture, difficulties present themselves, which no decision of the Church, no apostolical tradition, no consent of schools or of the faithful, no obvious necessity or reasonableness enable us to solve.

These difficulties are of the following kind: 1. to find a sense of 'Inspiration' natural to the word itself, distinct, and homogeneous; 2. a sense applicable to every portion of a collection of multiform writings; 3. a sense, which unites, as far as may be, the suffrages of theologians, who, in the absence of authority, have speculated on the subject in their own several ways.

§ 1

If I were asked what I meant by the Inspiration of a book of Scripture, I should begin with some preliminary remarks.

I should say, that Almighty God has directly revealed Himself to us in a history and in doctrines, which are beyond sense, reason, and any natural informant whatever, and which for this very reason are supernatural in the mode of their communication as well as in their matter. This history, these doctrines are called 'Revealed Religion' or the *res revelata*, and the announcement of them is the *revelatio* or the Word of God.

The Divine Word or Revelation, though a direct act of the Almighty, comes to us through Prophets and Apostles, preaching and writing. As contained in their writings, it is the Verbum Dei Scriptum. Hence those writings

---

[1] The deleted draft 'D' began:
I think no doubt can fairly be raised that in all ages of the Church, from the earliest to the present, it has been the general belief that Holy Scripture is inspired, and, as a consequence of inspiration, that it is free from all error. This has been the belief of Fathers, the belief of the schools, the belief of Bishops and people. When, however, so much being taken for granted, we proceed to inquire what is meant by 'inspiration', and what is meant by 'error', difficulties make their appearance which can scarcely be resolved; and we begin to understand the divine wisdom, which has guided the Church in Council in never introducing into her canons of faith either the word 'inspiration' or the phrase 'free from error'.
There is also another draft of this introduction dated 27 June 1861 which Newman deleted in pencil.

contain the Word of God, or, as is more commonly said, are the Word of God. As containing, then, the Word of God, or being the Word of God, they are emphatically called Scripture, and are divine, sacred, authoritative.

(This variation of phrase marks a variation of doctrine on the subject. If the sacred writings *contain* the Word of God, there is, by the force of the terms, a something in them over and above the divine Word, or a human vehicle; if they *are* the Word of God, then there is nothing in them human at all. In each case, they involve a direct act of the Almighty. In the former case, they are more properly said to be inspired; in the latter case, dictated).

It is the Church which has pronounced Scripture to be divine, sacred, authoritative; and it is the Church again, which by a divine light decides what is Scripture and what is not; or, as it is said, places a particular book in the Canon or catalogue of sacred books. She makes a particular book canonical. This she does on the ground of its being, or its containing, the Word of God, of its being (dictated or) inspired by the Holy Ghost. This gift then is that, which constitutes the divinity of a book of Scripture and its capacity or claim to be placed on the sacred Canon, its *forma*, if I may use the word, *canonicabilitatis*?

[Later notes in pencil:]

In *word* all agree — inspiration. What is inspiration? Why, first — it is not indirect inspiration, but direct. Inspiration is 1. a *direct* act, 2. of illumination, 3. in religious and moral matters, 4. of a *public* and ecclesiastical nature, for the information of all.

As far as words go there is no difficulty, as I have said already. *Inspiration* is that *forma* — but what is Inspiration? Nothing can show more strikingly the vagueness of the word than that dictation (which is a different thing) should be under it. [End of notes]

What we have then to inquire is, *what* is this *forma*? is it dictation or inspiration? Subordinate to this is the inquiry into the degrees or kinds of inspiration; and, as dictation is commonly considered one of these, the question before us in its simplest shape is; what is that Inspiration which constitutes a book such, that the Church is able to put it upon the Canon?

First, then, Inspiration is divided into inspiration proper and dictation. Of these Dictation, as the ordinary acceptation of the word tells us, is a process,[1] which one man gives the words, and another writes them down. Contrariwise to revelation, its primary meaning has reference to words, not to things. When Scripture is said to be dictated by the Holy Ghost, this means, in its strictness that the human authors are pens in the Hand of a Divine Writer; and secondly it may mean that the sacred text is the report, as it may be called, of a divine speech; Further, when Scripture is said to be *as if* dictated, this must mean, that, whatever be the process, the result is this, viz., that the sacred text must

---

[1] At this point, Newman wrote 'go on p.5' referring to a manuscript written on 21 June 1861, which now follows.

73

be regarded as the writing of the Almighty God. What is actually dictated by Him, ⟨Almighty God⟩, is as directly His, as the commandments graven on the stone tablets by His finger; and cannot admit of any defect, except such, (an important deduction of course) as is inherent in human thought and language. By what is as if dictated, is meant, I should consider, a writing inerrable in all its religious bearings. In consequence we may argue from the words of such texts, as being divine enunciations. Dictation is what has sometimes been called *inspiratio antecedens*.

Inspiration literally means a *breathing into*; it implies then besides itself that which breathes, and that which is breathed into. Thus Inspiration, properly considered, does not express ⟨imply⟩ so much as dictation, what is the subject acted on in inspiration, becoming the instrument of the agent in dictation. A prime minister dictates a letter, and inspires a newspaper.

Accordingly, dictation involves ⟨contemplates⟩ the substance of Scripture, and inspiration implies a quality of it. If we speak of holy men being inspired, we mean that their minds were exalted, enlarged and purified, intellectually and morally, by the Holy Ghost; if we speak of a book as inspired, we mean that a human composition is made the vehicle of a divine message. Dictation only requires the co-operation of the human will; inspiration presupposes the operation of the human intellect.

Inspiration proper accordingly admits degrees, but dictation does not; dictation has one sense only, but inspiration has many. It may be divided into moral and intellectual; these are distinct genera; it cannot, as I think, be divided into dictation and suggestion, though some divines would make dictation a kind of inspiration, viz. verbal, but by verbal is properly meant the case when human words are instinct with a divine sense, which will be noticed presently. As regards degree, it may be divided into plenary and partial, that is, extending or not extending to the whole mind or the whole writing, which is the subject inspired. Another division of passive inspiration, is into plenary and partial. By plenary will be meant an inspiration ⟨directly or indirectly God's⟩ so complete in its extent, that not a word occurs in the composition, but is there by the intention of the Holy Ghost; a prerogative which absolutely excludes formal error. Partial is, when only portions of a book are under this direct divine disposition.

It may be divided into verbal, and ideal; by verbal I mean an inspiration which directs, and thereby runs through the words, or the phrases, or the sentences, of the speaker or writer; but ideal a divine presence in the intentions? ⟨acts⟩ or words of the speaker and the composition of the writer. These two are cross-divisions; since a same work, for instance, may have partial verbal inspiration and plenary ideal, that is, may be divine as regards all *res et sententiae*, and sometimes or often in *voces et locutiones*.[1]

---

[1] Newman later noted in pencil:
'*N.B.* Observe this idea of inspiration brings in necessarily the doctrine of the double sense — so necessary in Prophecies, as against thesis such as Mr. R. Williams, in Essays and Reviews'. See *Essays and Reviews* London 1861, pp. 63 ff.

[Newman deleted the following paragraph]

It may be asked, if Inspiration may be ideal, how does it differ from Revelation? I answer, Revelation relates to the object which is revealed but inspiration to the instrument of the revelation ⟨agent and subject⟩. By inspiration from a Divine Power an object is first revealed to the person inspired, and then again, in his words or writings, mediately to others.

Here we are led on, from the meaning, etc. the meaning of the word *inspiration*, to consider its grammatical force; it is both an active word and a passive. We speak of 'inspiration of God' and 'inspiration of Holy men' or 'of Scripture'.

In the active sense it is an *impulsio* or prompting to act, to speak or to write; a suggestio, or supply of subject, thoughts, arguments, and arrangement, (say) in writing, and a presence or superintendence, or guardianship. These two latter have sometimes been called: *inspiratio concomitans*; or again sometimes, an *assistentia positiva* and *negativa*. Strictly speaking, however, a guardianship cannot be called *inspiration*, any more than dictation; for as dictation destroys the thing *breathed into*, so does an external assistentia or guardianship destroy the *breathing*; and this indeed is implied in the word *negativa*.

In the passive sense of the word it may be divided into actual and habitual, answering to actual and habitual grace. A man or book is actually inspired, when, or where, he or it is under the present operation of the divine gift. Habitual inspiration is a permanent endowment, implying a past *impulsio*, now virtual, on the part of God, and consisting in a certain capacity, independent of its present actual exercise. Such every book of an inspired writer must be, though of course it may be more (than this) viz. a result of actual grace. I understand habitual inspiration to answer very nearly to the inspiratio consequens of some authors.

Now to illustrate these various words in the senses proper to them:-

1. Revelation. St Paul says:- 'Neque enim ego ab homine accepi illud, neque didici, sed per revelationem Jesu Christi'. Gal. i. 12.

(And this revelation did not consist in words spoken or written: — 'Quod oculus non vidit, nec auris audivit, etc. ... nobis ... revelavit Deus per Spiritum suum'. 1 Cor. ii. Here the Spirit is contrasted, when revelation is spoken of, with sight and hearing. The same is implied, though the idea of words is introduced, in the 'arcana verba, which it was not lawful to utter,' when St Paul was caught up into Paradise 2 Cor. xii; and the voice of the seven⟨?⟩ thunderings, which St John was not allowed to speak of. Apoc. x.4.)[1]

2. We have one instance, out of many others, of absolute *dictation* in the words put into the mouth of the covetous prophet, which he would fain not

---

[1] Newman later noted in pencil: NB The speeches of Job's friends are inspired not as being God's words, but though they are not — they are inserted by God's direction for particular objects — showing particular characters, giving examples, being warning, etc. etc.

have said, but which he distinctly willed to say; 'Cui cum Dominus occurrisset posuissetque verbum in ore ejus, ait, Revertere ad Balac, et haec loqueris ei.' Num. xxiii. 16.

3. For *quasi-dictation* we may refer to the greater part of the book of Deuteronomy, in which the Law is recapitulated in the words of Moses. Such again are dogmatic sentences, as Verbum caro factum est.

4. Impulsio: Instances of inspiration, in the sense of an impulsio, instigatio, or prompting to write, are very frequent in Scripture. Thus we read in Isaias, 'Dixit Dominus ad me, Sume tibi librum grandem, et scribo in illo stylo hominis' viii. 1. And in Jeremias, 'Scribe tibi omnia verba, quae locutus sum ad te, in libro'. xxx. 2. And in Habacuc: 'Respondit mihi Dominus et dixit, Scribe visum etc . . . . .' ii. 2. And in the Apocalypse frequently: 'Scribe ergo quae vidisti etc. . . . .' i. 19.

5. For *verbal inspiration*, that is, instances in which the very *voces* or *locutiones* are so directed as to become the vehicle of a divine meaning, we may refer to Matt. iii: 'He shall baptize you' where St John might by fire have intended either the fire of suffering, or a spiritual cleansing as perfect as fire is in the case of metals, yet the Holy Ghost may have specially intended the word of Purgatory [and to] the familiar words in 2 Esdr. ix. 15: 'Panem de caelo dedisti eis', which, besides conveying a past historical fact, have a Christian meaning; or to Sap ⟨Wisd.⟩ xii [xiv].7: 'Benedictum est lignum, per quod fit justitia,' which literally refers to Noe's ark; or to Genesis xxii 'My son, God will provide Himself a lamb etc'., or to the speech of Caiphas, about one man dying for the people. And to the prophets generally, who rarely, at least in their Evangelical predictions, speak by dictation, but with a double sense. And in this will 'verbal inspiration' differ from dictation, that the former implies a double sense, and the latter does not.

6. Instances of inspiration of the substance or matter of what is said, in contradiction of verbal inspiration, are such as the words of Isaias in the Hebrew as reported by St Matthew in Greek, 'in veritate educet judicium', Isai. xlii, 3 and 'donec ejiciat ad victoriam judicium'. Matt. xii, 20. The general sense is one and the same, and that is the inspired truth, though the expressions differ from each other. So again, the second book of Maccabees, by the confession of the sacred writer himself, is composed by himself, but its matter is true and from inspiration.

7. Plenary: instances Job's friends.

8. For habitual inspiration it will suffice to refer to such passages as the prayer of Nehemias in 2 Esdr. ix. 6, etc., and St Stephen's speech in Acts vii, which are the personal speeches of inspired men.

These being the various senses of the word Inspiration, the question follows which of them belongs to a canonical book ⟨Scripture⟩; that is, Is a canonical book ⟨Scripture⟩ the Word of God, (as being) literally dictated by Him, or again as being the work of men who He had inspired, or again of those who were overruled to write what had a meaning beyond their own, or again, is it the Word of God up to a certain point ⟨standard⟩, or for certain purposes, or in its matter, or in respect to its absolute truthfulness?

§ 2

June 27, 1861.[1]

These being some of the various senses, in which the Inspiration of Scripture may be taken, I will in the next place set down some of the many definitions and accounts which have been given of Inspiration, and see in what they are incompatible, and what they have in common with each other, and how on the whole they assist us in deciding the question, in what sense Scripture is the Word of God. Calmet says, from p 2 'Fideles omnes de Scripturae inspiratione conveniunt; theologi de inspirationis *ratione* inter se non consentiunt'. How truly this is said, the following specimens of their teaching will show.

1 Inspiration is a *divine, physical force*.
Athenagoras says ὡς ὄργανα κεκινηκότε τὰ τῶν προφητῶν στόματα

2. Inspiration is *dictation*.
Billuart says, Probabilius videtur, ad rationem Scripturae sacrae requiri, quod non solum sensus et sententia, sed etiam singula verba sint a Spiritu Sancto dictata. de Fid, t 2 p 38, 9.

3. Inspiration is a *quasi-dictation*.
Ex Charmes says: 'Auctor principalis Scripturae sanctae est Deus ipse, qui eam Prophetis et Apostolis quasi dictando inspiravit'. p. 7. [p. 8]

4. Inspiration is a dictation *in everything, little and great*. Canus says[2]: 'Fateamur singula quaeque, sive magna sive parva, a sacris auctoribus, Spiritu Sancto dictante, esse edita'. ii, 17. p. 75.

5. Inspiration is a *prompting* to write and a *superintendence* in writing

---

[1] June 27, 1861. This draft was deleted:
These being some of the various senses, in which inspiration and its kindred terms may be taken, the question follows, which of them denotes the gift proper of the Holy Scriptures? which is to be accepted as the forma canonicabilitatis? which, in the absence of dogmatic decision in the matter, is adequate to the idea conveyed in the words, sacri, divini, and canonici, words which *do* belong to the books of Scripture *de fide*?
Now I proceed to set down ⟨detail⟩ a number of definitions or accounts of Inspiration, as they are given by theologians. This I do, not with a view of bringing out here their differences of opinion on the point, (for this was the last of three difficulties which I enumerated and will be the subject of the next section,) but in order to illustrate the second of them, viz the difficulty, even if a clear notion of inspiration be attained, of applying it in its simplicity and integrity to the whole text of a book so multiform as the Bible. And 1. Inspiration
1. Impossible to say that inspiration is *the same* in Prophets and in histories.
2. on the verbum Dei *and* verbum hominis.
3. on 'without error' being no more than canons of Councils
4. on so little light thrown by the gospel on the *whole* structure of the world.
[2] In the third fascicle of Document B, Newman had discussed Canus' extreme view on the inspiration of Scripture; he observed, 'And honestly carrying out this view the authorities at the Holy Office made Galileo touch the holy gospels and "abjure, anathematize, and detest the heresy of the movement of the earth".' [Newman continued] 'Nay these theologians who take this extreme view find it difficult to be consistent with themselves. Calmet can hardly be so considered whether he sees no material difference between the doctors of Louvain and Lessius.'

77

sufficient to secure *inerrancy* in what is written, even in *things not necessary to salvation*.

Marchini says: 'Inspiratio est singularis ex Spiritûs Sancti moventis ad scribendum impulsio, directio, et praesentia, mentem animumque scriptoris gubernans, qua errasse non sinit, efficitque ut scribat quae velit Deus'. p. 91. [p. 70] He says presently, 'res, etiam ad salutem non necessarias, in Scripturis, auctore Spiritu Sancto, esse exaratas'. p. 93. [p. 72]

6. Inspiration is an *adsistentia positiva* of the Holy Ghost, at least as regards the *res et sententiae* of Scripture.

Perrone says: 'Inspiratio sese extendit saltem ad res atque sententias, ut ipsi libri non modo immunes sint a quavis vel levi erroris labe, sed praeterea ut iis in omnibus adstiterit adsistentia positiva.' t 3 [2. ii]. p 71. and so Bouvier t 2. p 32.

7. Inspiration is a *special assistance* as regards matters of *faith and morals* and *essential facts*.

Bergier says: 'Par une inspiration particulière de la grace, il les a portés a ecrire, et les a dirigés dans le choix des choses; par une assistance spéciale de l'Esprit Saint, il les a preservés de toute erreur, soit sur les faits essentiels, soit sur le dogme, soit sur la morale'. in voc. [t 2 p. 331]

8. Inspiration is an *assistance* from the Holy Ghost, which enabled the sacred writers to *keep clear of serious errors*.

Holden says according to Perrone: 'Ad inspirationem plane sufficere, si Spiritus Sanctus ita scriptoribus afflet, ut graviores saltem errores ipsi praecaveant'. vid Perrone t. 3 [2. ii.]. p. 64.

9. Inspiration is an *assistance and guidance*.

Vincenzi says: 'Dei Spiritus Apostolos afflabat, tum eorum praedicationi, tum illorum scriptis adstando ac moderando', part i, p. x.

10. Inspiration is such, that Scripture, both *is* and *contains* the Verbum Dei.

Bellarmine first says: 'Propheticos et Apostolicos libros verum esse Verbum Dei'; and then continues, 'Libris, qui canonici nominantur, verbum Dei contineri'. de V. D. i. 1 fin and 2 init. The latter sentence is taken from the Council of Trent.

11. Inspiration is a divine *prompting or impulsion* to write what is definitely *contemplated* by the writer beforehand.

Ex Charmes says: 'Est incitatio quaedam interior, quâ quis impellitur ad aliquid fixum et determinatum scribendum, sive antea fuerit notum, sive non.' p. 9.

12. Inspiration, to satisfy its idea, need *not be more than impulsion and habitual inspiration* without any actual influence or present operation of the Holy Ghost at all; for so I understand an *after-approbation*.

Less[ius] says, according to the Louvain censure: 'Liber aliquis humanâ industriâ, sine assistentiâ Spiritûs Sancti scriptus, si Spiritus Sanctus, postea testatur nihil ibi esse falsum, efficitur Scriptura Sancta.' Perrone, [t. 2. ii.] p. 65.

Distinct, not to say divergent, as these accounts of inspiration are ⟨(seem⟩ (at first sight) to be, they are not more so than the impression made upon theologians and the account given by them of the general feeling of Catholic Schools towards them. For instance, by some it is said that

1. The common doctrine of divines is the doctrine of *dictation of the sacred text*. 'Est communis', says Billuart. Speaking of this doctrine quoad singula verba, Rabaudy says, 'Sancti Patres eidem veritati aperte favent'.

2. The common doctrine of divines, is *not* that of dictation, but that of the sacred *text's preservation from error*. Bergier says . . . . . [Quotation not inserted]

3. The common doctrine in the present age, is, that it is sufficient for the idea of inspiration, if it be, *not* dictation, *not* positive assistance, but only an *impulsion*, a *protection* from error, specially as *to faith and morals*, ⟨in materia fidei et morum⟩ and an *after-approbation*. Amort says, 'Communem nunc esse apud cordatiores Scripturae interpretes et Theologos sententiam, ad constituendum librum Scripturae sacrum et canonicum sufficere, quod Scriptor, ex speciali motione seu inspiratione divinâ motus, se applicuerit ad ea scribenda quae' (humanâ ratione) 'cognoverat, ita tamen ut ne irreperet error specialiter in materia fidei et morum'. p. 106. Dem. Crit.[1]

4. It is *not* sufficient for the idea of inspiration, ⟨(Inspiration it is not,)⟩ if it be made to consist in an *after-approbation*, or in a *special assistance* of the Holy Ghost, or in a *revelation*. Ex Charmes says, 'Deus scriptoribus sacris afflavit, non per simplicem approbationem eorum quae humanitus scripserunt; nec sufficit specialis Spiritûs Sancti assistentia; nec requiritur in omnibus divina revelatio; sed proprie dicta inspiratio.'

5. Of Inspiration *nothing* can be pronounced beyond this, *that there is Inspiration*. Reithmayer says: 'Que les livres canoniques soient divinement inspirés, c'est une vérité, sur laquelle tous les catholiques sont d'accord. Mais en quoi a consisté précisément l'inspiration de ces livres? Chaque mot a-t-il

---

[1] In the third fascicule of Document B, Newman had argued: 'Calmet holds . . . that "all the Scriptures are inspired and free from error, and contain nothing but the Word of God —" and says that this is the view of all Fathers and Divines. [Newman quoted from and referred to pp. 469, 480]. If this is not the view of all the Fathers and Divines, if there be a minority for any other view or views, their testimony proves nothing at all. . . . Contrast with this historical fact [Calmet's view], the opinion of Amort whose authority is great, as being a friend of Benedict the xiv, and as dedicating to that learned and wise Pontiff the work from which I am going to quote: [Newman then quoted from Demonstr. critic. p. 106 and concluded]

Down to the 16th century then there is one doctrine about the inspiration of Scripture, one and one only; in the 18th century too there is a doctrine "*communis* apud *cordatiores* scripturae interpretes et theologos"; but the former doctrine is that the very words of all Scripture are immediately dictated and inspired by Almighty God; the latter that some books of Scripture may be written "humano prorsus ingenio", with no antecedent motio or suggestion to write, and an assistentia only, for so I interpret "specialiter in materia fidei et morum"

How is it possible to reconcile these two views; divine inspiration and dictation in every word of all scripture, and no divine dictation or impulse or inspiration ⟨suggestion⟩ at all in whole books of Scripture? The possibility of elucidating ⟨interpreting⟩ the definitions of Trent by the Holy Fathers and the school of theology seems utterly to vanish in the face of ⟨with⟩ such a contrary in their decisions ⟨testimony⟩. It seems inevitable to conclude that there never was an apostolical tradition on the subject. When we consider the state of the evidence more closely, this conclusion grows upon us'.

été inspiré? Sur ces questions, et quelques autres semblables, il y a diverses opinions permises.'

6. About inspiration *all Catholics agree*; only some authors hold *different genera* of inspiration. Calmet says: 'Theologi, qui duo vel tria inspirationum genera statuunt, et cum Patribus Scripturam inspiratam et auctoritatis infallibilis esse conveniunt, ab iisdem Patribus non sunt secernendi . . . nulla apud ipsos? nisi vocum et locutionum varietas.' [Vol. 3, p. 475]

Now let us see whether we cannot reduce these opinions, various as they are, into one or two general formulas.

The canonicity of a book of Scripture, that is, its being the Verbum Dei, consists

1. in the fact that its writer was filled with the illuminating Spirit of Truth.

2. in the fact that its writer was urged, prompted, impelled to write it, — it, that book, definitely, — either by the natural providence or by the supernatural power of God, or by both together. So say Amort and Ex Charmes, taking this or that part of the whole proposition.

3. in the fact that its writer was assisted by the Illuminating Spirit, during the writing, either positively, or negatively, or in both ways. So Marchini, Perrone, Bergier, Holden, Vincenzi, Bouvier.

4. In the fact that its writer received an after-approbation upon his book from the illuminating Spirit. Thus Less[ius] and Amort.

I observe of these four solutions, that in each of them an external form is assigned as the forma canonicabilitatis, in fide formata caritate, charity is the external form of ⟨justifying⟩ faith. Being then homogeneous, they are compatible with each other and will combine, and thus we have a fifth solution; viz., the sacredness of a book of Scripture consists,

5. in the fact that its writer was filled with the Illuminating Spirit, was divinely prompted to write, was assisted in writing, and was granted after writing a recognition of his book.

Hence we have the formula: 'Inspiration, or that which constitutes the sacredness and the divinity of a book of Scripture, is the attestation of the Holy Ghost ⟨Illuminating Spirit⟩ to the book ⟨work⟩; for the inspiration of the writer, the prompting, the assistance, and the approbation by the Holy Ghost are all of the nature of an attestation.'

The defect of this definition by means of an external form is, that it does not solve the (very) question on which the (whole) difficulty ⟨everything⟩ turns, viz., (whether inspiration be inspiration proper or dictation), whether a canonical book is, or contains the Word of God; except by ⟨unless indeed⟩ answering that a canonical book is really never anything else, strictly speaking, than a work of man, though of man directed and guarded by the Holy Ghost, differing from dogmatic canon ⟨the definition⟩ of an Ecumenical Council, not in any intrinsic property, not in any greater authority or truth, but in the fact that on a more varied subject-matter it procedeed from an inspired author.

This certainly may be said [that] it is but ⟨And that accordingly it is but⟩ improperly called the Word of God, as being a transcript of the Word or Revealed ⟨in accordance with His Word,⟩ but neither dictated nor inspired except in the sense of habitual inspiration.

Let us then proceed to enumerate those answers which assign an internal or proper form for constituting a book of Scripture. Such are the following:

That a book is sacred and divine consists in its being

1. spoken or written by the Spirit of Truth,
2. dictated in its words by Him,
3. impregnated in all its parts with a divine sense by Him,
4. intended, disposed, and used in all its parts by Him,
5. preserved from all formal error by Him,
6. preserved from all substantial error by Him.

Of these, the first which may be called the *physical* doctrine ⟨view⟩, is that of the Ante-Nicene Fathers. The second, the doctrine of *dictation*, is that of Canus, Rabaudy, Billuart, etc., after the early Doctors of the Church. But what is most characteristic of the early Church and its Fathers, both Ante-Nicene and Post-Nicene, from St Justin to St Gregory I, is the third doctrine, which I have above called that of *verbal inspiration*. The fourth, which I have named the doctrine of *plenary inspiration* is that of *res et sententiae* and their *selection and disposition*, which is held by Suarez? Fr Perrone, Mgr Bouvier, Archbp Dixon, etc. The fifth is so much the common doctrine of theologians that Calmet seems to consider it the true and satisfactory one. The sixth is held by Holden and others, such as apparently Amort and Bergier.

These definitions, being internal, are not homogeneous with each other, and cannot be united or formed into one broader formula. If Scripture is dictated by the Holy Ghost word for word, it is not merely assisted quoad res et sententias; much less does it admit of accidental error. If it is only preserved from formal error, it is not actually impregnated through with a divine sense, much less the very utterance of God through a physical medium, the pen of a human hand. Differing then from each other in their idea of the inspiration, which constitutes a canonical book, they imply, if put together, in one formula that Scripture is not homogeneous, but that, although in all its parts possessed of one and the same authority, nevertheless it is not written with one and the same inspiration. And this perhaps is what Calmet means, when he speaks of writers who hold that there are different *genera* of inspiration.

The formula then, derived from investigating the internal or proper form of inspiration runs thus: the Bible is the Word of God *such*, by virtue of its being throughout written, or dictated, or impregnated, or directed by the Spirit of Truth, or at least in parts written, in parts dictated, in parts impregnated, in parts directed, and throughout preserved from formal error, at least substantial, by the Spirit of Truth.

(And at this point I leave this part of our investigation for the present).

[Note in pencil: 'From the first etc. of definitions it is proved that it is *a work of man*. In these, in *what sense* is it the work of God'.]

It is plain that a formula like this altogether satisfies the question which has led to this investigation. I asked what was meant by that inspiration which constitutes a book of Scripture canonical; and the answer, as this formula supplies it, is, that inspiration is in some books or in some parts of books a dictation, in others an impregnation or leavening of the human text, and at another time a divine composition and arrangement of pre-existing matter and in all cases a divine preservation from substantial, if not formal, error. In all cases it is the presence of a divine agency in the composition of the book. (It follows that (inversely) as the Divine agency is powerful, the human is subordinate, and as the divine withdraws ⟨withholds⟩ itself, the human prevails).[1] A book of prophecy or a gospel, a book of moral instruction or a psalm, and a history, will not have one and the same ⟨have different⟩ measure and mode of divine influence ⟨agency⟩. Such is the answer which we may derive from the combined ⟨joint⟩ teachings of those divines ⟨theologians⟩, who consider inspiration to be really a quality of the sacred text.

July 12, 1861. And this is the view which I shall attempt to prove from the Fathers and Divines, viz. that the *idea* of a Canon, with a definition of canonicity, is late. Malou denies that the Jews had a canon, or at least that we know it. St Jerome took it as he found the 4th century Rabbis asserted it. Till then 'Scripture' did not mean one and the same thing — it meant 'inspired' — a vague word — various[—] of inspiration. We cannot argue from what was included in the word 'inspired' used *here* by the Fathers, what they meant by it *then*, from the Prophets to the Maccabees. After St Jerome, there was the idea of a Canon, but the Jewish. This obtained till Trent — even now not finished.[2]

[Notes later inserted in the MSS at this point]

July 4, 1861.

NB There is a view I should like to pursue, if it be not an illusion, viz. that

---

[1] Above the brackets in pencil: 'This sentence under the chapter on "Error".?'
[2] A passage deleted in draft 'D' reads:
'The second reason for refusing to the language of the Fathers about Holy Scripture the full meaning which they at first sight carry with them, is found in the circumstance ⟨fact⟩ that the canon of Scripture was not so large then as it is now. The Fathers wrote before the Council of Trent united with the Council of Carthage in receiving the Deutero-canonical books. And it is known that they did not recognise various of the sacred writings which are in our Bible; and this uncertainty about the limits of Scripture was not removed till the decisions of the Council of Trent, even if it may be said to be quite ended now, as I shall presently shew, quote Bellarmine in Vincenzi p 1. It is not wonderful that the most important books of Scripture, as the Psalter or the Gospels, should be earliest recognised and universally recognised as divine; and it is not wonderful that a higher idea of inspiration (I do not say authority) should attach to them than to those which were of secondary importance. It is not wonderful then that, as the number of the sacred books introduced into the Canon has increased, the idea of inspiration has been lowered and that the divine operation necessary for a prophecy such as the book of Isaias has not been recognised as necessary for the writing of the concluding ⟨last⟩ chapters of the book of Daniel'.

the early (Ante-Nicene) Fathers quote Scripture differently from the Post-Nicene? and this difference founded on difference of schools of interpretation? Theophilus, Justin, etc., are they literalists? if so, they look on the books of Moses as *histories* — and find them just the antagonistic informations to what *especially* met the Ante-Nicenes, viz., that mythology, cosmogony, philosophy of the Ancients. Hence they speak of Genesis as a true and divine narration of *facts*. The Post-Nicenes on the contrary were not so much controversialists with Pagans (vide Civitas Dei?) and again they were spiritualists — hence *they* speak of Scripture, not so much as a history, but as a mystery — (Origen, by the bye, must be taken with them, and *Clement* is for ὄργανα as well as mysteries. What of Irenaeus?) and hence each word of Scripture has a profundity of meanings, etc. . . .

March 31, 1863. 'Unanimous Consent of Fathers'. This, I think, is (1) a decree of *discipline* — there is no anathema. (2) it is negative — viz., that you may not *oppose* that consent, not that you must teach *as* they do. (3) They have *changed*. Did we live in Ante-Nicene times, we should not have been at liberty to hold that the 'Sons of God', in Gen. VI were other than Angels, etc. etc.

V The Teaching of the Fathers, 1863, 1861

§ 3

It is generally considered ⟨understood⟩, that the Holy Fathers taught that Scripture was dictated by Almighty God, and is divine because its author is divine. Whether, however, they ascribed to every portion of their canon one and the same high inspiration, is not so easy to determine; their words apply principally to the Old Testament, and, of the Old Testament to the prophetical portions, according to the words used of the Holy Ghost in the Creed, 'Qui locutus est per Prophetas.' Hence too St Justin so frequently calls the Holy Ghost 'the Prophetical Spirit'. And I suppose, when Scripture is spoken of by the Ante-Nicene Fathers, the Prophets are mainly intended. It is very doubtful if we can argue from the Fathers saying that one book is dictated, that they thought another was. Did they look at scripture as a *whole* with one idea?

However, theologians commonly consider that the same high doctrine was held by the Holy Fathers as regards the whole of Scripture. Thus Canus, after saying, as I have quoted him above, 'singula quaeque, sive magna sive parva, a sacris auctoribus, Spiritu Sancto dictante, esse edita', proceeds, 'Id a Patribus accepimus; id fidelium animis inditum et quasi insculptum est; id itaque et nos, et Ecclesiâ praesertim ipsâ magistrâ et duce, retinere debemus'. — Lib. ii c 17 fin. p 75. And Calmet, after stating the opinion, 'Spiritum Sanctum sacris auctoribus adeo adfuisse, ut nihil omnino seu rebus seu dicendi modis scripserint, quod a Deo inspirante non acceperint', adds, 'Quam quidem sententiam Patres omnes, qui de Inspiratione egerunt, et omnes Theologi, qui usque ad decimum sextum saeculum scripsere, amplexi esse videntur'. [Vol. 3] p. 469. And not to speak of particular passages in the writings of particular Fathers, on which they would have a right to insist, they might fairly argue that the gift of the Spirit under the New Testament was greater than it had been under the Old, and that if the Prophets were but the organs of the Holy Ghost, much more were Apostles and Evangelists.

I set down some principal heads of the teaching of the Fathers on the Inspiration of Scripture, with instances under each.

1. Almighty God *speaks* in Scripture; or Scripture is His *voice*.

Thus St Clement of Rome, who in his first Epistle quotes from the New Testament as well as from the Old, speaks of the 'true ῥήσεις of the Holy Ghost'. 50 [45].

St Irenaeus, quoting the words in St Matthew 'The generation of Jesus Christ was in this wise', observes that 'The Holy Ghost said them through

Matthew'. iii, 18 [16]. p. 204. And again, that 'by Paul the Spirit bears witness to Abraham'. iv, 19 [18], p. 236.

St Theophilus. iii

St Clement of Alexandria calls the Scripture 'the voice of God'. Strom. ii. p. 362.

Tertullian calls certain? passages in the Gospels and Epistles, 'Dei voces'. Apol. 31. And he speaks of the 'enunciation of the Spirit'. de cult. fam., ii. vid also ad Uxor. ii, de Virg. Vel. 4, p. 175 and 15, adv. Hermog. 22, de Resurrect. 24, de Monog. 12.

The writer (Cajus?) quoted by Eusebius, Hist. Eccl. v. fin. speaks of 'the divine Scriptures as spoken by the Holy Ghost'.

Augustine Ep. 14 says that Scripture not only speaks the Truth, but that its words and phrases are from the Holy Ghost who dictated them.

2. The power of God played upon ⟨uses⟩ the sacred writers, as upon ⟨as⟩ musical *instruments*.

'The divine plectrum' says St Justin 'uses the just, as the lyre, κιθάρα 'ad. Gent. 8.

Athenagoras, as already cited.

And Theophilus says:

Clement calls the prophets? ὄργανα θείας φωνῆς Str. vi. 827. 33.

3. The Holy Ghost *wrote* Scripture.

'The Scriptures are written by the Holy Ghost' says Origen. Hom. xxvi in Num. (t. 2. p. 371)

'What is Scripture', says St Gregory, 'but the Epistle of the Almighty God to his creature?'

Epist. St Augustine says the same, Serm. ii in Ps. 90. n. 1. Enarr. in Psalm. 149. 5.

And Theodoret, that 'the tongues and hands of the writers are the very pens of the Holy Ghost'. Praf. in Psalm. 102 p 395

4. The Holy Ghost *inspired* the sacred writers.

St Justin says that Moses and the Prophets, the masters of our religion, have taught us, not all from their human διάνοιας ⟨reason⟩, but from the gift given them from above from God. ad Graec. 10 fin. vid also 8.

He speaks of the teaching, which Christians rely on, as 'not being vain fables or unargumentative words, but as full of divine spirit and βρύουσι ⟨germinating⟩ with power, and τεθηλόσι ⟨vigorous thriving⟩ with grace.' Ad Tryph. 9.

And he says that, in the most ancient times, there were certain holy men, 'who spoke by a divine spirit, and foretold the future, (prophets they are called) who spoke only those things which they heard and which they saw, being filled with a holy spirit.' ad Tryph. 7

St Theophilus says that the Prophets and the Evangelists agree with the Law, because they all, possessing the Spirit (πνευματοφόροι) spoke by the one Spirit of God. iii 12. vid also ii. 9 and 32.

He speaks of the Holy Prophets, 'as possessing, χωρήσοντες, the Holy Spirit of God'. 17.

In the passage I have referred to, ii, 9, in which the word πνευματοφόροι occurs, he also speaks of the Prophets as inspired by God himself, and so becoming taught of God.

St. Clement speaks of the 'God-inspired Scriptures.' Str. vii. 894. 33; 896. 1.

Origen says that the sacred books are 'no compositions of man, but from the inspiration of the Holy Ghost.' Philocal. 7

And afterwards ⟨in an earlier passage⟩ he says, 'Since the prophets speak? having received from His Fulness, there is not? anything in Prophecy, Law, or Gospel, or Apostle, which is not from the Fulness.' ibid. p 19.

Tertullian speaks of the Old Testament, as written by men 'spiritu divino inundatis'. Apol. 18.

He says that in the first Epistle to the Thessalonians 'majestas Spiritûs Sancti' suggests the words? 'of the times and seasons, etc'.

And he accounts for a rule of St Paul's, on the ground that 'prospiciebat Spiritus Sanctus dicturos quosdam, etc.' de Monog. 12. And he speaks of St Paul urging a point 'totis viribus Spiritûs Sancti.' de Patient. 12; vid. also de Virg. Vel. 4

What makes these passages still stronger than they are on the first reading is that they are founded on statements in Scripture, and therefore both illustrate the Words of Scripture on the subject of inspiration, and are corroborated by these words.

When St Justin says, 'Such things are announced to us by Moses and the other Prophets, as the Holy Ghost descending on them chose to teach,' ad Gent. 35 it is impossible not to connect the statement with St Peter's announcement that 'Holy men of old spoke as they were moved by the Holy Ghost.' 2 Pet. 1. When Origen says that 'the sacred books are no composition of man, but from the inspiration of the Holy Ghost,' Philoc. 7, he is repeating St Paul's words, 'all Scripture is divinely inspired.' And, when St Irenaeus says that 'the Holy Ghost said a certain thing by Matthew,' or St Clement of Alexandria calls Scripture the voice of God, or Tertullian speaks of the 'enunciation of the Spirit, referring to [space]' they are simply echoing such phrases of Scripture itself, as 'Thus saith the Lord,' and 'Well spoke the Holy Ghost by David,' or 'by Isaias,' etc. etc.

These and other Scripture statements on the subject of their own inspiration will come before us in their proper place, when we have to investigate the testimony of the sacred writers about themselves; here I refer to them by way of throwing light upon the doctrine of the Fathers and giving authority to their words.

5. This inspiration extended to historical facts.

For instance, the Creation, unless the passages be taken to mean the doctrine that there was a creation, not the history how and when.

St Justin speaks of 'the history, which from divine inspiration ἐπιπνοίας the prophet Moses wrote in Hebrew.' ad Gent. 12. And ibid 34, he speaks of θείας ἱστορίας, though this passage is not decisive of inspiration, for the word 'divine' may be contrasted to the cosmogony, mythology, and philosophy of paganism. (vid Pseudo-Justin 30. p. 592) 'Such things' he says again, 'are announced to us by Moses and the other prophets, as the Holy Ghost descending on them chose to teach.' 35.

'The Creation of the world' says Theophilus, 'has been described by Moses, the servant of God, through the Holy Ghost.' iii. 23. Speaking of the scripture ⟨sacred history⟩ of creation and the flood, he says, 'All these things the Holy Ghost teaches us, who is? through Moses and the other prophets.' ii. 30.

Tertullian speaks of the Holy Ghost as constituting 'the form? of His Scripture?, as regards the history of creation'. adv. Hermog. p 22

(N.B. the Hexaemerons?)

6. Scripture is full of mysteries.

'It is fitting' says Origen, 'to believe, that the Holy γράμματα ⟨Letters⟩ have not one κεραία ⟨title⟩ void of God's Wisdom.' Philocal p 19

St Irenaeus says that the whole Scriptures are spiritual, ii. 28. n. 3

St. Chrysostom says that 'there is not a syllable in Scripture without a profundity of meaning'. In Matt. Hom. i?

St Jerome will not allow the idea ⟨it⟩ to be true that the words of the Apostle, 'the cloak which I left, etc.' were spoken by Him without mysteries. ad. Pelagian, iii. And he says that 'the very letters and syllables of divine Scriptures are full of mysteries.' in Matt. ii ad Eph. iii

In these and in other passages, the Fathers bring out, as strongly as words can express, the doctrine that certain sacred books, as, for instance, the Prophets, are the Word, the writing of Almighty God, coming from Him immediately, and without any admixture of human imperfection in consequence. But then the question remains, and has to be answered, whether this high doctrine that Scripture [is] in no sense the word of man, is implied necessarily in those passages, or ⟨and⟩ how far; and again, whether it applies to every ⟨any⟩ book of Scripture whatever. Is any part of Scripture the work of that individual person whom the Holy Ghost moved to write?[1] I conceive

---

[1] An alternative version partly reads:

In these and other passages the Fathers bring out as strongly as words can express that certain sacred books as the Prophets, are ⟨Scripture is⟩ the word, the writing, of Almighty God, coming from Him directly, and without any mixture of error in consequence. But the question still remains, and presents itself for solution, does this doctrine that Scripture is the Word of God and in no sense the work of man, ⟨preclude it in any sense from being the work of man also?⟩ as deduced from *all* they say, apply to any books of Scripture but those about which they speak? The language itself, the dialect, vocabulary, syntax, is human, it is not written in the language of Angels — it does immediately address itself to the intellect — it is not conveyed in the medium of the lumen gratiae, or gloriae. In one sense then it is confessedly the word of man; and in an important sense, for human language involves a vast *entourage* of human ideas, associations, memories, sympathies, media of judgments; Scripture then, if not the language of a man, is at least the language of men; is it in some sense the language of a man also? Is it in any sense the word of the individual human person ⟨pen man⟩ whom the

the Fathers hardly ask themselves this definite question, as it might be asked in the Schools subsequently; and that for many reasons. First there was the veneration in which they held Scripture generally, as being the Word of God; and next their controversial position must be taken into account, relatively both to the Jews and the heathen. They were refuting the Jews out of their own books, and therefore not likely to disparage them; and again they were producing against the Jews Scriptures of their own, which they would at least equal to the Jewish Scriptures, and they were urging the heathen with the contrast between the Jewish Scriptures and the legends or speculations of the heathen world. Moreover, at a time, when the Catholic Church could not be appealed to as a patent fact in an extended establishment and a long and glorious history, and before there was that hierarchy of saints and martyrs, with the records of their lives and deaths, of which later ages ever have had advantage, the Sacred Scriptures, containing the particulars of so many miracles and prophecies was the definite instrument of controversy and note of the Revelation. And then too, it is further to be observed, that we have no right to apply what they said of one book to what they might have said but did not say of another, in those times when the idea of a Canon or Catalogue of sacred books did not present itself so definitely and precisely to the mind as it has done since.

Out of these and similar considerations I shall now enlarge on two; first the vagueness with which they used the word inspiration, and secondly, the vagueness of their notions about canonical Scripture.[1]

1. First let it be observed, that the Fathers were in the practice of using the 'inspiration,' 'divinely directed,' 'Spirit-instinct,' and the like, not only definitely of the gift of revelation and its authorized enunciation, but as moral gifts; nay, and when supernatural knowledge was intended by such terms, still not inerrancy in thought and expression, but of such a gift as ecclesiastical authors and holy men might ordinarily possess in any age of the Church, without any pretensions to have their works ranked with canonical Scripture. Thus, while Theodoret calls Isaias θεοφορος and St Caesarius gives the same title to David, St Ignatius, in his Epistles, takes it to himself as his special designation. And in one of those Epistles he distinctly declares that the Spirit was speaking by him, setting down at the same time what the Spirit said, like 'The Spirit speaketh expressly' of the Apostle. St Basil calls Prophecy θεοφορουμενη; but S Clement calls the true gnostic, θειας and θεοφορουμενος.

---

[1] Newman noted in pencil: 'N.B. the theological sense of inspiration is a *direct act* of illumination by God in *public* matters'.

Holy Ghost inspired to write? I conceive ⟨think⟩ the Fathers have not directly answered ⟨no thought of answering⟩ this question otherwise than in the affirmative. I conceive them to say, or at least to imply, I consider that, even if they did not say, that they would have said, if asked, that the Scriptures, though the writing of God, though sacred in its separate words, though full of profound meanings and spiritual mysteries, nevertheless was the word of man in another aspect, and in this aspect necessarily imperfect, from the imperfection first of human language, and secondly of the individual minds who wrote it.

S Cyril of Alexandria and St Gregory Nyssen speak of David and St Paul as θεόληπτοι; an epithet which the Pseudo-Areopagite uses of the Prelates of the Church.

A striking illustration of this remark occurs in the beginning of St Gregory Nyssen's Hexaëmeron. He professes his intention of harmonizing the apparent discrepancies in the cosmogony 'which', he says 'the great Moses has philosophized κατα θειαν ἐπιπνοιαν;' but he proceeds to tell us, that the work has already been done in substance? by the θεοπνευστος θεωρια of his own brother, St Basil, and he goes on to prefer St Basil's comment to the text of Moses, as being more perfect. The passage is a remarkable one, but too long to quote. He qualifies what he has said so far as to apply the same word θεοπνυεστος to the covenant, διαθηκη, itself, which he says, is superior to any? writing of St Basil; but he has already made the difference one of degree, and he says nothing which tends to a retraction of this broad statement.

So St Clement of Alexandria, speaking of his own work, says that he wrote οἷς ἐαν θελησῇ το πνευμα ὑπομνημασαι Strom. iv. p. 564, and that he will write further 'if God will and as God inspires.' ἐμπνεῇ. ibid.

If then the Epistles of St Ignatius or St Basil's Hexaëmeron are not in all respects divine, but are mainly human works, though St Ignatius speaks of the Spirit speaking through him, and St Basil's brother, himself a saint, says that his inspired comment on the first chapter of Genesis was to be preferred to sacred text, it does not exclude the idea of a human author from the work to which it is ascribed ⟨applied⟩.

Take again the instance of the Sibylline oracles. They are now considered to be forgeries, but the Fathers thought otherwise. They held, that certain heathen women had been inspired by Almighty God to prophesy of Christ, and in this they need not have been mistaken, though they were mistaken in thinking they possessed their prophecies. Thus St Theophilus speaks of the 'prophecy' of the Sibyl as 'having been a Prophetess among the Greeks and the other Gentiles.' Ad Autol. ii. 36 init. And in another place of 'the Sibyl and the rest of the Prophets.' ii. 38. St Justin says that the Sibyl 'from a certain powerful *inspiration* teaches by oracles (χρησμων)'. Ad Gent. 37. St Clement speaks of Almighty God as 'giving to the Jews Prophets, and in like manner having raised up the most illustrious of the Greeks, as native prophets proper to ⟨at home in⟩ their language,' and then he refers to an apocryphal work of St Paul which appeals to the Sibyl. Strom. vi. 5. fin.[1] St Jerome says that the Sibyl's power of divination was the 'praemium? virginitatis.' Adv. Jovinian. Even St Augustine Oppt. 2. (In Galat?), while separating the Sibyl from the Prophets of God, says that she spoke 'in spiritu'. And, though Lactantius, considered that that 'Spirit' was not from God, yet even he in one place, after quoting Chrysippus, says 'sed nos ab humanis ad *divina* transeamus', and then

---

[1] Newman also noted: N.B. Clement quoting an apocryphal work of St. Paul (over the page) for the *Sibyl*, shows that we cannot *rely* on the early Fathers when they give opinions about Scripture etc., as if they necessarily spoke for *apostolical tradition*.'

proceeds 'Sibylla dicit haec etc.,' vii. 23 as if the Sibylline verses could really receive a title which is the prerogative of Holy Scripture.

Now of course I do not mean to say that the Fathers put the Sibylline oracles in the same class of inspiration with the Jewish Prophets; on the contrary, they seem to have considered their authors ⟨them⟩ ministers of superstition ⟨pagan worship⟩ in spite of an inspiration such that it could not come simply from the evil spirit, (whom the mercy of God from time to time made use of, as of Balaam amid his superstitious altars); but it is on this very point I would insist. I mean that the Fathers spoke as controversialists, without any intention of enunciating dogmatic truths; and, as they did not mean to deny that the poems had a pagan origin, though Almighty God condescended to have spoken through them, and St Paul and St Clement of Rome appealed to them, so in like manner they may have held and professed the plenary inspiration of Holy Scripture, as they did, yet not intended thereby to deny that nevertheless it had a human aspect, while it was divine.

Take a stronger instance still. Bellarmine says that the present Septuagint text is so corrupt that it is quite another work from the original which the translators left. This seems to me an opinion advanced to cover a difficulty; (examine this) for other? writers speak differently. That the text, as Natalis Alexander says, 'innumeris in locis aberrat, a textu primitivo Scripturae sacrae,' (t. 3. p 459) meaning by the 'primitive text' the Hebrew, I suppose cannot be doubted; and the Fathers, as St Jerome, were aware? of this. The discrepancies were before their⟨?⟩ time, and they did not consider that they arose out of any corruption of text, or were mainly to be attributed to transcribers. Calmet says that we have the text which the Jews preserved before the Christian era, and which the Fathers quoted. He says: 'Versionem Septuaginta, qualis nostra aetate superest, *ipsissimam* esse quam apostoli et Patres legebant pariter et laudabant.' p. 71, and 'textum Septuaginta nostrae aetatis eundem plane esse, quem Judaei ante Jesum Christum servabant, et ab illis Christiani recepere.' p. 72.

This version, subducting the 'menda' of transcription, the Fathers considered inspired and inspired, not as the Sibylline oracles, in a different sense from Scripture, but in the same sense in which Scripture is inspired. St Irenaeus says: '*Unus idemque* Spiritus Dei, qui in *Prophetis* quidem praeconavit, quis et qualis esset adventus Domini, in *senioribus* autem interpretatus est bene, qua bene prophetae fuerant, ipse et in *Apostolis* annuntiavit plenitudinem temporum adoptionis advenisse.' iii. 25 [21]. And St. Augustine in like manner comes to the conclusion: 'illos Septuaginta eo Spiritu interpretatos quo et illa, quae interpretabantur, dicta fuerant.' De Conc. Evang. ii. 66.

And this seems to be held by a *consensus* of the Fathers, Bellarmine says (p. 127) that it is '*certissimum*' that the writers 'peculiari modo Spiritum Sanctum assistentem habuisse, *ne quâ in re errarent,* ut non tam interpretes, quam *Prophetae* fuisse videantur;' and he appeals to the 'communis sententia' of Philo, Josephus, Justin, Irenaeus, Eusebius, Clement, Epiphanius,

Chrysostom, Cyril, Tertullian, Augustine, Hilary 'et alii omnes.' Calmet does not go so far, but he says, 'celeberrime? semper apud Ecclesiam, et peculiari S. Spiritus? afflatu, ut vetustis quibusdam? Patribus creditum est, adornata;' [vol. I] p. 69, and then he refers to Clement (Strom. i), Justin (ad Gent. et Tryph), Cyril (Catech. 4), Irenaeus (iii. 25, (21)), Epiphanius, (Pond. et Mens), Chrysostom (In Gen. Home. 4), and Augustine, (doctr. Chr. ii. 15; Conc. Evang. ii, 66). Even St Jerome, who is more critical in dealing with the Septuagint than other Fathers, does not hesitate to say that the authors 'Spiritu Sancto *plenos* transcripsisse,' Calmet. And he considers, together with St Augustine and St Epiphanius, Bellarmine, p. 130, that, where the variations from the Hebrew are not the mistakes of copyists, that they are the work of the Holy Ghost.

Yet in spite of this St Jerome considers that every kind of error is not excluded from the Septuagint, Calmet [vol. 1] 75, by its inspiration. And Natalis Alexander, allowing that its authority would be destroyed, if its 'aberrations'? from the Hebrew endangered faith and morals, or argued fraud or ignorance in the translator, [vol. 3] p. 460, maintains that they matter not, 'provided they leave the faith uninjured,' which, I suppose, he means to imply as the state of the case.

Here then we have a work, the authors of which are full of the Holy Ghost, which is the word of that one and the same Spirit, who heralded our Lord's coming in the Prophets, and announced it in the Apostles, which is a translation made by the same Spirit who spoke the original, which is so inspired as to exclude error, which is the writing of Prophets rather than translators, which in its departure from the original Scripture was directed by the Holy Ghost, which, as Calmet tells us, 'canonica habetur adhuc penes Graecos,' [vol. 1] p. 73, but which nevertheless, in spite of its inspiration, is not without imperfections and is open to grave criticism. What is the explanation of this? Natalis Alexander gives it; he tells us, that the errors of the Septuagint matter not, provided they do not endanger faith or morals. So it seems, that a work may be written under the plenary inspiration of the Holy Ghost, in the judgment of the Fathers, yet at the same time may be so far human still, as not to be guaranteed against errors short of serious ones. Without putting the Septuagint on a level with the original Scripture, which at least St Jerome does not do, we may apply this general principle, thus elicited, to the interpretation of what the Fathers say of the Scriptures, New and Old. The strong language in which the Fathers speak of their inspiration, is no obstacle to their also holding, whether in fact they hold it or not, that the inspiration does [no] more than secure them from any faults except errors against faith and morals.

But this is not all. Let us consider the criticisms which the Fathers or Divines actually have made upon books of the Canon, or books which from the time of the Fathers have been received as canonical in certain parts of the Church, and on books, which might, or still may be made canonical by the authors of an Ecumenical Council. Of course it makes an essential difference,

whether at the time of their criticisms they considered the books which were the subject of them canonical or not; but, even when they did not, some light will legitimately be thrown by our review on the question before us.
[Undated and incomplete, but marked 'E'.]

I have already observed, on Calmet's authority, that the Septuagint version is canonical among the Greeks. Considering their rigid, nay their superstitious adherence to antiquity and the letter of tradition, we cannot be wrong in saying that the belief, on which that canonicity is based, has been uniform and uninterrupted in the countries which surrounded the Eastern Mediterranean and its adjacent seas, from the age of St Clement to our own. The word 'canonical' includes whatever inspiration is necessary for a sacred book. Yet we have found from Natalis Alexander, in the instance ⟨case⟩ of the Septuagint, that a canonical work need not, by virtue of its canonicity, be free from all mistakes, so that they do not compromise faith and morals.

This point may be illustrated still further. Consider the case of the third book of Esdras. 'Extra controversiam positum est', says Calmet t.i. p 591, after 'Sextus Senensis, Patres Graecos tertium Esdra, ante Nehemiam constitutum, tamquam canonicum habuisse'. It is quoted by St Justin, Tryph, St Clement, Strom 1, Origen, Hom   9 in Josue, St Athanasius, Orat. in Arian, Pseudo-Athanasius, Synop., (St Chrysostom), Pseudo-Chrysostom, 'et alii passim', says Calmet, [vol. I] p 593. It was also received by the Latin Fathers, as St Cyprian, ad Pompeian, and St Augustine, Civ. D. 18.36. Doct. Christ, 2.8. Ep. 3. and Pope Innocent. It is quoted? by Councils, as the third Carthage and Laodicene. 'Solemne est', says Calmet, with Greek and Latin Fathers to quote it against heretics, and to appeal to it in questions of faith. And it has nothing in it contrary to faith and morals. Its characteristic is that beautiful narrative, the contest of wisdom between these youths, which turns upon the celebrated adage, Magna est veritas et praevalebit; a narrative, which has been popular with ecclesiastical writers, ancient and modern. It keeps its place in the Greek canon; it was found in Latin, as well as Greek, MSS, editions, impressions, of the Bible down to the time of Sextus V.[1] St Jerome is sole exception to this consensus of authorities. He rejected it. He warns the Christian student? 'ne apocryphorum tertii et quarti Esdra somnus delectetur' [in Calmet, vol. 1, p 593.]; nor can it be denied that St Jerome is more critical in his judgment, and his standard of canonicity more exclusive than that of the other Fathers. He calls the histories of Susanna and of Bel and the Dragon 'fabulas'. He accuses ⟨speaks⟩ of the Pastor, which ⟨as⟩ I shall notice presently, (as 'Liber apocryphus, stultitia condemnandus'). of stultitia. He does not allow the canonicity of those books of the Old Testament, as Tobias, Judith, and the Maccabees, which are not in the Jewish Canon; and its absence from that Canon is his first and main reason against the book in

---

[1] Newman noted on the opposite page: 'The limits of Scripture are not drawn even now — by which I do not allude to the Fontes of Sextus, Canus, and du Pin (Malou [vol. 2] p 137) on the three rules for making a book canonical, vid Bellarmine p 52'.

question. His tone of thought ⟨He⟩ is not a fair specimen of what the Fathers thought consistent or not consistent with inspiration, and, if it is not to be accepted, as assuredly it is not, in the case of the history of Susanna or Judith, it must not be accepted here. Here there is a book, universally taken as canonical. It had then, in the judgment of the Fathers, all the qualifications necessary for an inspired book. What in fact has it? it is beyond all blame or exception as regards faith and morals; it cannot claim greater accuracy than this. St Jerome says that it is inconsistent with itself Calmet [vol. 1] p 593; and Calmet that it 'plurimum abhorret from the genuine history of Esdras, as it is contained in the Hebrew books and the canonical copies' [vol. 1] p 596. This inconsistency with itself, this contrariety with the first book of Esdras of the Hebrew canon, were no recondite facts, which it required learning or study to elicit. They were on the surface of the composition and were no scandal to the early Church. Is it not clear then that the Holy Fathers, in their requisites for canonicity, in their idea of plenary inspiration, contemplated directly instruction in faith and morals, and had comparatively ⟨very⟩ little sensitiveness on questions of historical fact. I am not speaking of what is doctrinally certain in this matter ⟨here⟩ ⟨true or not⟩; what may be lawfully asserted by a theologian now, and what may not; I am all along inquiring into the views held by the Fathers on the inspiration of Scripture, and the value and force of them; and I ask, supposing a writer now said, 'the Inspiration of Scripture does not necessarily extend to historical facts, but only to matters of faith and morals', what would he say more than a consensus of Fathers has virtually ⟨implicitly⟩ propounded in their recognition as canonical of the third book of Esdras?

Next, as to the fourth book, this has never been received as canonical, either in the East or in the West. It cannot, I think, be said to contain any thing against the faith, as far as it had been dogmatically defined in the early ages, but it abounds in errors in matters of fact, and in fables, properly so called, and almost professes to have been written after the coming of Christ. Yet in the first place it is used on various days in the Offices of the Church. This is a recognition on which Bellarmine lays stress in various places, when proving the Canonicity of disputed books. In the case of Baruch he says, p 41, 'Nobis persuadet (that it is canonical) Ecclesia Catholica auctoritas quae ... in pro festo Pentecostes palam lectionem ex libro Baruch, cum lectionibus aliorum librorum, legi jubet'. p 41. He says that the canonicity of the additional chapters in Daniel, p 43, is proved from the Council of Trent and the *use* of the Church, 'quod argumentum apud. ... Catholicos magnam vim habere debet'; and then he observes that the Hymn of the Three Children is read in the Mass on Ember Saturday, as well as at Matins on feast days; the histories of Susanna and of (Bel and) the Dragon in Mass in Lent. Now quotations of the fourth book of Esdras are introduced in the Mass at Pentecost, and in the paschal office for martyrs, communem martyrum. Moreover it is quoted as the work of a sacred writer in the Epistle ascribed to St Barnabas, by Tertullian de Praescr. init., as Scripture, by St Clement Strom. iv, as equal

93

to Jeremias, by Pseudo-Chrysostom as the writing of 'a Prophet', and by St Ambrose as the writing of one who was 'inspired by the Divine Spirit'. (Refer In Bon. Mort. xi, 50, de Sp. S. ii, in Ob. Satyr). Is it not plain then that, when the Fathers spoke of a book as inspired, the question of its being free from errors besides those against faith and morals did not distinctly come into their consideration?

Now let us pass on to the Pastor of Hermas. This cannot properly be called Apocryphal, for even now under certain conditions it is in the power of the Church to receive it into the Canon. I say so on the authority of Stapleton. '*Manet firmum*', he observes, 'auctoritatem hanc, ut sane? sit penes Ecclesiam Catholicam huius *temporis*, . . . si id ei Spiritus Sanctus suggereret, librum aliquem. . . . nondum in Canonem receptum, Apostolorum tamen tempore conscriptum, et nunquam hactenus Ecclesiae judicio reprobatum, ex. c. librum Hermae, discipuli Pauli, Pastoris nomine inscriptum, a multis antiquissimis Patribus, Clement etc. et citatum diligenter et egregie commendatum, vel Constitutiones apostolicas a Clemente editas, in numerum librorum sacrorum et certo canonicorum referre posse'. de Princ. F. contr v lib 9 fin. t 1. p. 333.

Now for myself I am not able to acquiesce in the belief that the Pastor is a work of the Apostolic age; but it is so considered by the greater number of theologians; it was so considered by most of the Fathers who have made mention of it, Origen expressly speaks of its inspiration; Clement speaks of the power in Hermas speaking divinely according to ⟨by⟩ revelation'; θειως τοινυν ἡ δυναμις ἡ ἐν τῷ ἑρμᾶ κατ' αποκαλυφιν λεγουσα. Str. 29 § 181 Irenaeus calls it 'Scripture' iv. 21.2; it is quoted? also by Tertullian and Cyprian and by Athanasius and Theodoret, though they testify to the fact that it had not been ⟨was⟩ included in the Canon. N.B. Prosper says that Hermas 'testimonium nullius est *auctoritatis*'. contr Collat. 30—but does auctoritas mean more than canonicity? (N.B. add opinion of modern theologians). On the other hand St. Jerome calls it 'apocryphus stultitiae condemnandus'; we may readily grant that this is an extreme and unfair judgment; and that he would of course have refrained from it had the book been introduced into the canon; but does it now show at least that a book may be called by the Fathers 'inspired' and 'Scripture', which nevertheless is not free from imperfection of every kind?[1]

---

[1] On the opposite page, Newman noted: 'N.B. As to St Clement's Phoenix, it was "secundum vulgi opinionem" — it was believed in by Tacitus, Tertullian, Epiphanius, Origen, Cyril. How is it more than believing "Terra stat"?' Newman discussed the point in greater detail and only partly deleted in draft 'D'; 'Now for myself I do not suppose there is sufficient evidence to assign safely the Epistle of Barnabas or the Pastor to the Apostolic age; but this is not the prevalent ⟨common⟩ opinion of Catholics; and will any one say that the idea of the inspiration necessary for a canonical book ⟨canonical inspiration⟩ would not be lowered in the judgment of every school of theological [thought], compared with what it is now, if these books were admitted by some future Council into the Canon?

Or to take the case of St Clement's first Epistle; this is doubtless the writing of St Paul's fellow labourer ⟨companion?⟩ the Pope who succeeded St Peter. Therefore it clearly is admissible according to the Church's divinely directed intelligence into the Canon. Therefore

St Jerome certainly is a severe critic; we know he rejected all books that were not in the Hebrew Canon 'Quod non habentur apud illos (Hebraeos) nec de viginti quattuor senibus sunt (i.e. the authors of the 24 books of the Hebrew Canon) procul abjicienda'. ad Domnion. Here however a remark suggests itself. St Jerome is one of those who is so earnest in maintaining that the very words of Scripture are full of mystery, and that there is a divine meaning in the most trivial observation of St Paul. But let it be observed, he was not speaking of our Canon; he was speaking in that tone of adoration, as I may call it, of any but [sic] the writings of such as Moses, David, Isaias, Matthew, John, and Paul. He was not speaking of Susanna or the Dragon, of Judith, or of the Maccabees.[1] We have no reason for saying that he considered all canonical books, as . . .

[The rest of the manuscript seems to have been lost.]

F   [Canonicity and Inspiration]

Melito ⎫
Eusebius ⎭ [Catalogues?] No. they did rather than give this Book?

The vagueness of the Fathers' ideas about a 'Canon' — they called them 'Scripture' and 'that' not already to a *book* or collection — they said that St Paul was inspired, and Hermas, and Basil — not [grouped?] them together, any more than if one said 'vox populi, vox Dei'. Peter the Hermit? 'the will of God'?

Then how stood Melito's 'canon'? Out of two diverse? 5th century? Eusebius?

[The whole crossed out]

[1] In the third fascicule of Document B, Newman wrote:
'Indeed, looking at the matter historically, we seem to come to this conclusion, that the higher we place the claims of Scripture on our faith, the more we contract its range, and the broader is its range, the less lower must be our estimate of its inspiration. The early Fathers, who spoke so strongly of dictation, seem to have contemplated specially, the Prophets, the Apostles, and the Evangelists, as men filled with the Holy Ghost, and writing on those subjects in which they would have especially exercise of the supernatural gift as Prophets, Apostles, and Evangelists. They did not contemplate such books ⟨works⟩ as Tobias, Judith, Ecclesiasticus or the Maccabees. But since the Council of Trent by divine guidance as [sic] fixed the canon with these books inclusively, it was to be anticipated, as is the case, that it would keep silence on the subject of inspiration, and that theologians should tend to a lower and a lower view of the requisite properties of a sacred and canonical book as such'.

our theory of inspiration must be so framed, that as to contemplate the possibility of this Epistle being in future time a portion of canonical Scripture. Now this Epistle speaks of the phoenix, as a real bird. It will follow that an error in natural history is no bar to our ⟨the⟩ belief in the inspiration of the writing which contains it; or that the inspiration of Scripture does not extend, as such, to the verification and guaranteeing of irrelevant matters of fact.

Reasonings ⟨Thoughts⟩ such as these doubtless pressed strongly upon the minds of the theologians who first received from the Church the Decrees of the Council of Trent; for from its date ⟨that era⟩, when the Canon was definitively enlarged commences the lower views of the inspiration necessary for a canonical writing. The Jesuits, the keen and active school to which the same momentous era gave birth, were the first to perceive and to avow the modifications necessary on this point in Catholic teaching'.

July 15, 1861

(1) The Fathers quote such books as were popularly of authority, and believed them written by the Spirit — but what exactly was the sense in which they were inspired does not appear. (2) At a time when there were prophets – Melito. A book was not necessarily canonical because inspired — canonical was an inspired book which the Church had recognized, and put forth as a rule of faith and morals. (3) We see this from the instance of Melito — viz. he and his churches quote various books — e.g. what? but still he did not therefore feel he knew what the *canon* was, and he inquired when he was in the East, and could of course find none but the Jewish of the Old Testament for none else had been put out. He does not find any Canon of the New. (4) So again Origen quotes various works as Scripture and as inspired, but when he comes to a question of *Canon* he falls back on the Jewish. (5) And so St Jerome — he is rigid about the Jewish canon — yet he *uses* and *appeals* to other books not upon it, and he implies the Church can *make* books canonical, which are not by reporting? that the Council of Nicaea put Judith on the Canon. (6) It would be the same with Epiphanius etc. (7) The Jewish Canon alone quoted in the New Testament. The Jewish Canon then was received in Palestine, Egypt, Asia Minor, Cyril, Amphilochius, *Hilary*, Council of Laodicea Anastasius Damascene Greg Naz Pseudo-Areopg. Pseudo-Athan. Synopsis Festival Letters Nicephorus Leontius

Hilary, Ambrose, Victorinus, Primasius, Bede. Hilary had been in the East and Italy, and Ambrose was [out of?] Gaul.

1. The point was, *not* that they were inspired, *but* that they were canonical. *Other* books were inspired. What was meant practically by *canonical* books is seen in Justin and Theophilus — they *appealed* to them both against the Jews and against the Gentiles, and the *Prophecies* both to Jew and Gentile. 2. Next came the Gnostic Controversy, which set Old T. against N. Hence Irenaeus 'One Author.' Also he used it, especially the N. T. *doctrinally* against the Gnostic Nestorianism etc. Also historically the facts of our Lord's life. 2a. about Clement Ignatius and Polycarp's use of it. For all these [purposes?] books must be canonical

N B. Just as each sacrament has its special grace, and as God's mercy fits things exactly to the need, so it might be expected that, in every subject on which a sacred writer was to write, he would be supplied according to his need, for that end which was canonicity, though sometimes in one way, sometimes in another.[1]

As to the *end*, next consider if not *faith* and *morals*.

July 16/61

---

[1] In the first fascicule of Document B, Newman had noted: 'St. Paul says "we carry this treasure in earthen vessels" — such is Scripture — it is; it is a literature, prompted by, inspired with, occupied with, a Divine Power; but like a sacrament, it has something earthly something heavenly; the treasure of grace, which extends all through it like an inward spirit, divine; the external vehicle, something only as regards style, sometimes in other respects'. [deleted]

First of all show that canonicity and inspiration are two different ideas, not necessarily connected. qu about the word γραφή

2. There was the gift of *prophecy*.

3. The Church has since distinctly declared the difference between particular revelations and canonical inspiration — also, that the private visions of Saints are not necessarily to be followed — but this was not clearly discriminated then. Hence e.g. Hermas.

4. Hence the question was⟨?⟩ whether Wisdom, Maccabees etc. Hermas etc. were of *private* revelation or public. The one having error, the other not.

5. Though there was a canon of the O.T., there was none of the New.

1861

1. I have been told to speak *in private* to such persons as are in perplexity. The consequence necessarily is that my own opinions are circulated with misapprehensions, exaggerations, etc. I wished two years ago to begin a course of Explanations, when I undertook the R. [Rambler] but this was not liked.

2. Two things must be observed, 1. it is very inexpedient for oneself to go as near the wind as possible in faith but 2. it is very wrong not to open the necessary faith as wide as possible for others.

3. I begin by declaring my belief in the H C Church as the oracle of Heaven, and submitting what I say to her correction.

4. Now as to Scripture, observe our position. It comes to us on the warrant of the Church. The questions of its inspiration, its interpretation is in her hands. If then I am asked such a question, I say what has the Church defined ⟨said⟩? We may not add to add [what is] de fide — tho' de fide? ⟨for reverence⟩ *Canons*? we may not add what the Schola says — and what particular doctors say — (qu. what they pronounce in arte suo, or what they say is *de fide*?)

NB On the *consistency of the Whole* — i.e. whether if inspiration is not accorded to historical facts, it does not weaken the confidence we have in the sacred writers' testimony to doctrines? — Is not this a matter of feeling? Let the one who feels it, therefore maintain the truth of the historical facts — but don't let him interfere with others who use their liberty. But the further question comes, viz if a person says, 'I *cannot* separate the two and therefore, since I *must* give up the historical facts, I must give up the doctrines too.'

1. On inspiration say, that a man may take Caietan — *but so that* he keeps in the temper to give it up if the Church rules it — but not expedient from difficulty of drawing the line and of keeping from incroaching on doctrinal assertions of N.T.

2. interpretation. *two* meanings, the first only known to the writer. E.g. out of Egypt and thus 'firmament on the whole cosmogony. Opposite theories Darwin etc.'

Guardian[1] June 5, 1861

It has pleased God to convey His revelation thro' the medium of the history and literature of a single nation.

There was no other choice but to describe many historical or physical or other phenomena; yet of these the human writers and earlier readers had no *scientific* knowledge. Hence to speak according to appearances was the one way to mislead no one.

Merely human writers would have *intended* to speak according to appearances.

They would have coloured their language by theory. *See Josephus on Gen. 1.*

Yet surely Genesis 1 has the air of teaching.

What does it teach? The *doctrine* of Creation?

Will that be enough? Perhaps so.

JHN

---

[1] In the Supplement to the *Guardian* of 5 June 1861, there was a multiple review of various pamphlets and books that had appeared in the wake of the publication of *Essays and Reviews*. Several of these were critical of the doubt thrown by the *Essays and Reviews*' authors on the doctrine of biblical inspiration.

Part II   Papers on Infallibility

Notes in preparation of my proposed Second Pamphlet to

PUSEY

on the Pope's Powers
which was superseded by Ignatius's Pamphlets to Ward.[1]

J H N

---

[1] See also, *Certain Difficulties felt by Anglicans in Catholic Teaching*, London 1907, vol. II, p. 17.

I   Introductory Notes, 1865, 1866

[A series of notes probably written during May, 1865.]
N B May 17, 1865

Thesis   The abstract principles of the Church are not necessarily equivalent to the concrete.

Abstract principles are those which are in force, in themselves and scientifically; concrete those which are to be received and practised in a given state of society as an oar looks crooked in the water.

E.g. Though it be true abstractedly that the true religion alone is to be allowed, yet in the concrete it is allowable to wish that there should be a general toleration of all religions.

Abstract principle 'Usury is unlawful'. Concrete 'Usury is lawful'. Abstract 'Toleration is unlawful'. Concrete 'Toleration is lawful'. Abstract 'Discipline must be enforced'. Concrete 'Discipline need not be enforced'. 'He who is born again overcometh the world'. Concrete 'He who is born again commonly does not overcome the world'. The theatre is another abstract principle.

In proof look at former times. 1. Consider usury — how different in the abstract command, and in the actual practice. Popes do not keep their abstract principles. That of the Monti di pieta.[1]

2. In the abstract are temporal great penances for sin. This in fact becomes suffering in purgatory. What a difference aspect and operation has the doctrine in fact!

3. Consider Novatianism. It was the pure gospel in the abstract — but if Popes had allowed that purity in the concrete, the Church would ever have been a sect, not a world wide power, as it was intended to be.

4. Take again 'turning the cheek to the smiter' — this is *perfection*. But can any state ever practise it? in practice it becomes a principle of perfection and the concrete principle is to resist evil even in a man's own person, as being a natural right.

5. Is not the very distinction of counsels and precepts part of the concrete religion, not the abstract.

6. When the present Pope says that 'he never meant the principles of the Encyclical to apply to England or Russia' what is this but to say that *in the concrete* principles are as changed as a oar ⟨stick⟩ seen in the water? for truth cannot change with the latitude.

The paper might *begin* with this (6ᵗʰ) as an introduction.

---

[1] *Montes Pietatis* were charitable institutions lending money at low rates of interest or even none at all, on the security of objects left in pawn. Several of these institutions received papal approval particularly from Leo X at the Fifth Lateran Council in the Bull *Inter multiplicis* (1515).

On vague conclusions in all matters of fact — as human liberty and grace, the extent and seat of infallibility.

On its being a question of historical fact whether an opinion is against all the Schola,[1] i.e. whether it is temerarious, which therefore when predicated of a proposition is not an infallible predication.

On the question of tutior pars in matters of infallibility being to be taken.

On the infallibility of the Church not being defined, much less ∴ that of the Pope.

Truths which defined on prescription as the infallibility of the Church sometimes are weakened by legal assertion.

Great scandal
Those who so write can have had little to do with souls
Unsettling consciences imperilling souls
A greater scandal or an increase of scandal if controversy
Hence men are held back
I believe the majority of us look with displeasure and amazement.
But a few noisy persons can do more

The passages look very extravagant — but so do all sentences of the kind detached from their context

The Infallibility of the Pope was an open question 30 years ago — vid Irish Bishops? Evidence on the Emancipation Question — again on the Maynooth Inquiry[2] When did it cease so to be? Ingemuit orbis etc.[3]

I never have been against the doctrine of the Pope's Infallibility — certainly strong acts from the beginning but I don't see that the munus pascendi requires infallibility. Benedict XIV against usury.[4] Say he is infallible then — yet it is now put on the shelf — its infallibility is on an abstract point and avails nothing practically i.e. as an act pascendi, of teaching practically, it is useless. It is an infallible truth, not an infallible command.

The gift has much more to do with abstract truths or such ⟨general truths as have⟩ general truths which have to be accommodated pro re nata. The Pope applies.

I don't see myself why an Ecumenical Council, i.e. the Pope in such council should not be *the* Oracle — the Pope enforces — supplies emergencies — and is guided extraordinarily when necessary being backed up by the Church — and the event shows he *has* been guided. That the whole Bullarium should be the word of God is an absurdity. The more we incline to the Papal infallibility,

---

[1] See also below, pp. 135, 147–9; *The Letters and Diaries of John Henry Newman*, London 1961 ff., XXII, pp. 98–9; *Difficulties of Anglicans*, vol. II, pp. 176, 337–8.

[2] See also, *Difficulties of Anglicans*, vol. II, pp. 186–94, 350–6.

[3] 'The whole world groaned and was astonished to find itself Arian', St Jerome, *Dialogus adversus Luciferianos*, 19.

[4] A reference to the encyclical *Vix pervenit* (1745). See also, *Letters and Diaries*, XXVII, pp. 132–4.

the more necessary are *forms*. Canus etc. give us *forms* etc. The anathema. I am told these are now superseded — this I cannot understand.

As to the haeresi proxima, scandalous etc. censures, Estcourt[1] by saying we *must be delicately* cautious of heresy supplies *the reason* of those censures. We go to the Pope to be *guarded* and *warned* — this is quite distinct from infallibility

Of course a Pope must speak *as if* he were infallible — every one in authority does — let alone so great a Power as the Holy See.[2] Why, a bishop does — a newspaper editor does. On the other hand *of course* we assent — it is correlative attitude.

[II]

Memoranda for P[usey] *Letter 2.*

Common sense tells us that what was an open question 30 years ago is an open question now.

It may be in the Providence of God, that, if the H[oly] S[ee] lost the temporal power, it should gain the definition of infallibility. I have never been against the Pope's Infallibility.

On the absence of Schools — on Railroads — on the 'Naturam expellas furca'[3] as exemplified in O'Mahon's life of Carrière.

The Rome School is liberal, but I. not history I don't forget F[r] Theiner — 2. not practical knowledge of heretics and of the world. Also, biassed by the party of the H[oly] S[ee] as Austrian tribunals in Lombardy were impartial except when politics came in. Secular Prelates in old time at least gave knowledge of the world. That is necessary for the *application* of the knowledge of the Cross.

Quote Perrone, end of Treatise on Church — about *slowness* with which Rome acts.[4]

If the Pope's briefs are infallible, much more are the Decrees of Trent — but Tournely and Amort say no, of the latter (though Veron or Holden says Yes).

---

[1] Canon E. E. Estcourt had a letter on the Book of Common Prayer and the Eucharist published in the *Weekly Register* of 2 December 1865, which was replied to in the *Christian Rembrancer* for January 1866, in irenic terms except for a charge of 'disingenuousness' in talking of heresy. Estcourt replied in the *Weekly Register* of 14 April 1866, stating clearly his views on the heretical content of the Book of Common Prayer. This reply was printed as an appendix to his *The Dogmatic Teaching of the Book of Common Prayer on the subject of the Eucharist*, London 1868.

[2] See also, *Letters and Diaries*, XXVII, pp. 286–7.

[3] Horace, *Epistles* I, X, 24. Joseph Carrière (1795–1864) was a Superior-General of the Sulpicians and an eminent moral theologian. O'Mahoney's *Life* draws attention to the Papal censure of some propositions of his writings and the suspicion of Gallicanism thrown on him.

[4] See also, *Apologia Pro Vita Sua*, edited by Martin J. Svaglic, Oxford 1967, pp. 238–40.

What is the real difference of de fide, and necessary to believe — according to Ward, in either case you are damned, if you do not believe.

If the Pope's briefs, the whole Bullarium? Benedict XIV's briefs? or are we to be ever picking out of it first one thing, then another?

The munus pascendi does not involve infallibility in the Pastor, but somewhere — i.e. in the Ecumenical Council.

Nor does infallibility help it — Benedict XIV's brief on usury may be infallible — but it does not *teach and direct* us.

Vincentius Lirinensis — the faith may increase intensive not extensive.

As to anomalies in passing the definition of Immaculate Conception vid 1st Council ὁμοούσιον adding to creed. 2. not in one place. 3. in one day. 4. St. Leo's interference.

Filioque Securus judicat etc.[1]

The Bishops' answers to the Pope were dictated by *the People*.[2] On the sensus fidelium vid Petus [Petavius] Incarn t 2 p 216 col 2.

The people have a special right to interfere in questions of devotion.

---

[1] Newman himself translated St Augustine's axiom as 'The universal Church is in its judgments secure of truth', *Essays Critical and Historical*, London 1919, vol. II, p. 101; see also, pp. 43, 108–9; *Apologia*, p. 110; *John Henry Newman and the Abbé Jager*, edited by Louis Allen, London 1975, pp. 18–20.

[2] *Pareri dell' Episcopato cattolico, di capituli, di congregazioni, di università . . . etc., sulla definizione dogmatica dell' immacolato concepimento della B. V. Maria*, Rome 1851–4, 10 vols. The Bishops' replies were popularized by Cardinal Thomas Gousset, *La Croyance générale et constante de l'Église touchant l'Immaculée Conception*, Paris 1855.

II   The Infallibility of the Church
and the Dogmatic Power of
the Pope, 1866

[III]

1866

What I wish to hold, and that on the ground that it has been the broad principle of Catholic divines hitherto is, that the subject matter of infallibility is the original depositum; that depositum (accepted by divina fides simplex or immediata) being viewed as including its logical outcome (accepted by fides mediata — Amort) and its concrete development (accepted by fides ecclesiastica — Tournely).

Whether a doctrine is or is not in that depositum the Church alone has the right to determine. She can determine it; and if it [she] did determine that the temporal power's necessity (e.g.) was in that depositum, she would thereby be certain that it was in it.

That she should make this categorical assertion of a doctrine, which she declares, being in the depositum or in other words 'de fide', is not necessary when she speaks by the mouth of an Ecumenical Council, because such great meetings being rare, the very fact of her speaking by some [such?] a solemnity, is equivalent to her saying that she is delivering the tradition of the Apostles, or explaining some doctrine of the depositum or dogma. Yet even in such Ecumenical Council she observes a definite form of enunciation in such declarations, and that is, the anathema — so much so, that there are divines who say that the decrees of Trent are not part of the dogma, as not having the anathema.

But, if even the enunciations of General Councils require some formula, rare as such Councils are, how much more do the Pope's pronouncements which are made at his pleasure every day of the year, as freely as his letters as a private doctor or his conversations with friends, or his answer to some address of congratulation, or his spiritual advice to some soldiers coming to take leave.

One should think that at the very least they require the anathema of contrary doctrine, in order to mark their dogmatic importance.

And accordingly we find divines laying down this condition broadly — Perrone says '*Dogmaticae* definitionis nomine, seu ... definitionis editae *ex cathedrâ* significatur Rom. Pontificis decretum quo proponit aliquid *universae* ecclesiae *de fide tenendum*, aut respuendum veluti fidei contrarium *sub censurae aut anathematis* poenâ'. t 2 [Part i]. p 516.

In the first clause, F^r Perrone lays down the condition which I first stated, viz that there should be a declaration that a doctrine is *de fide* — and in the second its equivalent, viz the *anathema*.

It is observable that he says 'sub censurae aut anathematis poenâ'. Yes — for in ancient times 'anathema' was used vaguely or rhetorically and may be taken to include under it all censures. Here there is a plain test of what declarations the Pope is infallible in, viz those in which he pronounces a proposition *de fide* and those in which he marks a proposition with a censure.

An anathema or censure is a well defined theological nota. It has many kinds, and if not limited to those existing kinds, it can only be extended under similar ones. These are qualifications of a proposition — affixed formally to definite statements. That a proposition should be formally censured, it is not enough that the Pope should denounce it in the fluent sentences of an Encyclical.

Take, by way of contrast, Gregory's Encyclical against Hermes.[1] There he distinctly says that the Sacred Office had declared his doctrines erroneae, scandalosae, haeresim sapientes etc. etc. And accordingly '*de apostolicae potestatis plenitudine* praedictos libros damnamus et reprobamus', he says.

Summing up then, I say, that the subject matter of infallibility is only that which the Oracle of infallibility declares to be in the depositum. It is in no sense at any time a new revelation, unless in the sense of *subjectivè* to Catholics here or there.

And by the depositum is to be understood the depositum in its logical outcome and in its concrete exhibition — an understanding which involves from the necessity of the case a certain pomoerium beyond what would be naturally called the depositum — for though in one sense the outcome and concrete form are included in the depositum, in another sense they are external to it. E.g. that 'the philosophy ⟨doctrines⟩ of Hermes is anti-christian', is outside or inside the depositum, as we please to view it. And so again 'the desirableness of not confessing venial sins is temeraria, perniciosa, etc'.—

But after allowing such pomoerium, to whatever extent, it is ever in its nature a portion of the depositum, whether the outcome, or the concretion, and never is distinct from the depositum.

To the above theory is opposed the new doctrine, stated in its boldest shape by Muzzarelli — viz that (not simply the Church in Council, when solemnities must be) but the Pope, who can speak when and how he will, is infallible in a province utterly distinct from the depositum, and related to it in no other way than Plato's philosophy may subserve the Mosaic revelation, the two coming from two distinct sources respectively, so that Muzzarelli uses the words 'new revelation'[2] and tries to interpret Suarez's 'new (subjective) revelation' into a countenance of his own view — and moreover that he

---

[1] *Dum acerbissimas* (1835).

[2] 'On ne peut donc nier que Dieu, par la bouche du Souverain-Pontife enseignant *ex cathedra*, ne fasse une espèce de nouvelle révélation'. A. Muzzarelli, *Opuscules*, Louvain 1827, translated from the Italian edition of 1826, p. 332.

exercises, as follows naturally, this infallibility without appealing to tradition, or the depositum.

[IV]

Four points to bring up

1. The infallibility is *never* an object only a *condition* — hence without revelation it cannot be brought into exercise.
2. The infallibility explains the revelation *interpretativè* — i.e. it explains what the Apostles *would have* said under circumstances, e.g. that Pius IX is Pope.
3. It is to be received *according* to what it says — and according to its limits. It does *not* say this host is consecrated — It does *not* say this book is true because it is clear of censures. When it says blasphemous it does not say heretical — when it says scandalous it does not say erroneous. It is infallible if the strength of the terms admits it *in se*; i.e. scandalous is hic et nunc.
4. Most important. I. as to subject matter, to decree the *Pope's* infallibility different from any other development, that it would be a *progress* — some people speak as if *they* believed *more*, who believed it. It is so in the case of the Bl[essed] V[irgin]. It would be so, if it were infallibility or no infallibility — but this is merely as to the *distribution* of a gift, — if I believe more of the Pope I believe less of the Bishops. It is robbing Paul to pay Peter. 2. as to *evidence* — no *growth* — merely the *extinction* of the Gallican Church. Rocaberti made up of regulars.[1]

Yet, if the Pope was made infallible de fide, I should have no anxiety about Providence finding some other safeguards of his acting with deliberation; just as (in another subject) now I have no ⟨I have never had any⟩ temptation to doubt that he is right in [maintaining?] defending his temporal right to territory, and that it is the Providential way for his safeguarding his independence (nay, as a point of doctrine that he is a sovereign in se independently of all territory, and has the right of being no one's subject). While I have never been anxious about his losing his temporal power ⟨his temporals⟩, being sure that, if Providence dispensed with one way, He would find another.

[V]

February 18, 1866 New idea of Composition.

1. I hope I have settled the difficulty of developments in my remarks on our Lady. After all, people rather will say, Was that great inquiry, Recueil of

---

[1] J. T. de Rocaberti (1624–99) was an active apologist of the papacy against Protestants and Gallicans, particularly the work of his fellow Dominican Noel Alexander. Newman was possibly suggesting that most of Rocaberti's 'evidence' came from the writings of the Regular Clergy.

answers of Bishops, December 8, 1854 only to define *so little*? Consider how few ⟨little⟩ are our definitions about the B[lessed] V[irgin].

2. Therefore you need not fear, our Lady in Eucharist, (which is indeed condemned) being made a point of faith etc. etc.

3. Cardinal Wiseman's passage in his Essays[1] He says that it is *clear* — and so are developments *clear* Anathema etc. etc.

and also 1. long preparation. 2. spoken to the whole world. 3. in matter of *faith*. 4. with an anathema or something to mark them.

4. However, I will not secure you against the definition of the infallibility of the Pope.

5. But I don't think it likely speaking under correction of the event.

6. But now on the other hand you must hear what we hold about the infallibility of the Church.

We never can acknowledge the Branch theory,
and what we can't leave out.

7. You will allow Church infallible etc. etc.

8. But you see you must allow '*This* is the Pope — *this* is the Church, etc', and we cannot go back from this.

9. Your first step is to draw up a profession of faith *such as we can accept* — and *then* ask for indulgence? *and then make terms.*

Some narrow the seat of infallibility so that it resides mainly or solely in the Pope, Bishops, Council, pastors and flock being only a sine qua non condition, or not even that; others expand it and place it in the Church as one living organism, the Pope as head and the Bishops ⟨body⟩ as his connatural assessor. And those who place it in the Pope, naturally confine the subject matter on which the infallibility exercises itself; while those who place it in the Pope in General Council, or in the Church generally, enlarge the range of subjects for which it is given

[VI]

February 20, 1866

Revelation is frequently so connected with some external fact that that external fact is the *subject* of the revelation. When St John B[aptist] said Behold the Lamb of God, he invests the natural fact (viz the visible Son of Mary) with a revealed meaning — and so we see with our eyes etc. A large society, a Head of it etc. etc. and revelation tells us that this is the supernatural Church.

But *who* is it that *applies*? the Church or the Revelation? St John B[aptist] *applied*, and *he* represents the *Church*. No, he is *both* revealer *and* applier.

---

[1] v. Cardinal Wiseman, *Essays on Various Subjects*, Vol. I, pp. 537–73, 'Ancient and Modern Catholicity'.

No — *this* is better — viz. Revelation, among other things, says, the acts, facts, and words by which the Church *brings* out or *applies* the Revelation are true, as also She cannot *do* things noxia etc. We believe them, not on the Church's authority, but because the Church is in them the *instrument* of the Revelation. She *reports* to us infallibly that a certain book is condemnable.

Or this: e.g. a dogmatic fact. It is de fide that she is right in condemning a book — *i.e.* we infer with more or less certitude that that book is heretical.

This is best. The Apostles could not reveal a mere set of ideas without application to facts — ∴ this application is implicit in the revelation — and the Church, as it infallibly ⟨faithfully⟩ conveys the revelation, infallibly conveys also its application. The twelve Apostles is a fact of revelation — that *this* is St Paul or St James, is the *application* of it. The Apostles at first were both inspired organ of the revelation and the infallible mode of its interpretation or conveyal or application.

If St John said *this* is the true *form* of doctrine, thus it should be reduced to writing, that book of Cerinthus? is bad, St Clement is the successor of St Peter, the Bl[essed] V[irgin] dwells with me at Ephesus, St Mary Magdalen is gone to heaven, he would speak as infallibly applying the revelation, or carrying it out in fact — and this application may be said to be implicitly contained in the revelation itself.

[VII]

February 21 [1866]

Here I come across the judgment of an old friend now occupying a post of great authority, and who has felt it his duty to combine authority and controversy in one publication. I have asked myself whether in that necessary collision which must take place I should speak without an express allusion to him or not — and I felt that, since, do what I will, I shall be considered to allude to him, I had better speak of him freely. The Archbishop's pastoral will to them who are his subjects necessarily be taken on its aspect of authority; to others it comes as a controversial paper.[1]

[VIII]

February 25, 1866

1. The Pope is the *initial* authority, doubtless — The question is whether he is the point of ultimate appeal.

---

[1] Manning's pastoral on *The Reunion of Christendom* was published at the beginning of February; see, *Letters and Diaries*, XXII, pp. 148–9; XXIII, p. 367.

2. St Victor, St Stephen, etc. prove it.[1] On pascendi gregem.

3. Were not their decisions afterwards confirmed in Council?

4. and doubtless the Popes have had a special instinct, Hence he is ever *consulted* — vid Cardenas [Part 3] p 3 col. 2, so that, independent of the duty of obedience, it would be very rash to take any opinion ⟨position of mind⟩ inconsistent with a judgment which they had expressed. And thus his advocates boast (as Perrone) that in *fact he never has* been wrong.

5. Some have thought that the *words* of their Bulls etc. prove (1) that they were *infallible* (2) that the *province* of their infallibility was larger than revelation.

But every authority must speak as if infallible. 1. even a schoolmaster. 2. and so, 'laying down the law' is a phrase taken from the Law to signify a sort of claim to infallibility. 3. The Anglican Church, not infallible, but never wrong. 4. Take again a Bishop's Pastoral — he the 'Doctor' of his Church — enlarge. No prerogative which the Pope has, (vid Council of Florence) which he *in terms* has not. His power bounded by the revelation, but so is the Pope's. A bishop goes out of this province and speaks peremptorily [illegible word] from the nature of the case, regendi, gubernandi, pascendi no one can answer him. And rightly so. St Ignatius 'Without the Bishop do nothing.' What a Bishop is to his Church — such the Pope to all Bishops and the whole Church. A Bishop of Bishops.

Yet a Bishop is not really infallible — nor does he *need* infallibility for government — he can gubernare, regere, pascere, without infallibility — and so the Pope.

6. It may be said that the Pope seems to appeal to himself and the See of Peter — but that is because by *divine right* he governs — because he has the strong presage that he will not be wrong, *because he has consulted* the Bishops beforehand, and perhaps altered or modified his prospective act at their suggestion, and because he *has to appeal to himself* in a way, viz in General Council.

[IX]

February 25 — Evening

The Church knows her depositum. She cannot mistake no part of depositum for depositum, or depositum for no depositum. She is infallible in action as far as hurting etc., the depositum goes.

Next 1 truths of revelation as necessarily evident

---

[1] Pope Victor (d. 198) attempted to suppress the custom of following the Jewish practice of dating Easter. Pope Stephen (d. 257) intervened in disputes in both Gaul and Spain, and was later involved in a long controversy with St. Cyprian.

2 truths in truths, i.e. implicit as well as explicit. These are de fide even before they are defined ⟨declared⟩ so to be, to those who see their necessity.

3 as the Church affirms the above, so it condemns opinions contrary ⟨contradictory⟩ to such opinions or any way inconsistent or prejudicial to such truths. In Cardenas [part 3] p 7 col I Jansenius's condemned propositions are condemned simply *on holy obedience*.

4 As an opinion may be inconsistent with revealed truth, without its converse? being *part* of revealed truth, it follows that there will be a whole class of wrong opinions which have no representatives among revealed truths.
The converse may also be wrong, or right without being revealed. Thus, if it is wrong to say that the Fathers are always in error without its being true to say that they are never in error and wrong to assert ⟨say⟩ that original sin without being revealed[?] that original sin is [?]

This is all previous to *words* etc., but now we come to the concrete expression of revealed truth.

[X]

February 26, 1866

My doubts about a second Pamphlet in continuation of my letter to Pusey are such as these[1] — arising from my feeling more and more the *extent*, *difficulty*, and *variety of views* taken, of the Treatise de Ecclesiâ and de Summo Pontifice.

I have not enough to say, nor would it be tanti, to write simply against *him*, unless I did something to establish a moderate view about the Pope and the Church, as against Ward, as in my first Pamphlet I had established a moderate view about the Blessed Virgin as against other extreme writers.

Now the case is very different of the former undertaking, from that of this new one.

The doctrine of Catholics about the Blessed Virgin is plain and simple; there are no varieties of opinion. I could lay it down broadly, and defend it, applaudentibus, quotquot sunt, Catholicis. All I had to animadvert on, was a certain extravagance of devotion in detail, and I could throw this off, as being foreign.

But, on the other hand, there is no one received doctrine on the Church, but several — several on the power of the Church, on the extent of the subject matter of its infallibility, and the seat of that infallibility. Whatever view I took, I could not, from the nature of the case, carry all Catholics with me.

[1] See also, *Letters and Diaries*, XXII, p. 167.

I should divide them into parties — some would be with me, and more would be against me; more, — for I could only take one view out of several or many views. There is no received English view — no books to appeal to.

Instead of taking all Catholics with me in a point of doctrine, to criticize points of devotion, I should be taking only some Catholics with me in a doctrine to attack another, and an authoritative view of the same doctrine. If I noticed that other view, Anglicans would say '*This* is your unity of creed' — If I did not, Catholics would say, I was ignoring what had at the time greater authority and popular acceptance than my own.

Moreover, I could truly and safely call certain devotions to our Lady, foreign, Italian; — but it will not do so to speak of a doctrinal view of the Pope and the Church, which is so highly sanctioned at Rome, and just now by the Episcopate.

I should not be writing against Pusey, but making a case against Ward, and every one would say so.

[XI]

February 26, 1866

Four heads.   The Church

1. General View. (1) sufficient for itself (2) *knows* its depositum (3) knows its boundaries (4) cannot say this is revelation which is not, nor is not that is (5) cannot do any thing which is really prejudicial to its depositum, whether by word or deed.

2. correlatives Scripture — Tradition ex cathedra revelation inspiration sine qua non — dogma divine faith. Nothing de fide which not revelation Veron etc. quoted by *Perrone* — *nothing by inspiration which not revealed* etc. etc. nothing etc. etc.

Note at end or after '4'

It is true that during the last 150 years a school have written which wishes to make inspiration the ⟨an⟩ *objectum* of faith, as well as revelation. What is *meant* by eccles. fides as distinct from divina? it is from grace, is supernatural etc. This seems to me contrary to the great tradition of teaching in the Church — down to Perrone, who refers to it in a note without speaking of it in text *at all*. De Lugo in a way Fenelon etc. etc. Suarez etc. Muzzarelli even *calls* it a new revelation, and says out the Church may reveal. To evade the difficulty of 'nothing de fide which is not revealed' they say it is not divine faith but ecclesiastical faith. This seems to me a shuffle Incredulus odi. I could much more easily believe the Pope's Infallibility.

3. On revealed truths etc., from the paper [IX] of February 25 evening.

AND THE DOGMATIC POWER OF THE POPE, 1866

4. On *certain* expressions — the ground of which is partly that the Church can do nothing to harm its depositum, and partly that it *interprets* the revelation ⟨depositum⟩ — as my paper of
Hence dogmatic expressions some de fide some not.
Here from overleaf — Fenelon etc:
March 4. Of course the Church can pronounce infallibly on any thing that will harm the faith, proposition or act — but can it pronounce on *positive* propositions? Cardenas gives one instance [part 3] p 6 col 1 (no — after all it is negative) — but there will be 100 negative necessarily to one positive.

[XII]

February 27, 1866

I am averse to it, 1. because it does not seem to be the old way. 2. because I do not understand a certainty which is more than moral and less than supernatural, and a faith which is neither divine nor human. 3. and for a third reason — because there has been a tendency of late to create a whole department of subjects on which it is to operate whereas at first it was, as far as I know, only and as a mode of explaining our faith in dogmatic facts, such as the heretical character of the Augustinus.

[XIII]

March 8, 1866

Since assistentia is all that the Church's infallibility proceeds from, and such assistentia, as though in matter of fact supernatural, might be brought about providentially, hence all the *laws* of its being secured are *human*. Hence, supposing the Pope the governing power it is *unlikely* he should be the infallible legislative or dogmatic — because human politics show us that it is a temptation too great for man to be both supreme and sole lawgiver and executive of the laws he has made.[1]
When we say that the Church infallibly protects itself, this means as a *whole*, and when it does so on principle. That the temporal power should at this time be kept is a point that the Pope and Church may be infallible in, from the deliberateness and principleness on which it is done — but this [needs?] applying to Vigilius, Honorius, John 22, and Paul III and Pius IV conduct towards England.[2]

[1] See also, *Letters and Diaries*, XXV, pp. 245, 262, 297.
[2] See also, *Letters and Diaries*, XXVI, p. 198.

[XIV]

March 30, 1866

NB.

Show how *very little* difference there is theoretically between the opinions of those who hold the Pope's infallibility and those who do not.

Consider

1. the great use of its not being defined is to *secure* the use of those *safe-guards* which are theoretically admitted by those who do hold it.

2. the real difference is practical and ethical — but *this* would remain *even though* it were *defined* — vid Carrière's life.

NB.

premise by saying it is not a question of centre of unity, doctor of the faithful, universal jurisdiction, etc.

[XV   Undated fair copy]

On the subject matter or objectum fidei materiale
which constitutes the credendum or dogma.

There are certain words which represent correlative ideas. These correlative terms are Revelatio, res revelata, verbum Dei, in materia fidei et morum, traditio, infallibilis Ecclesiae propositio, Ecclesiae magisterium, dogma, depositum, de fide, credendum necessario ad salutem, fides divina, supernatural certainty.[1]

The Revelatio is the supernatural act of God, the res revelata and verbum Dei is His revealed truth, res tradita as being now what it ever was, and so depositum, the infallibility of the Church is the instrument (or sine-qua-non condition) of ascertaining it, and therefore she is magistra fidelium, the dogma is the same truth viewed as? defined, the de fide is the same as proposed to us as necessary to be believed in order to salvation, and the fides divina is the supernatural habit and act of mind by which we internally assent to it; and it is synonymous with supernatural certainty.

The whole process consists of an act of revelation in the beginning, the truths then revealed once for all, and handed down, which are in consequence imperative on our internal assent, the Church's infallible proposition as bringing them home to our minds, and our reception of them or faith in them, with God's grace as its cause and their revelation infallibly conveyed to us as its motive.

There is nothing necessario credendum but what is de fide, for they are convertible terms. There is no object of fides divina, but the dogma. There is no action of infallibility except upon the res revelata — there is no act of

---

[1] See also, *Difficulties of Anglicans*, vol. II, p. 320.

supernatural certainty except upon the res revelata et tradita as an object. And so on — Every other act of faith except that which is exercised on the res revelata is principio, is an act of human faith — and has not the attribute of supernatural certainty. No declaration or proposition of the Church is infallible except those which relate to the res revelata. The proposition of the Church does not strictly enter into the object of faith — and so on.

Whether the infallibilitas Ecclesiae is invested in the Pope, or the Pope in Ecumenical Council, or in the Pope with or without the assent of the Catholic Episcopacy when speaking ex Cathedra, is a further question which I do not enter upon here. — But the main outline I have drawn out, and the series of correlative terms seem to me to be the teaching of divines in common.

The following passages, not carefully arranged, all tell in behalf of one or other of these several correlations.

1. Ecclesiam Christus instituit doctrinae *divinitus traditae* custodem, populorum ministram. Tale *magisterium infallibile* etc. Van Loo p 57.

2. Ecclesia Catholica, *Spiritu S. edocta* ex sacris literis et antiqua Patrum *traditione* docet etc. Concil. Trid. de Purgator. Sess. 25.[1]

3. Ecclesia, populorum *magistra*, sola est *revelationis* custos ac interpres *infallibilis neque aliam* doctrinae fontem agnoscit, praeter *solam* revelationem. *Omnes* theologi *consentiunt*, divinam Ecclesiae auctoritatem ipsis *revelationis* divinae *limitibus* contineri (and so Wallenburg in Van Loo p 182), easque *tantum* in rebus *fidei et morum infallibilitatis* permissione guadere. Van Loo p 148.

4. Vid the classical passage from Veron[2] which Perrone quotes and assents to t. 2 [i]. p 384. 5.

5. *Dogma* recte a Baronio definitur, 'omnis et sola doctrina quae in divinâ *revelatione* continetur et ab Ecclesiâ proponitur'. Van Loo p 52.

6. Christus Ecclesiae universum commisit *revelationis depositum*, in *hunc finem infallibilitatis* dote eam communivit, ut rite jugiter fungeretur munere quod ei demandavit. Perron. t 3 [2. ii]. 574.

7. Validissimae rationes ostendunt quod necesse sit aliquam constitutam divinitus auctoritatem esse, eamque *infallibilem*, quae divinam *revelationem* custodiat. Perrone t. I. p 224.

8. Tria habemus, 1. missionem *Apostolorum* ad gentes edocendas in *rebus fidei et morum*. 2. juge assistentiam Christi. 3. aeternum *Spiritûs* S. cum successoribus magisterium. ibid p 231.

9. Apostoli, sive Ecclesia, non solum habuit *revelationem* à Christo, sed à *Spiritu* S. *germanum sensum* ejusdem revelationis. ibid p 231.

10. Christus constituit Ecclesiam depositariam *revelationis, magistram* et *interpretem*, (i.e. revelationis) seu 'columnam et firmamentum veritatis'. ibid. p 391.

---

[1] See below, p. 131.
[2] 'Illud omne et solum est de fide quod est revelatum in *verbo Dei*, et propositum omnibus ab ecclesia catholica, fide divina credendum.' From the *Regula fidei catholicae* cap. I. §. I.

11. Regula *fidei divinae*, sive medium quo doctrinam *revelatam* ab hominibus cognosci oporteat, in solo Ecclesiae *magisterio* et auctoritate posita est. Van Loo p 37.

12. Ecclesia gaudet iisdem praerogativis, *infallibilitatis* nempe et auctoritatis, *ad* proponendam, custodiendam, ac interpretandam hanc *eandam revelationem*. Perrone t. 1. p 232.

13. Ecclesia custos et interpres *infallibilis* divinae sibi *traditae revelationis*. ibid. 258.

14. Ipse Deus prospexit *revelationis* suae incolumitati; *ad* dandam hominibus pleniorem cognitionem sui constituit ut haberetur juge, *infallibile*, visibile, et perpetuum *magisterium* in Ecclesiâ, cui *revelationis* depositum consignavit etc. ibid. p 387.

15. Ecclesia *infallibilis* prorsus est in iis quae ad *fidem moresque* pertinent, sive ut testis est, sive ut judex, sive ut magistra. Perrone t 2 [i.]. p 246.

16. Christus eam sibi suffecit ut testem, judicem, et magistram *earum veritatum* quas eidem *ipse commisit*, ac *propterea infallibilitate* instruxit. ibid p 256.

17. *Magisterium* et judicium in controversiis *fidei et morum* dirimendis, ibid p 269.

18. Objectum formale *fidei* est auctoritas Dei revelantis. Viv [part IV] p 31. S. Thomas docet *omnem* Fidem Divinam niti *soli* Deo *revelanti*. p 41.

19. *Objectum materiale Fidei* Divinae est omne et *solum* a Deo revelatum. Viv. [part IV] p 158.

20. *Fides divina* ultimate resolvitur in *solam* Dei *revelationem*. Ecclesiae auctoritas sub assistentiâ *Spiritûs* S. est *columna* et firmamentum veritatis. Viv. [part IV] p 158.

21. Assero Ecclesiae propositionem, seu regulam, non spectare ad objectum formale fidei, sed ad peculiarem *modum applicationis* ejus. Suarez t XI. p 48, 49.

22. Ecclesia est quidem *infallibilis* regula *fidei* nostrae; tamen hoc habet in quantum est veluti *organum* seu *instrumentum*, per quod Sp. S. loquitur. ibid p 49.

23. Si interrogemus cur Ecclesiae definienti credamus, respondebimus, quia habet *infallibilem* assistentiam Spiritûs Sancti; et si iterum interrogemus cur hoc credamus, respondebimus, quia Deus *revelavit*, cui credimus propter auctoritatem suam, non propter Ecclesiae auctoritatem, *licet* illa nobis *proponit* ipsammet revelationem. ibid p 49.

24. Ecclesia non accipit à Deo novas revelationes, sed explicat implicita. Viv. [part IV] p 55.

25. Quando Summus Pontifex suas *fidei* definitiones emittit, propria non edit, sed ea quae in *revelationis deposito*, per Scripturam et traditionem ad nos *derivata*, asservantur, profert. Perron. t 2 [i.]. p 519 [517]. *Infallibilitas* Petri in iis quae ad *fidem* pertinent. p 521.

26. Viva contrasts the belief in the Church and belief in the Revealer thus. Proponente Ecclesiâ existentiam *revelationis*, posse in nobis ab arbitrium dici

vel actum fidei *humanae* nixum *auctoritati Ecclesiae,* tanquam motivo, vel actum fidei *divinae* nixum *ipsi revelationi,* adhibendo auctoritatem Ecclesiae ut meram conditionem, non ut motivum. [part IV] p 44. I should maintain that faith in the Church is always human faith.

27. Omnino verum est, nullum posse esse dogma *fide divinâ* credendum, nisi illud a Christo *revelatum* sit, et perpetuâ *traditione* ab Apostolis ad nos pervenivit. Van Loo p 171.

28. L'Eglise professe, qu'elle ne *dit rien d'elle même,* . . . elle ne fait que suivre et declarer la *révélation* divine par la direction intérieure du *S. Esprit,* qui   lui est donné pour Auteur. Bossuet Expos. § 19.

[XVI]
On the dogmatic power of the Pope

1. The Pope is the initial authority — of this there is no doubt. I mean that prima facie what he says deliberately will be found to be dogmatic truth — that this at least may and should be taken for granted. The question is whether he is the point of ultimate appeal. vid Holden p 162. on the necessary power of the Pope, ut Caput, since Councils cannot be held every day, for the Ecclesiae paci et rei Xtianae bono.

2. The history of St Victor, St Stephen etc. proves that he is the initial authority. And it proves too that it is for him to *execute, protect, enforce,* apply the judgments of the Church. I think this is what is meant by his office pascendi gregem.

3. And it is difficult to read history without seeing that they have a wonderful instinct of what is true, and what is good for the Church. That it has never failed, or is infallible, is another question. But it exists; and it is just the gift necessary for one, who has the initiative, and is in arce et speculâ Catholic-itatis. His judgment in a particular case is to be trusted and followed, when he speaks as a Pastor and deliberately.

4. Some writers argue as if the munus pascendi involved infallibility. I do not see that at all. It involves a sort of infallibility in teaching somewhere, and that he is the ordinary enforcer of its teaching. But to enforce a point is not to rule it. If a Bishop were to put down Arianism in his diocese, he would be enforcing the Nicene doctrine, and he would be practically infallible, i.e. as being supported by a myriad of voices all about him and accordant with him, but he would not rule the doctrine. The ordinary pastio or pascendi actio of the Pope is enforcing old and known truths. This does not require infallibility, any more than a Bishop's enforcing them. The Bishop is the doctor of his diocese — the Pope of the Universal Church.

5. The Pope's munus pascendi consists very much more in directing conduct than in any dogmatic determination of points of faith and morals — and by aiming at the latter he may miss the former. E.g. (if it is right thus to

speak) Benedict XIV, sapientissimus Pontifex, has a dogmatic brief on Usury, which I believe neither at the time nor now (still more) has any practical use whatever. Its dogmatic principles are suspended in practice since the time of Pius VI, nay Scavini[1] says that Benedict himself practised usury, i.e. what *seems* like it at the very time of the Brief — I believe that is, that some saving clause was inserted to the effect that all these doctrinal principles were suspended *when* a particular state allowed of usury by its laws — and then Benedict, as a temporal monarch, *did* allow it by his laws. This of course must be accurately looked to — but, if so, what is the use of the Pope having an infallible judgment in his Briefs, supposing they are thus altogether in aere, or in nubibus, not touching practice, not reacting to what is real and tangible.

6. Some have thought that the authoritative tone and wording of the Bulls and Briefs showed that they were infallible enunciations — but I cannot admit this argument at all. Every one, who teaches, must by the fact that he is teacher, 'lay down the law', as it is called. Every schoolmaster speaks as if he is infallible. The Anglican Church was said by Steele, not indeed to be infallible, but never in the wrong. This is no mere witticism, it is the assumed fact necessary to its position, as a teacher. Every Bishop in his Pastoral speaks as if he were infallible, for he is the teacher of his flock; he speaks, from the nature of the case, as if no one could answer him. St Ignatius speaks of the Bishop of a diocese much in the same way, in which we speak of and feel towards the Pope — and as such strong expressions used of or by a Bishop do not prove him infallible, neither do the like expressions used of or by a Pope.

7. Nor [do] I see that his laying stress on the see of St Peter, 'this Apostolic see', proves more than that he inherits certain vast powers from St Peter — That he is by divine right the ordinary and perpetual teacher of the whole Church, that he has the right of pronouncing without being replied to, that he has a supernatural instinct about opinions, and practices and lines of policy, as they come across him — that he has the strong presage that he will not be wrong, because, as a rule, he has ever been right; that he is conscious he has consulted the Bishops of the Church, and is speaking in their name, perhaps has modified what he is putting forth at their suggestion; that he is at least a magna pars of the seat of infallibility, and in appealing to that seat is in fact appealing to himself, i.e. in another capacity, viz himself in General Council.

8. But if, all this being considered, the authoritative language of the Briefs does not prove the Pope's Infallibility, neither (still less) does the matter of them imply that he has the power of enlarging the bounds of the revealed dogma.[2]

---

[1] P. Scavini, *Theologia Moralis*, vol. II, pp. 258–9 on Benedict XIV and the Encyclical *Vix pervenit*.
[2] Newman lated noted:
Copied from Fr. Ignatius's Ryder book of extracts.
October 27, 1874.
Jacobatius de Conciliis
Lib. VI, p 241 Sed si esset dubium, an quod praecipitur (a Papa) sit peccatum vel non, dicendum est, quod si is cui praecipitur (mind, a *Catholic*) habet conscientiam, quod sit

[XVII]

On the principle of the authoritative enunciation of dogmatic facts.

The Apostles did not reveal a set of ideas without corresponding facts. They gave the world a religion, involving social intercourse and practical duties. They said, not only that our Lord was come, but they specified who, when, and where; — not only that there were organs of His revelation, but that Peter, John, Paul were those organs; not only that they had written treatises, but that St Peter's and St Paul's Epistles, and St John's Gospel were those treatises. All these assertions, that Peter was *the* Vicar of Christ, that the Apostles were the organs of His revelation, that this gospel, this epistle, was written by St John and St Paul, were dogmatic facts and portions of the infallible teaching of the Church. It was a dogmatic fact, that the Jewish Church had ceased to be the Church of God — and that the Church of the Apostles was. It was a dogmatic fact that St Ignatius was successor to St Peter in the see of Antioch, and that Simon Magus was a heresiarch. In other words, the infallibility of the Church not only guarantees and explains, but applies and interprets the revelation. So it did in the Apostles' days — so therefore it does now. Its determinations are concrete.

It will be seen that this doctrine does not enlarge the range of the Church's teaching. Nor does it introduce facts as such into the province of infallibility, but only certain visible and tangible and external phenomena, as far as they are the concrete expression of revealed doctrine. Decisions upon such phenomena are in a way implicitly contained in the revelation itself. They differ from logical developments — but, as to nearness to the directly revealed doctrine, it is not a more startling addition to the doctrine 'there are Saints', to teach that Ignatius, Polycarp, Clement, Hermas, Justin are in their number, than to teach that the Saints see the face of God before the resurrection. Rather, there is nothing to startle one in the doctrine that, whereas there are certainly are [sic] Saints, we know for certain some of them. And so with other concrete enunciations, or, to take a simpler case, what are *words* but a concrete development of dogmatic ideas? and *can* we do without them?

The question, however, at once arises what limit is to be put to this gift of infallibly carrying out the revelation into its concrete exhibition. I doubt whether any *principle* can be given sufficient for the purpose — and I consider that of some things we are infallibly certain, and of others not.

---

peccatum et injustum, quod praecipitur, debet deponere conscientiam; alioquin, si non potest illam deponere, nec se conformare cum conscientia Papae, *debet* sequi conscientiam suam propriam, et tolerare patienter si Papa eum puniat.

p 255 Sed ut cessaret etc.

Salmanticenses Dogm. t. VII p 183. The sufficient diligentia on the part of the Pope is necessary necessitate *medii*. Of course the presumption is always in the Pope's favour.

p 184 Ad salvandam indefectibilitatem quam Pontifex habet in docendo ex cathedra res fidei, non requiri aliquam perfectionem habitualem entitativam, aut modalem quae habitualiter determinet Pontificis intellectum, sed sufficere auxilia ei collata, *quando* definit.

Now to enumerate and distribute.

I say then, Revelation includes the expression of the revelation, that is the concrete corresponding fact, as a sort of complement to its dogma, or as quasi-dogmatic.

This expression or fact is threefold, being of events, acts, and words.

1. dogmatic events — e.g. that hic Jacobus is an Apostle — that Pope Pius IX is successor of St Peter; that the body of English Roman Catholics whom we see is a portion of the Church — that St Philip is in heaven, that certain Scriptures constitute the Canon.

2. dogmatic actions. that this infant has been regenerated by me by this baptism.

3. dogmatic words — that 'consubstantiality' is a revealed truth, of the Word of God — 'Deipara' of Mary.

And of course parallel negative expressions are dogmatic facts, or quasi-dogmatic also. E.g.

1. dogmatic events. Simon Magus was *not* an Apostle; that Cadalous was not Pope — that the Latrocinium was not an Ecumenical Council — that the Nestorians are not part of the Church.

2. This baptism made with wine did not regenerate.

3. Si quis *dixerit*, Non licere Sacerdoti celebranti seipsum communicare, A.S. Condemned Propositions that Jansenius's book is heretical.

I have spoken of these dogmatic facts, or concrete expressions of the revelation as themselves dogmatic or de fide, allowing only that the *line* cannot be drawn between such as are dogmatic strictly, and such as are not, but that they shade away from being dogmatic to being not dogmatic. Before explaining what I mean, I will observe that, if we please, we may deny *any of them* to be dogmatic or necessary to be believed, for not even 'that the work of Jansenius is heretical', which is the stock instance of a dogmatic fact, really is de fide — as may be seen by Chrissman's denial of it in his work lately reprinted 'Permissu Superiorum' at Wurtzburgh. (N.B. All I contend for is that they are received *either* by divine faith *or* human, either de fide *or* not necessary to be believed for salvation — not specimens of an intermediate class of credenda which may be enlarged indefinitely).

With this remark I set them down, as they occur in books of theology.

Amort gives these instances. 1. This host is consecrated. 2. This relic is true. 3. This Blood of Christ. 4. This Saint. 5. This Pope. 6. This definition of faith. 7. This heretic. 8. This erroneous proposition.

That Pius IX is the Pope is de fide according to the Fathers of the Society [of Jesus] — according to Amort

not de fide, but certain (i.e. a human certainty?) according to the Dominicans, and others, including perhaps Bellarmine.

That the Canonization of Saints is infallible and de fide, according to Tanner, Valentia, a Castro.

not de fide but certain by Suarez, Vasquez etc.

doubtful according to Lambertini.

Fides Ecclesiastica est assensus objecto, praestitus ob auctoritatem Ecclesiae circa rem nec directè nec indirectè pro *indubià* definitam. Amort de fid. t 1. p 305. How can you have a certain assent to an object which has not been pronounced '*indubium*'?

I have said that under dogmatic words come Condemned Propositions — here logic comes in — for they are generally viewed in their relation to a revealed major? premiss, and a certain minor etc. This of course introduces a large subject — and I must keep to that which is before me. (N.B. However Cardenas [part 3] p 9 formally distinguishes between the Pope's defining an article of faith, and defining a thing as certain. He says the distinction is *communis*. This must be looked at).

What I say is this, the concrete exhibition of the revelation is either implicitly a part of it, or not. If it *is* so, then the acceptance of it is de fide, and the faith which accepts is divine, being such, not only in its source, (gratia Christi) but in the substance of the act. If it be not, then its acceptance is not de fide, and the faith which accepts it, though divine in its source, is not fides divina. It bears the name of ecclesiastica, mediata etc., but whatever name be given it, it must ever be recollected that it is not correlative to a distinct subject matter or objectum materiale substantive and independent, but it belongs only to the concrete exhibition of the revelation, which is simply dependent on the revelation itself, and else it is not fides at all. To illustrate by an example — to believe in the *necessity* of the Pope's temporal power *for* his spiritual, never can be any thing higher than an act of human faith, because that tenet is not simply a portion of the development of the revelation into concrete form, but a simple independent proposition. On the contrary there are those who consider that 'that Jansenius's book is heretical' 1. is necessary to be believed in order to salvation (which it is not) 2. therefore, since it is not in the original revelation it must be so believed on the authority of the Church. 3. Therefore there is a distinct class of matters which (*not* being de fide, *not* of the original revelation), must and may be believed *simply* on the authority of the Church. 4. Therefore in particular the necessity of the temporal power, though not revealed from the beginning even implicitly, though not de fide, are necessary to be believed in order to salvation on the authority of the Church.

[XVIII. i]

Infallibility is correlative to revelation. (the verbum Dei). and to dogma. and to divine faith directly.

Dogma recte à Baronio definitur 'omnis et sola doctrina quae in divinâ revelatione continetur, et ab Ecclesia credenda proponitur' Van Loo p. 52.

Christus Ecclesiae a se conditae universum commisit *revelationis* dogma

⟨*depositum*⟩, eique praedicationem commendavit doctrinae suae; in *hunc* finem *infallibilitatis* dote eam communivit, ut rite jugiter fungeretur *munere* quod ei demandavit (i.e. munere of keeping the depositum et praedicandi doctrinam); ut autem fidem penes gentes omnes obtineret, virtute signorum eandem instruxit. Perrone t. 3 [2. ii] p. 574.

Per motivum formali quisque cognoscit non posse subesse falsum iis quae Deus *revelaverit*; per regulam proximam (Ecclesiam *infallibilem*) (in next sentence) pariter certus fit hunc vel illum *articulum* (dogma), omnesque etiam *fidei articulos, collectivè* sumptos, esse à Deo *revelatos*. ibid. Next sentence 'qui, abjectâ hac regula *infallibili*, sibi jus arrogat expendendi etc. *revelationis* objecta, ut inde etc. decernat quid *fide divinâ* credendum sit, is etc'. ibid.

Thus in defending *de facto* the inerrantia of the Popes in their decrees, he says 'Non de *quibuslibet* erroribus quaestio est, sed de iis *tantum* qui in decretis dogmaticis ex cathedra emissis, dum *universam* docerent Ecclesiam. Deberent 1 ostendere *fidei* errorem esse. 2 errorem definitionis dogmaticae ex cathedra' t. 2 [.i.] p 547.

Infallibility is correlative to revelation and to dogma and to divina fides directly vid 'Ecclesiastica consuetudo declarat' etc. Cardenas [part 3] p 6 col 2.

Perrone, t. I. p 221 etc. He enlarges at length on the need of infallibility, and the *only* use he puts it to, is the correct proposition of *revelation*, 'Ex naturâ rei, nisi a publicâ, external, ac *infallibili auctoritate* divina *revelatio* proponeretur, infallibiliter nobis constare non posset de identitate divinae revelationis. Cum *fides* non minus *divina et infallibilis* esse debeat in suo objecto quam in medio, patet *revelationem* nonnisi ab *infallibili* atque divina auctoritate proponi posse'. p 221. Nisi ab *infallibili* auctoritate *revelatio* proponeretur, dubii semper essemus etc. p 222. Validissimae rationes ostendunt, quid ... necesse sit aliquam constitutam divinitus auctoritatem esse, eamque *infallibilem* etc. quae divinam *revelationem* custodiat etc., p 224 Sequitur Xtum non aliam voluisse regulam proximam eorum quae et *credere* et *agere* deberent, nisi publicum, juge, ac vivens Ecclesiae magisterium. p 231 Patet connexum esse systema *auctoritatis* cum ipsâ *revelatione*. p 231 Tria habemus 1. missionem Apostolorum ad gentes edocendas in rebus *fidei et morum* 2. jugem assistentiam Christi. 3. aeternum Spiritûs S. cum iisdem successoribus magisterium. p 231 Apostoli sive Ecclesia non solum habuit revelationem à Christo, sed à Spiritu S. *germanum sensum ejusdem revelationis*. 231–2. Christus instituit Ecclesiam depositariam *revelationis, magistram* et interpretem, seu 'columnam et interpretem veritatis'. p. 391.

Regula *fidei divinae*, sive medium, quo doctrinam *revelatam* ab hominibus cognosci porteat, in solo Ecclesiae *magisterio* et auctoritate posita est. Van Loo p. 37, directly.

Ecclesia omnium saeculorum utitur seu gaudet iisdem praerogativis, *infallibilitatis* nempe et auctoritatis AD proponendam, custodiendam, ac interpretandam hanc eandem *revelationem*, utpote persona moralis, jugiter vivens usque ad consummationem saeculi. ibid. Perrone t. 1 p 232. (This passage might almost be quoted as a text). — necnon ad conservandam *revelationem* in sua primitiva puritate et integritate . . . et ad *regimen* in sua unitate conservandum'. And still better, the last sentence in the ch. p 235. 'Sola igitur etc'. 'Solam hanc ecclesiam custodem et interpretem *infallibilem* atque perpetuam esse divinae sibi traditae *revelationis*'. p 240. and sola idcirco etc. ibid. Also p. 258. Revelatio, infallibilitas, fides (divina), veritates (dogmata) are brought together in pp 294, 5, and the whole chapter. And look especially to p 335, where he speaks of *assistentia*, and limits it carefully, and connects definitiones *fidei*, revelatio divina, scriptura et traditio, ('*Nihil* Pontifex aut Concilia de suo obtrudunt, sed *testes* sunt doctrinae, quam Xtus docuit et Apostoli tradiderunt.' However, the assistentia is 'ut non patiatur in *errorem* labi'; but then he goes on again to connect it with *tradition*. p 336. And vid. the summing up p 387. I. non contentus *revelare* veritates (naturales rationabiles) revelavit praeterea (mysteria). 2. In the fulness of time, ipsemet prospexit *revelationis* suae incolumitati. 3. Ad homines retrahendos ab ignorantia, atque ad dandam illis pleniorem cognitionem sui, constituit, ut haberetur magisterium, juge, *infallibile*, visibile, et perpetuum in Ecclesia. 4. Huic Ecclesiae *revelationis* depositum consignavit, adsistentiam suam promittens, ne unquam in hoc ministerio vel deficeret vel erraret. 5. Christus instituit Ecclesiam, *depositariam* perpetuam *revelationis, magistram*, et interpretem, seu columnam.

[XVIII. ii]

Infallibility is correlative with revelation indirectly because infallibility is correlative to de fide or fides divina and dogma for fides divina is correlative to revelation.

De Ecclesiae *infallibilitate*. Dum Eccl. docendi munere fungitur, triplex officium exequitur, testis, judicis, magistrae. Testis in proponendis *fidei* veritatibus (i.e. dogmatibus. vid t. 3 [2.ii]. p 599 note) quas a Christo accepit; Judicis in dirimendis controversiis quae vel *fidem* attingunt etc; Magistrae, in ministerio quotidiano, quo vivâ voce et praxi fideles iis omnibus instruit quae ipsis intemerata doctrina et moribus informandis conferunt, eosque veluti manu ducit ad aeternae salutis iter capessendum. Perrone t 2 [.i.]. p 235 and presently, Magistra est in ministerio suo *exhibendo* ad homines rite informandos. p 236. But he sums up p 246 definitely. Ecclesiam *infallibilem* prorsus esse in iis *quae ad fidem moresque pertinent*, sive ut testis est, sive ut judex, sive *ut magistra*. And so, the Apostles did not use any *fidei* formulam, because praesto erant ope *vivi magisterii* ad res ipsas enuncleandas etc. p 249. Quod insequentibus eadem ratione per *jugiter vivum Ecclesiae magisterium* factum est, novis semper exorientibus haeresibus aut controversiis. p 250. *Christus eam sibi suffecit ut testem, judicem, ac magistram* EARUM VERITATUM QUAS

EIDEM IPSE COMMISIT, *ac propterea infallibilitate instruxit.* p 256. N.B. One instance of the infallible magisterium is the imposing the homöussion etc. 'Magistra infallibilis in ministerio quotidiano i.e. imposing points. Atqui neque judex infallibilis nec *infallibilis magistra* esset in docendo populum sanam doctrinam, nisi pariter infallibilis esset IN FACTIS DOGMATICIS.' p 269. Presently *magisterium* et judicium in controversiis *fidei et morum* dirimendis. p 269.

N.B. (Against P[usey]). What is universal must be revealed. (Securus judicat etc).

Ubi constans est, quod Ecclesia *universalis* veritatem aliquam speculativam aut practicam, ad religionem aut salutem spectantem, certo credat, de tali veritate constat, quod sit *revelata* à Deo in Scriptura aut Traditione. Exercit. Tolosan. p 181.

In t 2 [.i]. p 273 Perrone brings out clearly that whereas the Church is testis in *revelatione*, she is judex and magistra *neither directe nor indirecte* in (e.g.). *dogmatic facts*, but those facts are in divine revelation *ratione contradict-oriae doctrinae.* p 273. Look at Muzzarelli etc. in note p 275.

Omnino verum est, nullum posse esse dogma *fide divinâ* credendum, nisi illud a Christo *revelatum* sit, et perpetua *traditione* ab Apostolis ad nos pervenerit. Van Loo p 171.

Fides theologica (the theological virtue) significat actum vel habitum mentis assentientis *Verbo Dei* etc. Amort t 1. p 306.

Objectum formale *Fidei* est auctoritas Dei *revelantis*; *credimus* enim mysteria *Fidei*, quia Deus ea revelavit. Viva [part IV] p 31 A. S. Thomas docet, omnem Fidem Divinam niti soli Deo revelanti. p 41. Proponente Ecclesiâ existentiam revelationis, N.B. posse a nobis ad arbitrium elici *vel* actum fidei *humanae nixum auctoritati Ecclesiae,* tanquam motivo, *vel* actum fidei *divinae* nixum ipsi revelationi, adhibendo auctoritatem Ecclesiae, ut meram conditionem, non ut motivum. Viv [part IV]. p 44.

Fides divina ultimatè resolvitur in solam Dei revelationem. Ecclesiae auctoritas sub assistentia Spiritûs S. est columen et firmamentum veritatis; si tamen ea in motivum Fidei adducatur, non declinatur circulus. Viva [part IV] p 158 *Objectum materiale Fidei Divinae est omne et solum a Deo revelatum.* Viva [part IV] p 158.

[XVIII. iii]

Infallibility conveys as an instrument or sine-qua-non condition and Fides divina receives — not only the revelation but the expression of the revelation, as a sort of complement to the dogma, or as dogmatic.

Fides supernaturalis erga mysterium videtur nullatenus niti posse auctoritati Ecclesiae. Viv [part IV]. p 46.

Assero Ecclesiae propositionem, seu regulam, non spectare ad objectum formale fidei, sed ad peculiarem *modum applicationis* ejus. Multi sufficienter crediderunt sine propositione Ecclesiae, ut Adam, Abraham. Illi habuerent fidem ejusdem rationis cum nostrâ. Respectu nostri, Ecclesia non ingreditur objectum formale fidei. Suarez t. XI p 48. 49. Considerata (ut auctoritatis divinae) Ecclesia est quidem *infallibilis regula nostrae fidei*, tamen hoc habet in quantum est, *veluti organum seu instrumentum*, per quod Sp. S. loquitur. p 49. Pro objecto formali *Fidei* ponit (S. Thomas) primam veritatem, absolutè ponit divinam *revelationem* quocumque modo fiat. p 49. Licet credamus Ecclesiae definienti, si interrogemur cur illi credamus, respondebimus, quia habet infallibilem assistentiam Spiritûs Sancti; et si iterum interrogemus cur hoc credamus, respondebimus, quia Deus *revelavit*, cui credimus propter auctoritatem suam, non propter Ecclesiae auctoritatem, licet illa nobis *proponit* ipsammet *revelationem* Dei. p 49 (tamen Ecclesia est proxima et sufficiens regula credendi etc. ibid).

But he says too: Habet Ecclesia infallibilitatem proximam et immediatam, ex assistentia Spiritus Sti, *quae equivalet revelationi*, vel consummat illam. (Yes, but it presupposes the *existence* of the revelation) Quapropter, licet Ecclesia dicatur non docere novam fidem, quia *semper* explicat antiquam, nihilominus suâ definitione facit, ut aliquid sit nunc de *explicata et formali* fide, quod antea non erat. Suarez p 52.

Ecclesia non accipit a Deo novas revelationes, sed explicat implicita. Viva [part IV] p 55.

(Say) Anathema or censure — that is, propositions which either formally and directly oppose revealed truth, or are in some way or other inconsistent with it, either in themselves, or at least under circumstances.

Many authors make this 'expression' only de fide ecclesiasticâ, i.e. only certain with a human certainty (thus Suarez of the Pope, Bellarmine of Councils) not de fide divinâ.

Possumus distinguere duplicem ordinem propositionum, quae successu temporis explicitè creduntur. 1. Quaedam pertinent veluti ad *substantiam* mysteriorum, ut, quòd Xtus habuerit duas voluntates (et de hujusmodi credendum est, fuisse cognitas ab Apostolis, non tantùm implicitè, sed explicitè). 2. Aliae contingentes, quae tempore Apostolorum nondum evenerant, ut, quòd iste sit Pontifex, quòd hoc sit verum Concilium etc. (et haec non oportuit cognosci ab Apostolis explicitè, sed tantum in universali . . . Fortasse hoc modo in die Pentecostes non fuerunt edocti explicitè de omnibus mysteriis fidei, quoad particulares circumstantias, ut de modo vocationis gentium, de cessatione legalium et . . . multa de *futuris* Joannes in Apoc. intellexit, quae aliis revelata non fuere . . . Ita potest Ecclesia in his rebus cognoscendis proficere, *etiam cum certitudine fidei*, interveniente Ecclesiae *definitione*, quae (definitio?) propter assistentiam Sp. Sti vim habet revelationis (a virtual revelation) seu infallibiliter applicat *revelationem universalem ad particulare* objectum. (an *interpretative* knowledge in the Apostles, who WOULD HAVE spoken, if etc). Suarez, t. XI p 18.

which expression is threefold,
  the expression of facts, acts, and words.
The Church from its gift of infallibility has that instinctive sense of what is according to the revelation and what inconsistent with or injurious to it, that it can smite propositions, books, etc. It says that the book of Jansenius in 5 ways opposes true doctrine, or five true doctrines.
  1. a dogmatic fact; that this St James is an Apostle, that 'English Roman Catholics' are a portion of the one Church; that Pius IX is Pope; that a canonized saint is in heaven. 'Factum doctrinale est illud, cujus veritas habet connexionem essentialem cum veritate, unitate, aut honestate a Deo praestabilita Ecclesiae'. Amort [t. I] p 337. Of four kinds he says only the second comes into question.
  2. a dogmatic action. This baptism has given grace to this infant.
  3. a dogmatic word. 'Consubstantial' is true of the Word of God. Deipara of Mary. 'Meritoria causa justificationis passio Xti'.
and of course the negatives of such positive expressions.
  1. Simon Magus was not an Apostle. Cadalous was not Pope. The Latrocinium was not an ecumenical Council. That the Nestorians are not part of the Church. Jansenius's book is heretical.
  2. Baptism with sand or wine does not give grace.
  3. 'Si quis dixerit, non licere Sacerdoti celebranti seipsum communicare'. 'Jansenius's book is heretical'. (or under facts?).
  vid Montagnus de Censuris in Cursus Completus theol. t. I. p 1168.
  The various censures are enumerated in Viv. [part IV]. de Fide pp 96.7. Erronea est, quae opponitur conclusioni theol. *nondum definitae*. Temeraria, quae est contra communem sensum theologorum. Viva p 55. *Septem* censuras recensuit Concilium Constantiense in damnatione Wiclifi: haeretici articuli, erronei, scandalosi, blasphemi, piarum aurium offensive, temerarii, seditiosi. Perrone t 3 [2.ii] p 597 Abjeci sunt a Rom Pontif. — proximi haeresi, suspecti, male sonantes, schismatici, injuriosi, impii etc. ibid.
  Amort uses the term de fide (divinâ) [t. 1] p 313 p 335. (so do Suarez and Viva) mediata — which he seems to apply to these expressions — vid also Rabaudy. Vincent Ferr. Salmanticen. in Amort p 333. Vid St Thomas in Amort [t. 1] p 336 col. 2. Immediata is also *simplex* p 336. 'Fides mediata praestatur *Ecclesiae* in quaestionibus facti doctrinalis, ubi *infallibilitas* definitionis exigitur ad salvandam veritatem, etc. religionis'. p 346.
  Vid Perrone t. 3 [2.ii] p 599, 560 note; Veritates theologiae sunt 1. dogmata fidei. 2 conclusiones theologicae.
  1. Veritates fidei sunt (1) articuli seu *capita* fidei (2) dogmata 'in deposito revelationis', seu 'dogmata revelata'. (3) si definita ab Ecclesiâ sunt 'dogmata declarata'.
  2. Conclusiones theologicae (1) a praemissis immediate revelatis (2) ab unâ de fide, altera naturali lumine. Ambo mediate et indirecte pertinent ad fidem at least for those who see the deduction.

These supplemental acts of divine faith, are sometimes called acts of ecclesiastical faith, but, whatever name be given it, its characteristic is that they are not substantive acts so much as supplemental — and are not acts of faith in any thing beyond the revelation, but only in its expression — and therefore are acts of divine faith.

Fides Ecclesiastica est assensus objecto, praestitus ob auctoritatem Ecclesiae circa rem nec directè nec indirecte pro indubiâ definitam. Ista fides plerumque locum habet circa venerationem talium reliquiarum, Lectiones Breviarii, Martyrologia etc. Amort de fid. t. I. p 305.

They are sometimes regarded as engaged upon conclusions from a revealed major, and a minor physically, metaphysically or morally true.

'Ista fides (ecclesiastica ut supra) plerumque locum habet circa conclusiones theologicas, quas Ecclesia vel Summus Pontifex deducit ex unâ praemissa revelata et alterâ solum moraliter aut physicè certa.' Amort t. I. p 305.

(He calls this, from its motivum, fides mediata, towards the end of the page).

He gives 8 instances p 308. This host. This relic. This Blood of Christ. This Saint. This Pope. This definition of faith. This heretic. This erroneous proposition. (N.B. No department of infallibility directly from revelation.)

Conclusio theologica deducta ex unâ praemissa revelata, et alterà physicè vel moraliter certa, non est de fide, neque est articulus fidei, neque simpliciter loquendo pertinet ad fidem. Amort [t. 1] p 308, 9. (But then he understands by moraliter what others would call probabiliter, and by metaphysice what e.g. de Lugo calls moraliter. He quotes St. Thomas in proof, who says that it is not de fide that this hostia is consecrated, but humanae aestimationis, and he thinks that *physice* certa is not enough, because it may be false interveniente miraculo).

(It is an *applicatio* propositionis revelatae. p 311 col. 2, p 312 col. 2).

Conclusio theologica, deducta ex una praemissâ revelatâ, alterâ metaphysice certa est de fide. Amort p 309. He means by metaphysice what Canus means by certa lumine naturali, who says that, that the Nicene or Chalcedonian Council has not erred, is de fide, or that our priests are rightly ordained by true Bishops, that there is a true Eucharist in the Church now. On the principle that *Deus, revelando articulum, vult credi omne id, quod necessario et evidenter connectitur cum tali articulo.* i.e. p. 310.

'De revelatione virtuali seu mediatâ; i.e. propositione elicita per discursum ex unâ de fide, altera naturali. Estne credenda de fide. Suarez t XI, p 49 Distinguo. I. universalis de fide et particularis naturaliter. Omnis homo judicandus ergo hic Petrus. 2. Universalis naturaliter, particularis ex fide. Omnis homo risibilis. Christus est homo ergo Christus. p 50. As to the first the revelation is formalis, not virtualis, for all particulars are included in this universal? nay some of the second too, as Christ had a rational soul, for all men have? But a revelatio *tantum* virtualis or mediata, does not suffice for faith (I wish he would give an instance). In that case 'Conclusio sequitur debiliorem partem'. Ergo non potest ille assensus esse assensus fidei, p. 51. Assensus *sic* elicitus ex discursu ille non est in substantia sua supernaturalis. ibid.

An possit conclusio theologica credi Fide Divina, quamvis non sit immediate et formaliter revelata. Multiplex potest esse hujusmodi conclusio. 1. ex duplici praemissâ revelatâ, ut S. Matthaeus accepit Spiritum Sanctum. *Est de fide communiter.* 2. ex praemissa universali revelata et minore metaphysice aut physice certa; ut Petrus est redemptus. Est de fide, secundum Suarez, Lugo, Valentia, Tanner. 3. ex unâ revelatâ et alterâ moraliter evidenti, ut Tridentinum habuit Spiritum S. *Est de fide secundum Lugo, Valentia.* 4. ex unâ revelatâ et alterâ probabili, ut Xtus est in hac hostiâ. *Non est de fide communiter.* Viva [part IV] p 52.

That this (Pius IX) is the true Pope — is de fide according to Amort [t. 1] p 313 col. 2, according to Fathers of the Society [of Jesus] generally, according to Viva p 58 — not de fide, but certain, by Dominicans and others including perhaps Bellarmine, (who says of Councils, de Concil auctorit. e.g. 'naturali solum evidentiâ aut solum fide humanâ haberi, concilium Nicaenum etc. fuisse legitime congregatum, at hoc sufficere quod definita ab illis habeantur de fide') — Vid the lists of names in Amort p 313. Eo prorsus modo, quo revelatum est *hanc numero Ecclesiam esse veram Dei* ecclesiam, ita prorsus revelatam est hunc numero Pontificem esse vere Xti vicarium. Viva p 63.

Canonization of Saints.

1. (from Benedict XIV, through Amort) not infallible.

2. not de fide that infallible — Suarez, Vasquez, Rabaudy, Vincent Ferr?, Bannes, Salmanticenses, Raynaud etc.

Yes — de fide — Tanner, Valentia, a Castro, etc.

Papa ex Cathedrâ obligans totam Ecclesiam ad invocationem et solemnem cultum Sancto exhibendum est infallibilis. Amort [t. 1] p 332.

Those who do not say that it is de fide, say that it is *certain* etc. etc. p 333. Suarez, Vasquez etc. Lambertini *leaves it doubtful* till the Pope decides. p 333.

De fide est, eos, qui canonizati sunt, esse Sanctos. Viva [part IV] p 58.

Infallibilis est Pontifex, non solum quando praecipit (honesta) sed quando *approbat.* Cardenas part 3. p 2

[Separate note]

The Pope infallible, not in the canonization, but in the commending cultus etc. i.e. in the act, not in the doctrine. Amort t 1 p 333.

[XVIII. iv]

Papa docens ex Cathedrâ.

Hunc terminum complexum, Papa etc., prout Theologi ab aliquot saeculis loqui amant, diversimodi ab iis explicari:-

Quidam intelligunt Papam loquentem ad *totam* Ecclesiam in *materie* fidei et morum. Verùm . . . Papa potest edere Bullam doctrinalem in materie f. et m. eamque inscribere ad omnes Episcopos et fideles totius Ecclesiae, *quin eos obligat* ad credendum.

Alii, Papam loquentem ad etc. etc. *eos obligando* ad credendum definita. Melior explicatio, verum non sufficit; quia, si Papa in *primo post electionem* convivio, sine adhibita morali diligentiâ et maturo examine, etc. vellet statim super mensam definire etc. pauci Theologi qui ejusmodi definitionem adorare vellent pro infallibili oraculo Sp. S.

Itaque intelligo, Papam post adhibitam moralem diligentiam de sensu Scripturae et uniformis traditionis Ecclesiarum, etc. Amort. [t. 1] p 216 [p. 316]. vid also p 335 col. 2.

(N.B. Amort says p 327 'Natio Gallicana juxta stylum Ecclesiasticum, conficit quartam Ecclesiae partem'). (He allows with Baronius p 329 that Liberius fell, but did not *teach* heresy).

Errare non potest ex assistentiâ Spiritûs Sancti, in definiendis illis quae ad *fidem*, ad religionem, et ad ECCLESIAE REGIMEN spectant. Viva [part IV] p 64.

(Perrone insists in various places that the infallibility, whether of Pope or Church, does not exclude the 'media ad veritatem assequendam', quippe, non per modum infusi doni, sed per modum praesidii sive assistentiae, Deus illam promisit. t 2 [i] p 541. Vid also p 253.

Perrone says that the Pope exerts his infallibility as one *with* the body, quatenus unum cum ea corpus constituit, ut unitatis centrum. t 2 [i]. p 517. Vid however p 545. Therefore, not *simply* as successor of St Peter, or Vicar of Christ, or *in* as well as ex Cathedrâ?

Question. When the Pope condemns the absolution of any absent person (Cardenas [part 3] p 8) *what* does he directly condemn? is it the act? and only the doctrine, 'an absent person may be absolved' *indirectly*, as contained in the act? This double view of the decree as prohibitory and declaratory is treated by Cardenas pp. 8. 9. He says the decree is *both*.

Suarez etc. and Cardenas (p 8) say that the Pope *cannot but* deliberate before making a decree.

Cardenas p 9. formally distinguishes between the Pope's defining an article of faith, and defining a thing as certain. The passage should be looked at. He says it is *communis*. He says 'Sunt multa omnino certa, in quibus Pontifex errare non possit, quamvis non perveniat ad certitudinem articuli Fidei'. col. 2. But then I should say that they *related* to the faith, and were so pronounced to be and defined by the Pope. I don't like to admit a certainty less than a certainty of Faith, yet not human, though it *may* be understood to be a certainty which proceeds from grace, but of which the *substance* is not supernatural.

Damnare est verbum aequivalens τῷ definire, decidere, declarare. p 9. So *I* should say.

N.B. The infallibility of Church or Pope, implies the existence and use on his part of Scripture or tradition, but, even though he did not produce it, i.e. the instrumenta ⟨indicia⟩ traditionis, we must believe that he *has* used it, on the ground of his infallible magisterium. Perrone de Concept. Immac. and also his Praelect. Theol. t. 2 [i]. p 545 fin.

Non nisi ex Ecclesiae testimonio et magisterio certo nobis constare potest quidnam sit dogmaticae et divinae traditionis etc. Van Loo p 59 note and so on, p 63. Traditionibus dogmata fidei non posse tanquam primario certitudinis fundamento, quid à vivo Ecclesiae magisterio unicè mutuantur. Also p. 78.

On the *conditions* of an infallible definition.

Cardenas [part 3] p 6 col 2. 1. from the Pope *immediately not from S. Congregation*. 2. ex Cathedra tanquam Caput et Magister. 3 cum maturâ deliberatione.

'loqui ex Cathedrâ', 'docere Ecclesiam', 'loqui Ecclesiae', 'loqui ut caput Ecclesiae'. these four synonyms. Cardenas p 7 viz 'quando decretum edat pro universa Ecclesiâ'.

Definiunt vel approbant tanquam credendum vel observandum ab universâ Ecclesiâ. ibid.

Quando *obiter* et per transennam Pontifex aliquid *decernit*, etiam in materiâ Fidei, et morum, tunc *non* loquitur ex cathedrâ, neque ut caput Ecclesiae; ut Nicolaus de baptismo in nomine Xti. ibid p 7.

Loqui ex cathedra may be merely a *praecipere*, a giving a *praeceptum* ad *observandum*, as is plain all through p 7.

And so too, the Pope being considered the channel of infallibility.

'*Irreformabilis* pontificii primatus in *fidei morumque* judiciis'. Perrone t 2 [i]. p 515. Then, speaking of the Gallicans, 'Irreformabile ante ecclesiae consensum censetur ideo esse ab hujus articuli auctoribus judicium Summi Pontificis in *dogmaticis decretis*, quia ipsi minime *infallibilem* esse existimant in suo judicio ejusdem auctoritatem. Communis autem Catholicorum sententia est, Rom. Pontem ejusmodi *infallibilitatis* praerogativa à Xto Dom. praeditum esse, ita ut errare nequeat, cûm, tanquam supremus Ecclesiae Primas, aliquid *de fide* credendum aut tenendum universis christifidelibus proponit. *Dogmaticae* definitionis nomine, seu def. is editae *ex cathedra*, significatur Rom.i Pont.is decretum, quo *proponit* aliquid universae Ecclesiae *de fide* tenendum, aut respuendum veluti *fidei* contrarium sub *censurae aut* anathematis poenâ. p 516. Quando suas *fidei* definitiones emittit, propria non edit, sed ea quae in *revelationis deposito*, per *Scripturam et traditionem* ad nos *derivata*, asservantur, profert, p 519 [517]. *Infallibilitas* Petri in iis quae *ad fidem* pertinent. p 521. Si Pontifex in suo ac solemni *magisterio* in rebus fidei errare posset etc. . . .

Christus nobis praecepit ut *magisterio* Petri in iis praesertim quae ad *fidem* pertinent, N.B. (to include ecclesiastical faith?), nosmetipsos subjiceremus ... p 522. Even, when he insists that, since we must *obey* his definitions, there is no *real* obedience without internal assent, he does not go beyond *de fide*. P 544, 5.

[The following notes and longer extract were written by Newman at the same time as document XVIII and possibly even before it. But although they might not be in the proper chronological order, they have been reprinted here for convenience.]

NB The condemned propositions by Innocent XI have nothing to do with interior assent. Vid Language of the Pope. Cardenas. t 2 [3]. p 7.

On Irenica,
    vid Van Loo p 15 and Liebermann there quoted — referring to Veron and Holden and Bossuet.
    Perrone — Methodologia?
    Polemica. Van Loo p 36, the Wallenberghs and Veron and p 52 Chrismann.

    Ecclesiam esse illud cognoscendi (doctrinam vel medium vel regulam fidei motivum seu regulam fidei) medium sive regulam, docent Catholici, quam Christus instituit doctrinae divinitus traditae custodem, populorum minis-tram. Tale *magisterium infallibile* etc. Van Loo p 57.
    Directly. 'Ecclesia Catholica, *Spirtu S.* edocta ex *sacris literis* et antiqua Patrum *traditione* docet'. Conc. Trident. de Purgatorio Sess. 25.
    Trident. de Purgatorio Sess. 25.
    Ecclesia, tanquam populorum omnium ... *magistra*, sola est *revelationis* custos ac interpres promissione divinâ *infallibilis* — neque alium doctrinae fontem agnoscit praeter solam revelationem, hoc est sacras literas, et Traditionem tum scriptam tum oralem ... Ecclesia de illis (quae à philoso-phiâ etc pendent) *proprie* non judicat, ... quippe quae solius doctrinae *revelatae magistra* et judex est. *Hinc omnes theologi consentiunt, divinam Ecclesiae auctoritatem ipsis revelationis divinae limitibus contineri,* and so Wallenberg in Van Loo p 182, *eamque tantum in rebus fidei et morum infallibili-tatis promissione gaudere* etc. Van Loo p 148 *vid the classical passage* in Veron which Perrone quotes and assents to t. 2 [i] p 384–5 and vid Viva. It follows p 149 that '*argumenta* quibus Ecclesia utitur neque ad fidem pertinere, neque ulla divinae auctoritatis praerogativa muniri'. He refers to Gotti t 1. p 32.
    Hence about false propositions.[1] The Church damnat eas, non eo quidem quod de illis in se judicat, sed eatenus, quatenus illa veritati revelatae sunt

---

[1] See also, *Difficulties of Anglicans*, vol. II, pp. 333–4.

opposita. p. 149, and so on, an *important* passage. For the *contrary* to these passages have no sanction from the *Church* in consequence of the condemnation.

[XVIII. v]

The correlation of Revelatio, dogma, infallibilitas, fides divina etc. (continued).

Illud omne et *solum* est *de fide* Catholicâ quod est *revelatum* in *Verbo* Dei, et propositum omnibus ab Ecclesiâ Catholicâ, fide *divina credendum.* Veron. Reg. c. 1 § 1 init.

Fides divina est credere propter auctoritatem Dei *revelantis,* in quam *solam* auctoritatem *tota* resolvitur. . . . Propositio fit per pastores etc. *Nec enim* aliter fieri potest, ut talibus *credendis* singuli fideles *astringantur.* ibid. (aliter i.e. except as 1. *revealed* by God. 2. proposed by Pastores etc.)

He prefers the word 'Catholic' faith to divine faith — because theologians differ as to which *is* divine. And some hold certain things must be believed by *divine* faith, without saying such things are believed by Catholic faith, and that they are heretics and to be removed from the Altar and Church communion, who do *not* believe them.

Fides divina, quae sit etiam *Catholicâ, sola* est de quâ Paulus, 'Corde creditur ad *justitiam,* ore autem confessio fit ad *salutem*'. § 1 But duo debent conjunctim adesse, quo doctrina aliqua sit Fidei Catholicae; alterum, ut sit *revelata* à Deo, alterum, ut sit *proposita* ab Ecclesiâ. Si utrumque adsit alicui doctrinae, illa Fide divinâ Catholicâ credenda; si alterum desit, seu revelatio, seu propositio Ecclesiae, non est Fide divinâ Catholicâ credenda. § 2.

Cum nihil sit de Fide Catholicâ, nisi revelatum per Prophetas, Apostolos, et Auctores Canonicos, sequitur, Nihil esse de Fide divinâ, quae novimus ex revelationibus factis post tempora Apostolorum, ... *etiamsi* approbatae forent tales visiones a quibusdam Conciliis etiam Universalibus, quales aliquae referuntur in secundo Niceno etc. Fides, quae haberi potest ex iis *humana est.* § 3.

Sequitur insuper, nihil fide divinâ credi ex ullo miraculo facto post tempora Apostolorum, in confirmationem cujusvis doctrinae, nullumque horum miraculorum fide divinâ esse necessario credendum; . . . etsi talia miracula contineantur in Bullis Summorum Pontificum Romanorum canonizationis Sanctorum. § 3.

An assensus ob revelationes *privatas* sint assensus supernaturales et divina, et Fidei Divinae, quia videntur fieri ob auctoritatem divinam revelantis . . . . illa est quaestio problematica inter Theologos. Probabilius censemus, talem assensum non esse divinum, sed pure humanam, quia solvitur in pure humanam auctoritatem. Talis fides non est theologica, et longe longius non est Catholica. § 3.

Nullam consequentiam, deductam ex propositione aliquâ Fidei et aliâ evidenti lumine naturae, per formam logicam, sufficientem esse fundando Fidei Catholicae articulo. *Fides* ex *auditu*, auditus per *Verbum Dei*, non per consequentiam. Certum est varias esse sententias doctorum Catholicorum, an quod sic sequitur ex Scripturâ sit de Fide? — Asserunt Vega, Canus — alii negant. Distinguunt alii, Si ex duabus Scripturae, illam esse de fide, nunquam si ex unâ, et aliâ evidenti lumine naturae. Alio modo distinguit Vasquez, assensum conclusionis illius, quae deducitur ex praemissis, non esse Fidei, quae tamen, medio discursu vel instrumento aut potius proponente, splendet doctrina divina virtualiter contenta in praemissis, esse assensum fidei. Sic inter nostrates certum est *problematicum* solum esse, an quod sequitur de fide, sit de fide. *Consentiunt* ergo omnes non esse de fide *Catholicâ*, id est, non esse talem doctrinam, cui omnes *sub poenâ haereseos* teneantur assentiri tanquam de fide; et *si quis contrarium* diceret, novator ipse *valde culpandus* foret, novum dogma ingerens, etc, oppositum sentientes damnans, hoc ipso ipsemet *temeritatis* in re gravissima damnandus, et *censurâ ecclesiasticâ percellendus*. § 3.

And Holden, Jure secludimus à numero de necessitate credendorum, quidquid theologorum tantum modo consequiis fulcitur. p 170 Nullae decretales Rom. Pontificum in corpore Juris Canonici, nullae Juris canonici, sufficientes sunt fundando articulo fidei Cath. aliquot erroris arguendae sunt. Veron § 4 p 364. 6. Holden p 171.

Papa, quocumque modo loquens, etiam ex cathedrâ, non est Universalis Ecclesia; ergo quod ab eo proponitur . . . non est doctrina fidei Catholicae . . . Si quis contrarium doceret, novator ipse foret, et censurâ percellendus, quippe novi dogmatis inventor. . . . Opinionem, Pontificem etiam ut Pontificem posse esse haereticum et docere haeresim, si absque concilio definiat, et de facto aliquendo accidisse, non assentimus Bellarmino dicenti videri erroneam et haeresi proximam, quanquam hoc ipsum non nisi nutans dicit termino illo 'videtur'. § 4.

The difference between saying that a point is de fide and de fide Catholicâ, in Veron's work, I suppose, is this; that the point de fide is one, which, being certain, *may* be believed or *is* believed by fides divina i.e. by grace; but fides Catholica is the actual *promise* of grace, and the condition of gaining heaven. And thus the 'de fide' will belong to such truths as God may make known to one and not to another — which is how *other* writers express it. Non dicimus sic definita non esse de fide, sed non esse de fide catholicâ, seu non esse doctrinam, quam omnes, quo sint Catholici, tenere debeant, tanquam de fide, cujusque contrarium sit haereticum, et removens à gremio Ecclesiae. Omnes nihilominus concedunt, gravis esse auctoritatis, quod à Pontifice Sanctae Sedis docetur, and that it is temerarium discedere a pronunciatis à Papa proponenti ex cathedrâ. § 4.

On Gregory III's admitting of divorce in a *decretal*, Bellarmine says, 'Posset etiam dici, Pontificem ex ignorantia lapsum esse, quod posse Pontificibus accidere non negamus, cùm opinionem suam aliis declarant', § 4. but then (though this is another matter) such 'ignorance' on the part of Gregory shows that up to that date the Church, neither in doctors, people, or traditions, had taught that divorce never could be. Decretales fere omnes responsa sunt particularibus data, non toti Ecclesiae, in quibus responsionibus particularibus concedunt omnes Papam posse errare.

As to the capita before the Canons in the Tridentine Council, I think Tournely and Amort say that they are *not* de fide. But Vasquez says, Quicquid in capitibus traditur ante Canones à Concilio pertinens ad doctrinam, est Catholica fides. 3 part. disput. 207. cap. 3. Veron says generally that in the capita, id solum et totum est de fide, quod definitur. Solum dispositivum arresti seu contenti in capite est canone est de fide, motivum vero arresti, seu ejus probationes, non sunt de fide. Ver. § 4. Quidquid per modum *prooemii* vel clausulae viam decreto praemunientis, nequaquam habet definitionis virtutem. Sicut neque probationes — multo minus quae dicta sunt obiter. *Nihil praeter nudos canones.* Holden p 203.

Plurima continentur in conciliis etiam universalibus, quae non sunt de fide, scilicet quod in eo est *obiter* dictum. § 4. Vid Bellarmine too t 1 lib de clericis cap 28 and Holden p 153.

Nunquam hactenus damnavit Ecclesia sub excommunicationis poenâ eos, qui aliquid pertinaciter at absolute asseruerint, nisi ea id damnet tanquam errorem contra fidem. Vasquez apud Veron § 4.

Pertinaciter aliquid asserere est post definitionem id scienter affirmare. Vasquez ibid. Non sunt proprie haeretici qui sentiunt Pontificem non esse supra omnia concilia, licet Lateranense sub Leone X diserte et ex professo docuit Pontificem esse supra omnia concilia, et reprobavit contrarium decretum editum in Concilio Basiliensi, (quia) Concilium Later. rem istam non? *definivisse proprie*, ut decretum fide Catholicâ tenendum, dubium est — et ideo non sunt haeretici, qui contrarium sentiunt. Bellarm apud Veron § 4.

Objectum debet esse *definibile* de fide. E.g. Bellarminus lib 4 de Rom. Pont. cap 41 concedit Joannem XXII errasse cum docuit, etc. haec enim quaestio ad fidem non pertinet. Similiter doctrinae, legum aut philosophiae studia spectantes, non sunt definibiles de fide. Veron § 4.

Concilium generale errare potest in quaestionibus de facto. § 4. 12.

Longe longius abest esse de fide, hanc vel illam excommunicationem esse validam. § 4. 13.

Ut Concilium Trid. abstinuit à termino infallibilitatis in Ecclesiâ, ita licitum cuique ab eo abstinere. Nec nos ergo utamur, nec sapientiores in fidei rebus simus Concilio. Res significata per ipsum terminum est de fide. Veron. in fine operis.

[XIX]

Securus judicat orbis terrarum

When we say that the Church infallibly protects herself, this means when regarded as a whole, and when she does so on principle. It need not be so as regards particular, undeliberate, and local acts. If, as now, she lays down by the mouth of her chief Pastor with the assent of a great number of Bishops, that the temporal power is at present necessary for the spiritual, we may well believe that she is stating a fact in providence ⟨providential fact⟩, which it would be wrong to doubt. But this would not necessarily apply to such acts as the conduct of Paul III or Pius IV towards England; nor again to the conduct of Vigilius, Honorius, John XXII etc.[1]

On narrowness etc.

Holden says, *plurimi* siquidem sunt, qui . . . . non solùm consecutiones dubias, sed opiniones passim concertatas, ad *fidem* necessarias tuentur. p 173.

[XX]

The censures

'Temerarious' is sometimes explained by de Buck p 279. Viva [part IV] p 55 to be what is opposed to all divines of the Schola. It is then the declaration of a question of fact. Has the Church the gift to declare infallibly a matter of fact? Of course it may declare facts *authoritatively*, but from its position and its gifts. These invest its decision with high authority and more than probability; but it is not therefore de fide.

'Offensive to pious ears', 'scandalous' — these too are declarations of matters of fact — and, moreover, facts, which necessarily vary with the time and place.

Cardenas says that the Condemned Propositions of Innocent XI, concerning which he writes, have no concern with interior assent — that is, they may be held, I suppose, privately, or at least need not be condemned inwardly. vid the language of the Pope in Cardenas t. 2 [part 3] p 7.

The reverse of wrong is not necessarily right. It does not follow then, because the Church condemns a proposition, that she affirms the opposite, or contrary. The Church, says Van Loo, p 149, condemns false propositions, non eo quidem quod de *illis in se* judicat, sed EATENUS, quatenus illae veritati revelatae sunt *oppositae*; and so on. As truth is one and error manifold, there may be a thousand propositions, condemned or capable of being condemned to one dogma — and they are only condemned as opposing that dogma — so that their letter does not admit of being argued about or deduced from.

---

[1] Partly quoted by G. Biemer, *Newman on Tradition*, London 1967, p. 181.

It has to be considered, however, whether, since the Church can infallibly condemn a proposition, why it cannot infallibly approve a proposition, i.e. say it is CONSISTENT with the truth? this is not usual. The instance Cardenas gives [part 3] p 6 col. 1 is negative, not positive.

As Cardenas says 'Damnare est verbum aequivalens τῷ definire, decidere, declarare p 9 he says that infallibility extends non solum quando praecipit honesta, sed quando *approbat*, as well as when damnat. part 3, p 2.

Fr de Buck[1] in the Études Rel. Hist. February, March, 1866 says Les propositions contradictoires des propositions condamnées, meritent à divers titres d'être qualifiées de pieuses — mais les contradictoires de propositions *impies, blasphematoires*, ou *heretiques* sont *seules de foi*. Les autres censures n'imposent pas la même obligation. Cependant les docteurs sont d'accord pour affirmer qu'elles créent toutes des *devoirs de conscience*. Si une proposition est condamnée sous un rapport, sous ce rapport elle est digne de condamnation; et elle est, quant a la *practique, improbable*. Ainsi, si scandaleuse, et offensive pour etc. elle doit être considérée comme telle, and *comme improbable pour la pratique*. De Lugo (de fid. d 20. n 134) Moya etc. croient qu'on ne peut *pas inférer de là que la proposition soit fausse*. vid La Croix II, n. 204 Vasquez, Suarez, Noris, Noel Alexander, et presque tous les theologiens modernes remarquent, que plusieurs propositions de Baius n'ont été proscrites qu'à cause de la censure qu'il y avait jointe, ou de l'âpreté avec laquelle il s'exprimait. vid Clerc de Beauberon. De Gratiâ apud Migne t 10. p 904.

Si (in Concilio Generali) propositio non sit *directe* et *expresse* in terminis revelatae et Catholicae Fide dogma, proindeque nec illi propositioni oppositum, quod damnandum et anathematizandum est, sit ex *adverso* et *conceptis verbis* Fidei revelatae et Catholicae contrarium, aliis et aliis *censuris*, pro rei merito, affici et prohiberi solet; quibus tamen, sicut et caeteris omnibus supremi hujus tribunalis decretis, *religiose obtemperandum* esse fatetur omnis vere Catholicus. Holden p 147.

Fr Buck thus enumerates the Censures p 279.

Les croyances pieuses peuvent se subdiviser par opposition avec les diverses qualifications, notes ou censures théologiques. 1. impious and blasphemous. 2. heretical. 3. savouring of heresy. 4. false. 5. erroneous. 6. scandalous and pernicious. 7. temerarious. 8. dangerous. 9. ill sounding. 10. captious.

Vid an enumeration in Viv. de Fide pp 96. 7. and in his Damn. Theses.

Septem censuras recensuit Concilium Constantiense in damnatione Viclifi: Articuli 1. haeretici. 2. erronei. 3. scandalosi. 4. blasphemi. 5. piarum aurium offensivi. 6. temerarii. 7. seditiosi. Perrone t. 3 [2. ii] p 597.

Adjecti sunt a Romano Pontifice. 1 proximi haeresi. 2 suspecti. 3 male sonantes. 4 schismatici. 5 injuriosi. 6 impii. ibid.

vid Montagnus de Censuris in Migne's Cursus. t 1. p 1168

Holden de Resolutione Fidei p 290

---

[1] See *Letters and Diaries*, XXII, p. 188.

Haeresim sapiunt/Haeresi sunt proximae propositiones quae reperiantur oppositae vel Fidei Catholicae articulis, vel iis veritatibus quae ex revelatorum dogmatibus certissime et evidentissime, *nemine refragante*, consequi dignoscuntur. Temeraria est, non, comparatione facta ad interna et intrinseca principia, sed *ad externam aliorum auctoritatem*, and so Viva p 55 — auctoritatem vel ratione (universalis) jurisdictionis, vel verae et Catholicae Christianorum (unanimis) aestimationis, vel numericae recentiorum Theologorum multitudinis, but this *last kind of authority is doubtful*, for he says Qui, cum problematice ac dubie profiteantur se omnia disputare, *pro nihilo prorsus* habenda est eorum auctoritas. p 293.
And so he goes through Erroneous, False, Scandalous, Offensive etc.

[XXI]

On the new doctrine that a thing may be so certain that it must be believed under pain of damnation, though it is not *de fide*.
If this only means that a person, as an individual, must believe under pain of damnation, whatever he knows to be revealed from God ⟨above⟩, this is an axiom. Thus Saints are bound to believe what comes to them by a particular revelation. But what is now maintained is far [more] than this — it is that certain doctrines, though not revealed in the beginning, are so certain that they have a formal claim on all men, a universal claim for belief, and that no one can be excused from believing except on the plea of invincible ignorance. That is, a new department of necessary truths (I mean, truths abstractedly and in themselves necessary to be believed in order to salvation) is added to the credenda, though not technically to be called de fide.
1. I object to this as a novel doctrine, unknown to our great dogmatic writers of whatever school, who teach that that alone has a universal claim on our faith which was given in the beginning.
2. I object to it, because it has grown, quite gratuitously out of the doctrine of the imposition on us of 'dogmatic facts'. It is argued 'dogmatic facts' are necessary credenda, yet not de fide. Ergo other doctrines may be such. I deny the premiss. I consider, with many writers, that dogmatic facts *are* de fide — and I propose to prove this, i.e. prove that this may be probably held, and therefore that the contrary proposition cannot be assumed as a premiss in argument.
3. I object to it as an unmeaning distinction and an evasion. What do you mean by de fide, but what is necessary to be believed in order to salvation? And is it not absurd to speak of a certainty which is more than moral and less than supernatural? or of a faith which is neither divine nor human, but something between, or mixed up of both?
As to the *authority* which is in its favour.
First, it must be considered how many divines go as far as Muzzarelli in

declaring that declarations of Pope or Church, not founded on immemorial tradition from the Apostles, are *infallible*. How many, or do any divines venture to say that they are received (according to God's will), that they *can* be received by *divine faith*. What is more common to say is, that such declarations are 'certain', which seems to me a shuffle. Thus Cardenas 'Sunt multa omnino certa, in quibus Pontifex errare non possit, quamvis non perveniat ad certitudinem Articuli Fidei'. [part 3] p 9. col. 2. Now 1. does he mean by inerrantia, infallibilitas. If so, he is contradicted by the great body of divines, who, as in passages above quoted, make infallibilitas and revelatio ab initio, ad traditio, correlatives; with Bossuet 'L'Eglise professe, qu'elle ne dit *rien* d'elle même . . . . elle ne fait que suivre et declarer la *révélation* divine par la direction intérieure du S. Esprit'. Expos. 19. And 2. Certitude is a point. I am certain of the dogmas of faith by divine faith. What is that degree of certainty which is short of it? is it the effect of divine grace? is it a human certainty? is it what is called a moral certainty? He says his opinion is 'communis'. Let me for argument sake allow this — but then what is there to hinder me from saying 'Distinguo — there are two kinds of certainty — speculative and practical. These declarations of the Church or the Pope are but *practicè* certa?' Does he mean to say that the opinion is communis that they are speculativè certain?

Viva seems distinctly to contrast, in faith in dogma, the act of divine faith, and the human faith which at the same time we may (if we please) exercise towards the Church. 'Proponente Ecclesiâ existentiam revelationis, posse a nobis ad arbitrium elici, *vel* actum fidei humanae *nixum auctoritati Ecclesiae*, tanquam motivo, vel actum fidei divinae nixum ipsi revelationi, adhibendo auctoritatem Ecclesiae ut meram conditionem, non ut motivum.' [part IV] p 44.

[XXII]

Holden de resolutione Fidei.

Quotuplex est subjectum veritatis Christianae genericè sumptae? [p. 42] He means by subjectum, the materiale objectum — truths as held by the mind.

There are four classes.

1. Veritates divinae et Catholicae, quae immediatè innituntur revelatione divinâ, quaeque per traditionem universalem descendunt. p 43. Hujusmodi sunt omnes articuli fidei, qui vere sunt articuli, sive in solo intellectûs assensu, sive in operatione externa siti.

That is the depositum.   and the dogma.

Duo requiruntur ut veritas Christiana sit dogma Fidei *Catholicae*. 1. a Deo revelatum et ab Ecclesia universa pro revelato receptum. 2 per traditionem p 45.

Ergo Sanctum Petrum fuisse Romae, B.M.V. corpus assumptum fuisse, quae revelata non sunt, ab articulis Fidei Catholicae *excluduntur*. p 148.

Omnis fidei divinae assensus revelatione *divinâ* (but then this will take in *private* revelations, and is not confined to revelationes traditae ab Apostolis) innititur. p 45.

2. Veritates quae dici possunt pure Catholicae, quaeque, licet non sint propriè divinae et revelatae, nec dogmata Fidei divinae et Catholicae p 45, attamen universali innituntur traditione. Such as the history of the Jews in Scripture — that the Scripture is the word of God (Surely Scripture itself says this) — that St Peter was at Rome — that Lent is an Apostolic tradition. (Surely this under dogma *as being* an Apost. trad).

He says p 157, that, though these secundae veritates are not revelatae, they may be so mixed up or united with them, that they cannot be denied without incurring excommunication. In his fundatur Christiana fides. p 46. Hae sunt certissimae, quibus omnes Christiani *tenentur* assensum praebere — sed non possunt fundare fidei divinae assensum, i.e. it is a human certainty. Si has liceret in dubium revocare, rueret prorsus Christiana fides. p 46.

3. Veritates pure canonicae, quae serviunt Ecclesiae pro regula — quibus ideo obedientia aliqua debetur; hujusmodi neque ex universali traditione neque ex revelatione divinâ, immediatè et explicitè habentur. [p. 43]

4. Veritates theologicae, nempe per evidentes consecutiones ex principiis fidei, seu veritatibus 1 et 2. Perpaucae hujusmodi dignoscuntur. [p. 44]

He says p 149 that, if by implicitè is meant per illationem, only theological truths can be reached, not revealed, apparently holding that only explicit doctrines come down to us by tradition, so that even an Ecumenical Council cannot turn an implicit truth into a dogma. Theologicae quidem scientiae rationem habebunt hujusmodi veritates, privatorum hominum discursu detectae ac sustentatae; quae, *tametsi* postea *quovis modo* definitae ac decretae fuerint *ab Ecclesiâ*, potiorem *nunquam* acquirunt *certitudinis* gradum, licet majorem haberent auctoritatem. p 149.

He mentions two other senses of implicitè, viz confusedly, and indirectly; we believe the Athanasian doctrine, in Scripture, confusedly — and we believe it, in believing what the Church teaches, indirectly. The words confuse and indirecte are mine. The three senses of implicitè will be confusè, illativè, and indirectè. He considers that Councils can only define ⟨declare⟩ what was already revealed confusè. vid p 152 which he allows to include an *immediate* inference. But General Councils have ruled points in which the illations were distant and scientific — and then they do not command our internal assent. Verumtamen, quando ad evitandum Schisma, et pacem in Ecclesiâ conservandam, definitae fuerint hujusce naturae et conditionis veritates, eorum decretis *obediendum* (acquiescere, obtemperare, obsequium praebere, obedire contrasted with faith in infallibility p 162. 3) esse novit unusquisque Ecclesiae Catholicae vere filius. p. 153. Since the Pope claims no *higher* gift than that which all accord to the Church, it would follow from this (according to

Holden), that the Pope cannot claim more than obedience, not an internal assent, to any proposition which was not either revealed, and contained confusè (not illativè) in revelation. Vid St Jerome next page. In eis in quibus errare *potest* Synodus Oecumenica, a fortiori Summus Pontifex. p 206. He [Holden] proceeds more definitely. 'An liceat *hujusmodi* decreta interno saltem mentis actu in dubium revocare. Cui respondeo, quod imprudentis et superbientis animi judicium esset haec dubitatio, aut *saltem* hujusce dubitationis *publica significatio* . . . . An discipulus supra magistrum? . . . At objicies *contingere posse* singularem aliquem vel paucos inveniri, qui lumine caeteros omnes antecellant . . . . Si hoc supponere fas est, *caute* valde et cum summâ humilitate hujuscemodi (viro) licebit Ecclesiasticae Hierarchiae doctores privatim admonere.' [pp. 153–4]

Quaeres adhuc teneatur quisquam ad *internum* divinae fidei actum, quem nec semper fortassis in ejus potestate (N.B.) situm novimus? Quamdiu sane arbitretur quisquam hujusmodi fidei actum lumini naturali et rationi oppositum et contrarium esse, (!) nequaquam poterit ad illum eliciendum astringi. p 154 and then he goes on to speak of the deference due to authority, and (if I understand him) that the rei veritatis cognitio may make an act of faith (!) in the Church a duty. So far is he from thinking that any declaration of the Church (and therefore of the Pope) p 161 binding on our internal assent unless it has reference to some point implicitly (confusè) contained in the depositum.

Quod nequeunt Concilia Generalia, nequit Summus Pontifex. p 160. Dixisse novimus S. Hieronymum, 'Auctoritas orbis major est urbe'. p 161.

He says that, if by the Pope speaking ex cathedrâ be meant, juxta sapientissimorum quorumdam theologorum sententiam, the Pope sitting and presiding in General Council, it would be easier to prove that his decretum nulli prorsus sit errori obnoxium than if it be not meant. pp. 161, 2.

[XXIII]

July 10, 1866[1]

Infallibility
of the Church in teaching doctrine,
whether in faith or morals.
i.e. in teaching speculative truth.

Head
1. She is   §1. sufficient for herself. as everything is which has life —
                  self-conservation.

by a divine   2. knows her depositum
assistentia   3. knows its boundaries

[1] Partly quoted by Biemer, *Newman on Tradition*, pp. 180–1.

The great
maxim is
'Securus
judicat
orbis
terrarum'

4. never will be allowed to say that that is revealed which is not, nor that that is not, which is.

5. or (*do* any thing) act in any way by word or deed which is prejudicial to the depositum, which is not useful or necessary to it. (e.g. her *act* in silencing a controversy, in erecting a religious order, may be infallible)

6. She knows what opinions are agreeable or serviceable, and what are contrary or hurtful to the depositum.

7. She cannot, from the nature of the case, increase its depositum.

Head 2. Her infallibility is *referable and ministrative to,*[1] and bounded by the original revelation and depositum. In the process of its teaching and carrying out its teaching, the following provisions are correlative. Revelatio, res revelata, verbum Dei, materies fidei et morum, traditio, Ecclesiae infallibilitas, propositio, magisterium, dogma, depositum, de fide, credendum necessarie ad salutem, fides divina, supernatural certitude. (N.B. The only limitation I see here to this correlativeness is, that the magisterium Ecclesiae (besides relating to faith and dogma) includes the prerogative of *precepts* in aid and maintenance of speculative truths — vid Head I. § 5).

Head 3. Her infallibility enables her to pronounce ⟨determine⟩ Directly What *belongs* to the original revelation, or is de fide.
1. what is an article of the original revelation.
2. what is contradictory to the original revelation — i.e. what is impious, blasphemous, heretical.
3. what is implicit in the original revelation.

Head 4. Indirectly, what is *related* to the original revelation.
1. what is congenial, and serviceable to the original revelation, that is, pious opinions.
2. What is prejudicial to the original revelation — that is, next to heresy, savouring of heresy, ill sounding.

Head 5. Indirectly — what is the *carrying out in fact* of the original revelation.
1. concrete events — as that Pius IX is Pope.
2. concrete actions — as I have, as an instrument, regenerated this child.
3. concrete words — as the consubstantial — or the deipara.
And the negatives of these as
1. Cadalous was not Pope.

[1] 'vid overleaf.
[where Newman added:]
(N.B.) to be entered on another paper.
The main point I wish to ascertain is, whether I may not hold
1. The Church's infallibility is *wholly* ministrative custos, testis, judex, magistra, to the depositum — and does not exist except as far as she is custos, testis, judex, magistra depositi.
2. That none of her assertions must be received under pain of damnation, except such as are declarative and definitive of the depositum).'

2. This child, only baptized in wine, is not regenerated.

3. The Augustinus of Jansen opposes five points of faith.

[This page was crossed out.]

Head   Though the Church cannot increase the depositum fidei, there are two
3.   ways in which it can make positive enunciations beyond it, (viz by
        stating the *relations* of other propositions to it). In the first place (from
        its prerogatives under Head I) it can affirm that certain propositions are
        injurious to it. It does not affirm or deny their predicates of their
        subjects — but it affirms that the propositions, as they stand, are
        inconsistent with or injurious to the depositum. That is, it can con-
        demn propositions.

        N.B. perhaps a cross division would be better here.

3.   propositions *related* to the depositum, (1) favourably. (2) hostilely, i.e.
        (1) development or (2) condemned propositions.

4.   development in fact or in the concrete.

Head   And next she can enunciate that certain other propositions are more or
4.   less connected with or congenial to the depositum; necessarily con-
        nected, or probably so, or morally so, and therefore absolutely true, or
        certain, or probable, as the case may be. And again she can enunciate
        concrete propositions or carry out the depositum into concrete fact
        — under this head come dogmatic facts.

[XXIV]

July 10, 1866

General Considerations.
against the possibility or probability of defining
the Pope's Infallibility[1]

Supernatural facts necessarily have a degree of vagueness about them, as
far as they are supernatural. Thus, not to refer to the Divine mysteries, such
is the operation of grace upon the soul — and its adjustment with human
liberty. Such then may be the seat of infallibility. It will be sufficient, if we
here can gain such knowledge as is a warrant for believing or not believing.
May not the 'Securus judicat orbis terrarum' supply the test, subsequent to an
ecclesiastical decision, whether that decision is infallible or not. (Of course we
must define the orbis terrarum. I mean by it that rounded circumscribed
definitely distinct body, which has one polity, one organization, one government, one administration. There is only one such Christian body in the world,
for the Greeks, the Monophysites, Nestorians, etc., have no mutual inter-
dependence, and the Church of England so far as it has these characteristics is
a part or function of the State).

---

[1] See: Newman's letter to Ryder, 16 July 1866, *Letters and Diaries*, XXII, pp. 261–3;
Newman's letters to Pusey, March 1867, *Letters and Diaries*, XXIII, pp. 98–100, 104–7.

Ought the tutior pars to be taken in questions of infallibility? — and is there a 'tutior'? Does not some author say that it is a worse heresy (or an equal one) to make that de fide which is not, than to make that not which is?

Since the infallibility of the Church has not been defined, it must be defined, if any thing on the subject is defined, before we come to define the infallibility of the Pope. This is at least an argumentum ad hominem against those who, holding the Pope's infallibility, wish it defined. And it is a presumptive argument that it will not be so — and a deliberative argument that it ought not to be so, since the Church's infallibility is not. And it is a case in which, as in the case of the Church's infallibility, it may be said that prescription is a better title than a judicial decision.

There is very little *theoretical* difference between the *opinions* of the maintainers of the infallibility of the Pope and its deniers. They both hold that he is centre of unity, teacher of the faithful, possessed of universal jurisdiction. They both hold that, when his decision is generally accepted, it binds. The question merely turns on this, *whether* that acceptance is necessary as a *condition* of his decision being accepted as infallible. Where then does lie the difference between the parties? it is *ethical and practical*. How then would the definition of the Pope's infallibility, if made, change the state of things in these respects? It would leave things ethically just as they are, it would be injurious practically. I say this even granting, even professing to believe myself, that the infallibility of the Pope admits of definition.

1. That the ethical difference between the two parties would always remain is plain from such considerations as we see in the life of Carrière. See what Cardinal Wiseman says (I think in his lives of the 4 Popes) on Ultramontanism being simply 'a personal affection for the Pope'.[1]

2. That it would be a practical misfortune is plain from this — that, *while* it is not defined, the Pope has to act as if it were not part of the revealed dogma. Hence he has to consult the Bishops before hand, and be sure that he is acting with them. If it be said that Providence might find other means of securing due deliberation and caution, etc., I answer that this indeed is true, but we must judge of the future, and decide for the future, by probabilities. In the same way, Providence may supply the want of the temporal power, still we must act by the *appearance* that it is necessary for the spiritual. In the same sense I say, that the non-definition of the Pope's infallibility is, in the present state of things, a necessary safeguard for the due exercise of that his gift, even if he has it.

This consideration has the more weight, when it is borne in mind that the Church's infallibility is in its nature and mode ⟨cause⟩ a divine *assistentia*, not in any sense an inspiration. Its direct antecedents and causes are simply human, historical considerations, prudential motives, logical arguments. The apprehension then of opposition from the Bishops, of protests, of national movements, is just one of those providential securities for cautious decision,

[1] Cardinal Wiseman, *Recollections of the Last Four Popes*, p. 16.

143

of which the (exercise of the gift) attainment of infallibility is the result. The consulting beforehand Bishops and their flocks may enter into the idea of what is meant by a Papal decision ex cathedrâ.

Pursuing this line of argument, we may say that, for the very reason the Holy Father has the fulness of the *governing* power it is *unlikely* that he would have the infallible legislative or dogmatic authority; for, the ordinary constitution and working of the ecclesiastical system being carried on solely? by human laws, and the result only being overruled, we have a right to judge of what is likely or not by our political experience, and to say that such union of legislative and executive powers in one person is not like[ly], as being, as human politics teach us, too great for man to sustain, and a temptation to abuse.

People sometimes put together the extreme views on the Cultus B.M.V. and on the Pope's authority, and look at them complacently as proceeding from one advanced state of mind, on the one hand more devout, on the other and as if this must be *allowed*, more believing. But 1. as to the Cultus to me it is no increase in devotion, but in sentimentality, etc. etc. 2. as to the Pope's Infallibility it is *not believing* MORE, to believe it. The question is about the *seat* of Infallibility. He believes as *much* who gives it in a measure to the coetus Episcoporum, as he who gives it to the See of Peter. It is a mere question of the distribution of a gift. If I do believe in the Pope, I do *not* believe in the Bishops — and I rob Paul to pay Peter. Yet Archbishop Manning in his Pastoral falls into this fallacy.

[XXV]

December 12, 1866

There are three reasons for appealing to the Pope and three ways of receiving his words.

1. As the witness of Roman Tradition.
2. As the possessor of an *instinct* of Christian truth, so that *primâ facie* he is likely to be ever right, and to decide the matter by simply speaking.
3. As the administrator of the canon of the Church and the *enforcer* of her doctrine and customs in *practical matters*. This is so natural to the Pope, and so intimately his prerogative, that men often spontaneously look for a directive in practice, even when he never lays down doctrine, i.e. he only *means* it for a 'practical instruction'. E.g.

Eugenius IV gave a practical instruction about the Sacraments — though in the *form* of doctrinal *teaching*.

Benedict XIV laid down the abstract doctrine about usury, and it was mistaken for a practical instruction. (This surely is just the reverse of the former).

Pius IX laid down a doctrine about the necessity of the temporal power for the spiritual, and it was taken for a practical instruction.

III   Notes for Ryder, 1867

May 29, 1867

The first thing is to have a clear idea of Ignatius's position.[1] I understand it to be as follows:

1. That the Apostles committed vivâ voce the whole depositum to the Ecclesia docens which succeeded to them.

2. That this depositum was not a certain set of propositions simply, such as the Creed, but a body of doctrine, large, fruitful, various, which the Church (Ecclesia docens) was supernaturally empowered to receive and retains as by a *habit* of knowledge, and which it brought out in this part or that part of it, according to the necessity of the moment, without being able to say, whether that part which it brought out was or was not a *logical deduction*. It was received as a whole per modum unius, and such truths as were not actually spoken in terms by the Apostles existed in it, not so much implicitly and logically, as formally (?) ⟨virtually (?)⟩.

3. That the Church's infallibility necessarily (from what has been said above) went further than this for it was implied in the power of preserving the depositum that it had the power of guarding it. A navigator is not really such, who does [not] know of the shoals and rocks and currents through which he has to steer — and thoroughly to understand the deposit, implies a knowledge of what will interfere with it, prejudice it, injure it. This conservative infallibility Ignatius speaks of at p 24 in the words 'truths which are certainly involved in the Church's indefectibility'.

4. That the Church's infallibility takes cognizance not simply of abstract, but of concrete matters; that it pronounces not simply on doctrines but on facts. Faith does not embrace matters merely of the unseen world, but of the unseen world as realized in this world. It was not enough to believe that our Lord had given the deposit to his Apostles, but that hic Peter, hic James, hic John were in the number of those Apostles — not enough that the Church should be able to teach that Christ is God, but, as the (necessarily only way of teaching in the case of beings who communicate with each other by language) that to pronounce infallibly that this or that *proposition* is divine truth, e.g. the consubstantiality of the Son; not only to denounce Jansenism but to condemn the book which contains it.

In these three ways the depositum must be regarded, if you would enter into Ignatius's meaning — 1. It is a depositum in the same sense as the

[1] H. I. D. Ryder, *Idealism in Theology*, London 1867.

145

Kantian or Comtian system might be a depositum; not as a text which admits of deductions, but a living idea and body of doctrine. 2. It is a depositum which for its security requires certain pomoeria. 3. It is a depositum which must be realized in the concrete. And the Church is infallible in her teaching of the depositum viewed in all these three respects. And she claims infallibility in these three respects, and those who do not accept her claim and her decisions in these three respects are (at least material) heretics.

The only question is as to the limits of this claim and its subject-matter in these three respects. Mr Ward professes distinctly to *define* it, Ignatius says it cannot be defined — but 'solvitur ambulando' in each particular case, by the Church's *actual claim.*

Thus whether our Lord's risibility or non-risibility is within the depositum, or the condemnation of the risibility or non-risibility be within the conservative power of the Church, is decided by the fact of its Church's defining or condemning. And so, before the Church condemned the book of Jansenism, it was not clear whether she could pronounce on the subject-matter of a book.

Meanwhile, uncertain as the limits may be, when the Church has not herself drawn them, the pietas fidei acts on all declarations of authority, whether of the Pope, or Councils, or the Schola etc., though they be not distinctly matters de fide, and are not such because Lex dubia non obligat — the pietas fidei, I say, acts so far as this, that a Catholic will take them for granted and does not doubt them, though till they are put forward as de fide, he cannot make a distinct act of faith about them.

[XXVII]

June 24, 1867

I suggest the following in order to give you ideas.

1. I am glad to have to acknowledge the courteous style of Mr W[ard]'s pamphlet and article[1] — and will frankly say that, had his tone always been such, I should have written of him and his writings in a different manner myself.

2. I am glad to find from his explanations, that we do not differ from each other in so many matters as I had feared.

E.g. He has repudiated the intention, certainly conveyed in his language, of imputing mortal sin to all persons who, with perfect knowledge, refuse to admit the falsity of propositions noted with the minor censures etc. etc.
    other instances.

---

[1] W. G. Ward, *A Letter to the Rev. Father Ryder on his recent pamphlet*, London 1867. The first review article on the controversy 'F. Ryder and Dr. Ward' appeared in the July issue of the *Dublin Review*, vol. IX (1867), pp. 154–62.

3. Also, by his silence on my 4th head, I understand him to admit the justice of my remarks on his treatment of the Galileo case.[2] He gives it up.

4. Also, by his passing over my *second* head, I consider him to allow my right to hold the correlativity of de fide, the depositum and the Church (or Pope's) infallibility — nay, I go further — and think that, by his silence, I may claim him as holding the correlativity of tradition and infallibility — so that he would, if asked distinctly, allow that, however wide may be the province over which the Church's infallibility extends, she never exercises it without a tacit reference to tradition as the medium of her exercise of it — even though she does not, and is not bound to, mention the express channels or records of the tradition — in such sense that we are bound to believe that tradition *there is* for what she says, though she neither says it, nor we can discover it; and that it is only on this *condition* that she can exercise infallibility. This is an important point to clear up, and I trust I have interpreted him rightly.

5. Two of my headings then he passes over — two remain, and to these his remarks are confined. (1) The dogmatic character of all Encyclicals etc., and (2) of the minor censures made upon propositions. In other words, he does not allow that the Church can speak *solemnly* without speaking with her *infallible* voice.

6. *This then is the main proposition* to which I shall direct my attention — viz. to show that there is a department of teaching, in which the Church speaks, authoritatively indeed, but not infallibly.

Prove it — Amort — Tournely etc.

+Give instances — as St Gregory's denunciation of 'Universal Bishop', etc.[2]

7. This being thus shown, I now come to the two particular instances, which I gave of it, viz. Encyclicals etc. and the Minor Censures.

8. (1) Encyclicals.   +to come in here?

9. (2) Minor Censures.   I have no difficulty in admitting their infallibility, *except* as a difficulty ⟨matter⟩ of theory — etc. etc.

10. Thus I am led to the more accurate discussion of the *Principle* — the Church has whatever infallibility she claims — the point being this, *what* is the token or evidence of her claiming it.

viz (1) either her saying a proposition is de fide

(2) or marking it with an anathema, taking anathema in a vague sense as including censures (or some censures) under it. (Do the minor censures come under the word 'anathema' is a question to be decided).

11. If, however, other tests *besides* de fide or anathema are to be admitted, this must be done on the authority of the *Schola*; which *determines* BOTH *the proof* that a pronouncement is infallible or not, *and also* what the meaning of the pronouncement is.

---

[1] See, *Idealism in Theology*, p. 13. *Letter to Ryder*, p. 34.
[2] See also: *Essays Critical and Historical*, vol. II, p. 273; *The Via Media of the Anglican Church*, London 1901, vol. I, pp. 183-4, 188.

12. Thus I am brought to discuss the justice of an objection made to me that, instead of letting the Pope interpret his own words, I put the Schola as a sort of Pope over him. I answer that my opponents put *their own private judgment as a Pope over* him — and that the question is, whether he shall be supposed to speak by theological rule, by the rule of traditional phraseology, of the Schola and of the Bishops as interpreters, or by such interpretation which the rude intelligence of the lay mind gives to his words. (I referred to this, when in my pamphlet I spoke of the Pope's words being thrown *upon the public prints*, etc).[1]

Here the cardinal proof is the interpretation of the Damnatae Theses — as Viva's work — how differently they turn out from what they seem!

13. And now I go on to speak of the utter unwarrantableness of saying that the doctrine of invincible ignorance can be applied to cases of theses which are de fide or dogmatic.

It is quite true that I *may* have that evidence of the obligatio of a point, which is not dogmatic, i.e. defined, which makes it a duty to me to believe it — nay there may be cases, when the evidence is equivalent to that of a private revelation. In such cases I *may* perhaps believe ⟨take with⟩ divine faith. But commonly speaking divine faith only exists as to objects which are included in fides *divina Catholica*, the *public* doctrine of the Church. I conceive that Mr. Ward or I hold the doctrine of the Pope's Infallibility, *not* with fides divina, because that infallibility has not been defined, but with a certainty indeed, but a certainty short of it, a certainty of *opinion*. (This almost important point. It destroys, if it can be maintained, Dr Murray's application of fides divina, as a habit).[2] It is *not* then heretical *not* to believe it — *but* invincible ignorance is a term appropriated to one kind of *heretic*, viz the material.

14. And now I must before concluding make one or two explanations which are due to Dr ⟨Mr⟩ Ward. First of these is the passage in my Pamphlet about Sixtus V.[3] Now here I say in the first place that a legitimate argument in favour of my thesis was *derivable from* it — viz etc. But having said this, I have no hesitation in stating that, as it stands, I have been guilty of a confusion of thought etc.

There is one complaint of Dr Ward's on which he has already been good enough to take my explanation — but I mention it here, because he has in fact made it in his Pamphlet — viz Petrus mendacio nostro non eget etc.[4]

Again

etc. etc.

Father Ignatius Ryder.

---

[1] See: *Letters and Diaries*, XXIII, p. 254; *Idealism in Theology*, pp. 18–19, 62–3.

[2] 'Habitus fidei divinae definiri potest *Virtus theologica, qua homo, ob auctoritatem Dei, omnibus ab eo certo revelatis firmiter assentitur*. Haec fides est vel *pure divina* vel *divina-catholica*.' P. Murray, *Tractatus de Ecclesia Christi*, Dublinii 1860, vol. I, p. 7. See also: W. G. Ward, *The Authority of Doctrinal Decisions*, London 1866, pp. 110–12; *Idealism in Theology*, pp. 24, 29–30, 41, 43–6, 64–6; *Letter to Ryder*, pp. 14, 21.

[3] *Idealism in Theology*, p. 17; *Letter to Ryder*, 28–9.

[4] *Idealism in Theology*, p. 15; *Letter to Ryder*, p. 35.

[XXVIII]

July 9, 1867

It is necessary to keep distinctly before us what the point in controversy is between ourselves and those who side with Dr Ward.

The ultimate point is this, Are Catholics obliged, are they under the *obligatio*, to give an internal assent to Encyclicals, Allocutions etc., as such?

Dr Ward etc. asserting it, are bound to prove it; else, our liberty is in possession. It is not enough to prove that there are grounds for holding it as a probable opinion, and that therefore they have a right to hold it, and to think it safer to hold it, and act upon it themselves. It is not enough to give reasons for saying that 'infallibilitas Ecclesiae extendit ad Encyclicas Pontificias', such as to justify themselves in holding it, but they have to establish on a moral demonstration, that this tenet is so evidently in the objectum fidei materiale, as to be ex obligatione universali.

This demonstration may be conducted in (e.g.). three ways.

1. By the express decision of the Church, as the doctrine of two wills in Christ, or the word ὁμοούσιον, has been declared to be included in the objectum fidei.

2. By the consent of divines, as when we maintain that the substantial truth of Scripture, or the eternity of punishment, has the unanimous suffrage of the Schola.

3. By argument.

Of these three modes of demonstration, which do Dr Ward's friends adopt? There is no other possible to them but the third.

As to the first, of course they cannot pretend that the infallibility of Encyclicals as such, is defined.

As to the second, it is most important to bear in mind that this doctrine is unheard of till late centuries. This is not any proof that it is not true, because it may be a development of the Depositum. But such developments, even though in the objectum fidei, do not become generally obligatoria till they have some public recognition. In saying this, I am not denying that a consent of modern divines, clear, perfect, and lasting through centuries, might not almost obliterate a contrary consent in former times — but it must be recollected, that even in the case of the Immaculate Conception, no one asserted that the doctrine was binding on our internal assent *till* the Definition in 1854.

Now then when we come to the third mode of demonstration — a demonstration which must be stronger than that which existed for the Immaculate Conception up to December, 1854 — (and consider how very strong an argument there was *for it*,) what is it?

First they have to get over the modernness of their doctrine. It is hardly mentioned till the time of the Jansenist controversy.

We can trace the authors in whose writings it arose, etc. etc. It is not generally received now.

The Church again, so far from enforcing it, allows of such works as Muratori's,[1] Chrissman's[2] etc.

---

[1] See John Henry Newman, *The Idea of a University*, edited by I. T. Ker, Oxford 1976, p. 418, and note on p. 662.
[2] See footnote below on p. 155.

IV   Letter to Flanagan, 1868[1]

Among the mass of theological papers left behind by Cardinal Newman, of which it is hoped before long to publish a comprehensive edition, are the pages which follow on the theory of development in doctrine. They have been consulted from time to time by students, but recent discussion makes their publication a matter of urgency. They constitute Newman's clearest and shortest explanation of the matter, and seem to provide as direct an answer as could be hoped for to the questions raised and left unanswered in Dr. Owen Chadwick's learned and sympathetic study *From Bossuet to Newman : the Idea of Doctrinal Development.*[2]

The paper here printed for the first time came to be written as a result of the controversy over the extent of infallibility, in which the young Ignatius Ryder challenged the extreme views which W. G. Ward was preaching in the *Dublin Review* and elsewhere as the only orthodox ones. Henry Ignatius Dudley Ryder, born in 1837 and grandson of Henry Ryder, the first evangelical to become a bishop, first of Gloucester, and then of Lichfield, was the son of Newman's friend George, who became a Catholic with all his family in 1846. Ignatius received part of his education in Newman's Oratorian community, which he joined in 1856, becoming eventually, on Newman's death, its second Superior. Newman has described how Ignatius Ryder came to him of his own accord, begging him to write about infallibility, confessing his dislike of Ward's tyranny in the *Dublin Review*, and offering his help. When Newman put the matter off, Ignatius brought a sketch of his own, which became the first pamphlet in the controversy, *Idealism in Theology*, published in April 1867. 'When it was found to need further explanation', Newman wrote on 29 January 1868, 'he got ready a second, published at the beginning of this month, which promises to be quite successful, and to have done a great work in shattering the intolerable dogmatism of the Dublin. It was natural that, though every part of both pamphlets was the work of his own mind, that at first they, or at least the first pamphlet, was attributed to me . . . Gradually this opinion has been set right; still he has had the advantage of my name, and his pamphlets have come from this Oratory, and must have had my sanction'.[3] Few people can have followed the Ryder-Ward controversy with greater interest than John Stanislas Flanagan, the parish priest of Adare in Co.

---

[1] The following text, notes, and introduction first appeared as 'An Unpublished Paper by Cardinal Newman on the Development of Doctrine' in *The Journal of Theological Studies*, New Series, vol. IX, part 2, 1958.

[2] Cambridge University Press, 1957. See e.g. p. 195.

[3] John Henry Newman, *Autobiographical Writings*, ed. Henry Tristram (London, 1956), p. 265.

Limerick. Born in 1821, he had already become a great figure in Irish social life, when he suddenly departed to study for the priesthood at St. Sulpice, leaving it before ordination, to join Newman's Oratory, in 1848. He was a considerable theologian and devoted to Newman, but found community life irksome, and eventually, in 1865, returned to work in Ireland. He always remained on affectionate terms with Newman and the Oratorian community, notably with Ignatius Ryder, to whom he had for a time taught theology. He was consulted while the first pamphlet was being composed, and wrote his encouragement after it had appeared, and also his fears. 'You are engaged in a great battle, the end of which it is hard to see. My own opinion is that huge efforts will be made to have you put down, and if possible, condemned authoritatively — It is quite evident that everyone considers you as the Father's [Newman's] spokesman, and as representing the opinions of his school.' In this letter, written on 21 June 1867, and later in the correspondence, Stanislas Flanagan confessed how puzzled and perplexed he himself was, and how difficult he thought it would be for Ignatius Ryder to prove his case. These perplexities came to a head after the publication of Ryder's second pamphlet, *A Letter to William George Ward, Esq., D.Ph. on his Theory of Infallible Instruction*, in January 1868.

There Ryder maintained, against Ward who wished all the doctrinal instructions in official papal documents to be infallible, that this was the prerogative only of the *Depositum*, in which he included not only the original explicit revelation, but all later developments. Ryder wrote on pages 6 and 7 of his *Letter*:

The *depositum* delivered by the Apostles to the Church is not a set of barren propositions *simply*, but a body of doctrine — large, fruitful, various. It is not adequately represented by the result of what I will call the *Divine Recollection* of the Church, according to the promise, 'He will bring everything to your mind, whatsoever I shall have said to you', by the gradual gathering in and canonizing by the Ecclesia docens, of the scattered Apostolic traditions preserved in particular churches: such truths, for instance, as the inspiration of certain Books of Scripture, or the Immaculate Conception. It contains, not only these explicit revelations, to which some theologians, most unphilosophically, as I have ventured to maintain ('Idealism', p. 46), would restrict the term *de fide*; but the whole logical outcome of these Divine truths, whether elicited by comparison with one another, or with truths absolutely certain naturally. When I speak of a '*logical* outcome', I do not suppose that unassisted human reason can always verify the process; because the full force and significance of the divine premiss can seldom be more than partially comprehended; nor, indeed, does the Church necessarily make these pronouncements in a logical form. . . .

And seeing, moreover, that the Church is not merely the depository of a collection of barren propositions, but the guardian, interpreter, and dispenser of what the Fathers have called a divine philosophy, it is obvious that she must be strictly infallible wherever a mistake would be equivalent to a failure of her mission. Hence she is infallible in what Father Newman has called her pomoerium, which is only saying that, since her work lies in the concrete, she must have elbow-room.[1]

Flanagan's reaction on reading Ryder's second pamphlet is given in the following letter from Adare, dated 12 February 1868.

My dear Ignatius,
     I can't tell you how many fruitless attempts I have made to write to you. I have torn up at least half a dozen beginnings of letters to you, because I was interrupted and unable to finish them — If I fully agreed with you and believed in your fundamental theses I should merely have to tell you that I consider your pamphlet a triumphant defence of your 'Idealism', and an unanswerable reply to Ward's Letter — By your 'fundamental theses', I mean your statements at pp. 6 & 7 with regard to the 'depositum' and 'pomoeria' — These are my great crux, and I kick against them almost as violently as against anything in Ward, Knox, or Murray. I know that, unlike them, you do not impose upon any one an obligation of believing in your theory, but it makes me feel uncomfortable and uneasy to find that you, after studying so closely and diligently the whole subject, have found it necessary to adopt this theory, and to condemn as 'unphilosophical' that which I have clung to with extraordinary tenacity all my life. Then I am thrown into a state of positive dismay when I reflect that it is more than probable the Father [Newman] has given his imprimatur to your theses. Not only am I unable to find in his published writings the theory you advocate, but in conversation with him I always understood him to admit (1) that he would not assert that the Apostles did not know *explicitly* all the truths of the depositum, and (2) that he would not say that the Apostolic See had not also an explicit knowledge from the beginning of the full contents of the depositum — From these admissions of the Father [Newman] I had taken for granted that there was no insuperable *historical* difficulty to maintaining what you call the theory of the 'unphilosophical theologians' — That theory I took to be as follows:
     (1) that our Lord taught the Apostles explicitly all the truths of faith, according to the texts — 'Ille vos docebit *omnia* et suggeret vobis *omnia* quaecumque dixero vobis' — and, '*omnia* quaecumque novi a Patre *nota feci vobis*'. —
     (2) These truths exclusively form or make up the 'depositum', *which* the Apostles delivered to the Church.
     (3) For the safe custody of the depositum in its integrity, and the faithful teaching of the divine truths contained in it, Our Lord promised and endowed the Church with the gift of infallibility —
     (4) This gift of infallibility secures (*a*) that not one of these divine truths should ever be lost, and (*b*) that no human addition whether of number or accretion should ever be made to them.
     (5) To the custody of the depositum in this sense the promised gift of infallibility was limited.
     On the point, then, of the correlativity of Divine Faith and Infallibility you and I would be perfectly in accord — But you maintain that the Depositum 'is not adequately represented by the result of what you will call the Divine Recollection of the Church ... by the gradual gathering in and canonizing of ... the scattered Apostolic Traditions' — When Our Lord said 'omnia quaecumque novi a Patre nota feci vobis'

---

[1] See *Apologia*, Uniform Edition, p. 257: 'I enlarged just now upon the concrete shape and circumstances, under which pure infallible authority presents itself to the Catholic. That authority has the prerogative of an indirect jurisdiction on subject-matters which lie beyond its own proper limits, and it most reasonably has such a jurisdiction. It could not act in its own province, unless it had a right to act out of it. It could not properly defend religious truth, without claiming for that truth what may be called its *pomoeria*; or, to take another illustration, without acting as we act, as a nation, in claiming as our own, not only the land on which we live, but what are called British waters.'

He did not mean that he was making known to them all these truths explicitly, but only 'all' in *principle* or *germ*, so that the depositum contains 'the *whole logical* outcome of these Divine Truths, whether elicited by comparison with one another, or with truths absolutely certain naturally' — All the logical conclusions, therefore, according to you, which the Apostles in the first instance, and the Church afterwards, have deduced from the original revelata are as truly a portion of the contents of the depositum, as those original revelata themselves, and the Church is infallible in the process of deduction, and these logical conclusions are all objects of divine faith — I can't tell you what a profound repugnance I have to this view of the depositum, and if the Father [Newman] says it is the only one which accords with history and theology I shall have to recast all my notions of the fundamenta fidei. Of course what you mean is that the action of the Church, that is of the human mind, infallibly assisted by the Holy Ghost, on the primary immediate revelation is analogous to the action of the natural reason on the axioms or first principles of, say, Geometry. . . .

Flanagan concluded his letter with the words

> Do write to me and say if the Father does bona fide hold your maximizing theory. If he does it will be a sad floorer to me personally — and a great shock — . . . .

Needless to say Ryder at once showed this long letter to Newman, who immediately wrote the essay now published for the first time. It was sent to Flanagan, who pungently described its effect on him in a letter of thanks written on 10 March 1868:

> My dear Ignatius,
> I can't tell you how grateful I am to the Father for his exceeding great kindness in writing out that long paper for me. Thank him for it a thousand times. May I keep it? If not, of course I count on his allowing me to make a copy of it — It is to be the basis of my belief about the depositum from this time forth, and now that the old ground has slipped from under my feet, it is a comfort to have a new foundation to build upon. I had firmly believed all my life that the depositum *was*, just what he says it was *not*, and what in the nature of things it could not possibly be, viz. — 'a list of articles which could be numbered' — To find out now that I am wrong, and that I have all along been clinging to a false proposition on a fundamental point like this, is a great shock! and I can't help feeling very indignant, and very much disgusted with my old friends the scholastics, who have led me astray. . . . I feel so angry with them that I could kick them out of my shelves. . . . I wish the Father would write a treatise on de Fide, and I never would open one of their folios again.

Newman's manuscript is still kept in a cupboard in his room at the Birmingham Oratory, and numbered A. 43. 12. It consists of four folio sheets of white rag paper, folded double, sewn together, and written on both sides.

C. STEPHEN DESSAIN

Febry 15. 1868

I dare say I have not been consistent or logically exact in what from time to time I have said about the extent & subject matter of the Church's Infallibility, for it is a very large question and I never have set myself formally to answer it.

Certainly I have ever thought that the logical deductions of truths in the Depositum were capable of definition and made portions of the Dogma of faith. For those deductions come under the head of Developments; and it is now going on for 20 years since Stanislas wanted me to say (saying it was what was received in France) that developments generally, though notoriously existing, continually coming to light, and indefinitely & without limit numerous, were necessarily external to the dogma, and incapable of definition. This admission, I understood him to say, would reconcile him to the Essay I wrote on the subject; but I recollect I would not make it.

I have no reason to suppose that since that time I have been reconciled to a view of the subject, which I would not admit then.

As to the Apologia, it must be recollected that it was not a didactic work — nor did it contain a statement of my own personal views about infallibility, but was addressed to Protestants *in order to show* them what it was that a Catholic fairly undertook in the way of theological profession, when he became a Catholic. I myself, for instance, have ever held as a matter of theological opinion the Infallibility of the Pope; but I carefully abstain from asserting it in the general view which I give of Catholic doctrine. I felt I should be as obviously wrong in setting down theological opinions, when I was declaring the Church's doctrine as such, as I have thought Archb^p Manning obviously wrong in introducing into his Pastorals the Pope's Infallibility; and I think I bore in mind, as I wrote, because I have ever remembered, our Bishop's remark that what made F^r Faber's book on the Holy Eucharist so unsettling to Nuns was that he mixed up dogma with theological opinion, and that in a popular work theological opinions ought to be kept under. It was for this reason that I introduced into my statement two or three sentences from Chrismann, which professed less about the province of Infallibility than I held myself.[1] It was for this reason that I spoke so vaguely about the Pomoeria. I myself hold that the doctrines which may be considered as belonging to it are in some cases of obligation & in others not; but which are such & which not, is decided by theological opinion & it varies. Such, for instance, would be the infallibility of canonization — to him who thinks it infallible, it is such. And there are two motives, short of fides divina, which occasion silence & acquiescence on such points, or at least very cautious & restrained avowals in opposition to them: the pietas fidei (which I think I did not refer to) and the duty of obedience. It was for the same reason, that, in speaking of condemned propositions, I did not expressly say, whether the condemnation was infallible or not, because a distinct assertion could not be made without turning a statement of 20 pages into a volume. All I did, was to say that such condemnations from their general character constituted no great burden for our faith to bear.

[1] Philip Neri Chrismann was an eighteenth-century German Franciscan, from whose *Regula Fidei Catholicae et Collectio Dogmatum Credendorum* Newman quoted in the first edition of the *Apologia*, pp. 392–3 (Ward's Oxford edition, p. 345): 'Thus, in illustration, it [infallibility] does not extend to statements, however sound and evident, which are mere logical conclusions from the Articles of the Apostolic *Depositum*; again, it can pronounce nothing about the persons of heretics, whose works fall within its legitimate province.' Newman withdrew this after the first edition, as he explains, because it was an extreme, and he wanted a representative view. Newman learned, too, that the first proposition was open to objection. Chrismann minimized, but his work was included in Migne's *Theologiae Cursus Completus* in 1841, the quotation from him occurring there vol. vi, p. 941. The Wurzburg edition of 1854 was put on the Index in 1869, after the paper now published was written.

In the second edition I withdrew the two sentences from Chrismann because they seemed too strong an *assertion*, & to be taking a side, — where as I wished to be vague. No two theologians perhaps can exactly agree where fides divina ends, and pietas and submission begin. No two thinkers can say how far the habit of the day extends and where it stops. For instance, if I were to say that the inspiration of the text of Scripture was not a point de fide, I should be saying what I believe to be true — but to say so would not correctly exhibit & represent the current opinion; it is a consideration of comfort to individuals who are perplexed, but, if forwarded prominently, might perplex and unsettle those who have no difficulties. I cannot bear tyrant majorities, and am tender about minorities; but I have no wish that minorities should kick up their heels, and throw the majority into confusion.

So much on what I have said in my Essay on Development & in the Apologia; I don't recollect having said any thing on the subject elsewhere. What I have said in conversation, I cannot of course recollect; but one conversation I recollect having with Father Knox, either at Littlemore or after he had seen Brownson,[1] which remains on my memory, because I have ever repeated it to myself; and perhaps I have got the substance of it somewhere in writing, tho' not printed. The immediate subject was how St Hilary or St Irenaeus could use expressions or make statements about the Holy Trinity or the Incarnation, which the great subsequent Catholic development of doctrine afterwards discarded, without his failing in a real apprehension of the doctrine itself. And, as what I maintained in the case of these Fathers as regards those cardinal doctrines, I should maintain in the case of the Apostles as regards all doctrines whatever, I have ever meant the explanation which I gave of the state of mind of St Hilary as regards the Incarnation to apply (mutatis mutandis) to the state of mind of St Paul as regards (say) the Immaculate Conception. — I say 'mutatis mutandis', because the Apostles were inspired, and the Fathers were not.

Now as to the Apostles: — What do we mean by a man's being *master* of any subject, say science? What is meant by *knowing* the Aristotelic philosophy? Does it mean that he has before his mind always every doctrinal statement, every sentiment, opinion, intellectual & moral tendency of Aristotle? This is impossible. Not Aristotle himself, no human mind, can have a host of thoughts present to it at once. The philosophy, as a system, is stored in the *memory*, deeply rooted there if you will, but still in the memory, and is brought out according to the occasion. A learned Aristotelian is one who can answer any whatever philosophical questions in the way that Aristotle would have answered them. If they are questions which could not occur in Aristotle's age, he still answers them; and by two means, by the instinct which a thorough

---

[1] Thomas Francis Knox became a Catholic with Faber in November 1845, and shortly afterwards visited Newman at Littlemore. He then travelled in America, where he visited Orestes Brownson, who attacked Newman's *Development of Doctrine* so violently at this time. He joined the Oratorian community in 1848, and was one of those sent to London in the following year.

Aristotelic intellect, the habit set up in his mind, possesses; next, by never-swerving processes of ratiocination. And as a thoroughly grounded anatomist knows whether the smallest bone or bit of bone shown him is human or not, so the perfect Aristotelian will know whether this or that opinion, sentiment conjecture, generalization, negation, is Aristotelic or not. In one respect he knows more than Aristotle; because, in new emergencies after the time of Aristotle, he *can* and *does* answer what Aristotle would have answered, but for the want of the opportunity did not. There is another point of view in which he seems to have the advantage of Aristotle, though it is no real superiority, viz that, from the necessities of the interval between Aristotle and himself, there has been the growth of a technology, a scientific vocabulary, which makes the philosophy easier to remember, easier to communicate and to defend — nay, which enables him to view it as a whole, per modum unius, with a grasp of mind which would be superior to the view taken of it by any equal intellect, or in other words, caeteris paribus, and, if not more vigorous than Aristotle's grasp, because of the superiority of Aristotle's vigorous creative intellect. Such a technology with its explanations bears up his intellect, as corks a swimmer, as a pole a rope dancer, as a belt a runner, and keeps him from accidental mistakes, momentary slips, from which Aristotle's more vigorous perspicacious intellect was the safeguard. It keeps his learning well about him, and at command at any moment, as being a sort of memoria technica, both as embodying elementary principles, and as condensing the tradition of a thousand questions and answers, of controversies & resolutions of them, which have taken place between Aristotle's time and his.

Such a scientific apparatus has its evils; for common minds, instead of throwing themselves into the genius and animus of the philosophy, will make the technology the beginning and end of their study; and will be formalists, pedants, bigots, and will be as little made philosophers by their verbal know-ledge, as boys can swim because they have corks or run because they have belts. I am not concerned with an inconvenience which is accidental & indirect, and no fault of technology itself: — its advantage is obvious. Take, for instance, an instance in theology, — nay, I had better pass on at once to theology, for the sake of which these remarks, already sufficient for their purpose, have been made, — let then the words be taken 'Spiritus Sanctus superveniet in te, et Virtus Altissimi &c' — what person of the Blessed Trinity is meant by 'Spiritus Sanctus'? I conceive that an Apostle would have answered promptly, emphatically, 'The Third' — so has answered the Church, but some of the earlier Fathers, I think, answer, 'The Second.' Why do they say 'The Second?' because they were not individually perfect theolo-gians; why is an Apostle, why is the Church able to decide the point? because each, in his or her own way, is a perfect theologian — the difference between them being that the Apostle answers promptly, the Church uncertainly, at intervals, for what the Apostle is in his own person, that the Church is in her whole evolution of ages, per modum unius, a living, present treasury of the Mind of the Spirit of Christ.

Now to continue the contrast between the Apostles and the Church. The Apostles did not merely know the Apostles Creed; what knowledge could be more jejune, unless the meaning of each separate word of it was known in fullness? They must know all and more than all about the word 'Son of God,' which the Church has enunciated since their time. And so of every article, & portion of an article. What then is meant by the Depositum? is it a list of articles that can be numbered? no, it is a large philosophy; all parts of which are connected together, & in a certain sense correlative together, so that he who really knows one part, may be said to know all, as ex pede Herculem. Thus the Apostles had the *fullness* of revealed knowledge, a fullness which they could as little realize to themselves, as the human mind, as such, can have all its thoughts present before it at once. They are elicited according to the occasion. A man of genius cannot go about with his genius in his hand: in an Apostle's mind great part of his knowledge is from the nature of the case latent or implicit; and taking two Apostles, St Paul & St John, according to their respective circumstances, they either may teach the same thing in common, or again what is explicit in St Paul might be latent in St John and what is explicit in St John may be latent in St Paul.

But how could such a knowledge, partly explicit partly implicit, and varying day by day as to what was the one and what the other, be transmitted to the Church after them? Thus: I believe the Creed (i.e. the Deposit, I say Creed as more intelligible, since it consists of Articles) was delivered to the *Church with the gift of knowing its true and full meaning.* A Divine philosophy is committed to her keeping: not a number of formulas such as a modern pedantic theologian may make theology to consist in, but a system of thought, sui generis in such sense that a mind that was possessed of it, that is, the Church's mind, could definitely & unequivocally say whether this part of it, as traditionally expressed, meant this or that, and whether this or that was agreeable to, or inconsistent with it in whole or in part. I wish to hold that there is nothing which the Church has defined or shall define but what an Apostle, if asked, would have been fully able to answer and would have answered, as the Church has answered, the one answering by inspiration, the other from its gift of infallibility; and that the Church never will be able to answer, or has been able to answer, what the Apostles could not answer, e.g. whether the earth is stationary or not, or whether a republic is or is not better than a monarchy. The differences between them being that an Apostle could answer questions at once, but the Church answers them intermittently, in times & seasons, often delaying and postponing, according as she is guided by her Divine Instructor; and secondly and on the other hand, that the Church does in fact make answers which the Apostles did not make, and in one sense did not know, though they would have known them, i.e. made present to their consciousness, and made those answers, had the questions been asked.

I have taken notice of this particular superiority (so to call it) of later times over Apostolic, when speaking of Aristotle in illustration, and now I must notice that other point of superiority, which lies in the existence and know-ledge of scientific phraseology. Had St Paul been asked whether our Lady's conception was immaculate, or whether she was born in original sin, is it wrong to say that he would have been puzzled by the words 'conception', 'immaculate', and 'original sin'? Is it detracting from his perfect knowledge of all that which the Church in after times has developed and shall develop to the end, if I allow he would have kept silence and have left the question un-answered? is it more than saying, that scientific phraseology was not among the languages which were comprised in the Pentecostal gift? — But if he had been asked, whether or not our Lady had the grace of the Spirit anticipating all sin whatever, including Adam's imputed sin, I think he would have answered in the affirmative. If he never was asked the question, I should say he had in his mind the decision of the Church in 1854 in confuso or implicitè. I speak under correction.

One other question I must notice. What is meant by the *mind* of the Church? or of the Apostles committing their philosophy to the Church, yet not to each individual Father & Doctor? for the Church is not a person, as an Apostle is, but is merely *made up* of Fathers & theologians, and how can they altogether have one mind, which is not the mind of each? It is no answer to this question to say that the mind to which the Depositum is committed, is the infallible mind of the Pope, unless indeed we considered him infallible as an Apostle at all times, whereas we only say that he is infallible ex Cathedrâ. However, the theory of his infallibility will illustrate the question, and serve to answer it. We all know how different a boy's or a man's state of mind is, when he is in an idle, relaxed, careless mood, and when he is put on his metal. A boy in a class will make gross mistakes, because his mind is not roused; threaten him with some punishment, and he, as it were, wakes up, and to your surprise knows a great deal about the matter on which he is questioned. In like manner we never could take a friend's conversational sayings even in his own province of thought for his deliberate enunciations. I conceive then that the Depositum is in such sense committed to the Church or to the Pope, that when the Pope sits in St. Peter's chair, or when a Council of Fathers & doctors is collected round him, it is capable of being presented to their minds with that fullness and exactness, under the operation of supernatural grace, (so far forth and in such portion of it as the occasion requires,) with which it habitually, not occasionally, resided in the minds of the Apostles; — a vision of it, not logical, and therefore consistent with errors of reasoning & of fact in the enunciation, after the manner of an intuition or an instinct. Nor do those enunciations become logical, because theologians afterwards can reduce them to their relations to other doctrines, or give them a position in the general system of theology. To such theologians they appear as deductions from the creed or formularized deposit, but in truth they are original parts of it, communicated per modum unius to the Apostles' minds, & brought to light to the minds of the Fathers of the Council, under the temporary illumination of Divine Grace.

I put all this on paper with great diffidence, though it is the view I have entertained for so many years.   J H N

Works and Editions cited in Newman's Papers on Inspiration and Infallibility

AMORT, EUSEBIUS. *Demonstratio Critica Religionis Catholicae.* Venice 1744
  Theologia Eclectica, Moralis et Scholastica. 4 Vols. Bologna 1753
BANNES, DOMINICO. *Scholastica Commentaria . . . in D. Thomae.* Venice 1687
BELLARMINE, ST. ROBERT. *De Controversiis Christianae Fidei.* 4 Vols. [Volume I
  containing *De Verbo Dei*] Paris 1608
BERGIER, N. S. *Encyclopédie Méthodique. Théologie.* 3 Vols. Paris 1788–90
BILLUART, C. R. *Cursus Theologiae.* 3 Vols. Brescia 1836–38
BONFRÈRE, JACQUES. *In Totam Scripturam Sanctam Praeloquia,*
  in J. S. Menochius, *Commentarii totius Sacrae Scripturae* II. Venice 1743
BOSSUET, J. B. *Oeuvres.* 12 Vols. [Volume 3 containing *Exposition*] Paris 1743–7
BOUVIER, J. B. *Institutiones Theologicae ad usum Seminariorum.* 6 Vols. Sixth Edition.
  Paris 1846
CALMET, A. *Dissertationes in Vetus et Novum Testamentum.* 3 vols. Würzburg 1789
CANO, Melchior. *De Locis Theologicis.* Padua 1734
CARDENAS, J. *Crisis Theologica Bipartita, sive Disputationes Selectae ex Morali Theologia.*
  Venice 1694
CASTRO, ALFONSO a. *De Iusta Haereticorum Punitione.* Lyons 1556
CHRISSMAN, PHILIP NERI. *Regula Fidei Catholicae et Collectio Dogmatum Credendorum.*
  revised by P. J. Spindler. New edition. Würzburg 1854
DAVIDSON, SAMUEL. *Sacred Hermeneutics developed and applied.* Edinburgh 1843
DE LUGO, JOANNIS. *Opera Omnia.* 6 vols in 3 [*De Fide* in Vol. 3] Venice 1751
DENZINGER, H. *Enchiridion Symbolorum et Definitionum.* Würzburg 1856
DIXON, JOSEPH. *A General Introduction to the Sacred Scriptures.* 2 vols. Dublin 1852
Essays and Reviews. [Various Authors] London 1860
EX CHARMES, THOMAS. *Compendium Theologiae Universae.* Macerata 1828
Exercitationes Theologicae Tolosanae. 2 vols. Toulouse 1714
FERRER, ST. VINCENT. *Opera, seu Sermones de Tempore et Sanctis cum Tractatu de Vita
  Spirituali.* Augsburg 1729
HOLDEN, HENRY. *Divinae Fidei Analysis.* Paris 1782
JACOBATIUS, D. *De Conciliis,* in P. Labbé and G. Cossart, *Sacrosancta Concilia* XXIII.
  Venice 1728
LAMBERTINI, P. [Benedict XIV] *De Servorum Dei Beatificatione.* 15 Vols. Rome 1787–
  92
MALOU, J. B. *La Lecture de la Sainte Bible.* 2 vols in 1. Louvain 1846
MANNING, H. E. *The Reunion of Christendom. A Pastoral Letter to the Clergy etc.*
  London 1866
MARCHINI, J. F. *Tractatus de Divinitate et Canonicitate Sacrorum Bibliorum.* Turin
  1777
MIGNE, J.-P. *Theologiae Cursus Completus.* 28 vols. Paris 1837–46 [Contains works by
  Montagnus, Clerc de Beauberon, Chrissman and others]
MUZARELLI, ALFONSO. *Domino Temporale del Papa, Opuscolo.* 1789
NATALIS ALEXANDER. *Historia Ecclesiastica Veteris Novique Testamenti.* 8 vols. Paris
  1730
O'MAHONY, T. J. *Joseph Carrière, St. Sulpice and the Church of France in his time.*
  Dublin 1865
PALLAVICINO, SFORZA. *Vera Oecumenici Concilii Tridentini . . . Historia,* corrected
  edition. 3 vols. Augsburg 1769
PERRONE, J. *Praelectiones Theologicae.* Second edition. 8 vols. Rome 1840–4
  De Immaculato B. V. Mariae Conceptu Disquisitio Theologica. Rome 1847

PETAVIUS, D. *Opus de Theologicis Dogmatibus.* 6 vols in 3. Antwerp 1700

POTTER, J. *Praelectiones habitae in Scholâ Theologiae apud Oxonienses.* Oxford 1754

PUSEY, E. B. *The Church of England a Portion of Christ's One Holy Catholic Church, and a Means of Restoring Visible Unity. An Eirenicon, in a Letter to the Author of 'The Christian Year'.* Oxford 1865

QUETIF, J. and ECHARD, J. *Scriptores Ordinis Praedicatorum Recensiti.* 2 vols. Paris 1719–21

RABAUDY, BERNARD. *Exercitatio de Scriptura Sacra, seu de verbo Dei scripto, eiusque revelatione, et de modo, quo fuerit inspirata,* in F. A. Zacharia, *Thesaurus Theologici Supplementum I.* Venice 1764

RAYNAUD, THEOPHILUS. *Opera Omnia.* 19 vols. Lyons 1665

RYDER, H. I. D. *Idealism in Theology, a Review of Dr. Ward's Scheme of Dogmatic Authority.* London 1867
    A Letter to William George Ward, Esq., on his Theory of Infallible Instruction. London 1868
    Postscriptum to Letter to W. G. Ward, Esq. London 1868

SALMANTICENSIS, COLLEGII. *Cursus Theologicus.* 12 vols. Lyons and Barcelona 1679–1704

SALMERON, ALFONSO. *Opera Omnia.* 16 vols. Cologne 1602–4

SCAVINI, P. *Theologia Moralis.* 3 vols. Brussels 1847

STEELE, SIR RICHARD. *An Account of the State of the Roman Catholick Religion.* Second edition. London 1716

SUAREZ, F. *Opera Omnia.* 23 vols in 11. Venice 1740–51

TANNER, ADAM. *Universa Theologia Scholastica.* 4 vols. Ingolstadt 1626–7

TIRABOSCHI, GIROLAMO. *Storia della Letteratura Italiana.* 8 vols in 15. Modena 1787–94

TOURNELY, H. *Cursus Theologicus Scholastico-Dogmaticus et Moralis.* 10 vols in 5. Cologne 1752–65

VALENTIA, GREGORY of. *Commentariorum Theologicorum.* Second edition. 4 vols. Ingolstadt 1592–1603

VAN LOO, BERNARD. *Introductio in Theologiam Dogmaticam.* Rome 1859

VASQUEZ, GABRIEL. *Commentariorum ac Disputationum in primam partem S. Thomae.* 4 vols. Lyons 1631

VEGA, A. *Tridentini Decreti de Iustificatione Expositio, et Defensio.* Alcala 1564

VERON, F. *De Regula Fidei Catholicae,* in A. & P. de Walenburch, *Tractatus . . .,* [see below]

VINCENZI, A. *Sessio Quarta Concilii Tridentini vindicata.* 2 parts. Rome 1842 & 44

VIVA, DOMINICO. *Cursus Theologicus.* 8 parts in 2 vols. Padua 1755

WALENBURCH, A. & P. de. *Tractatus Generales de Controversiis Fidei.* 2 vols. Cologne 1670

WARD, WILLIAM GEORGE. *A Letter [to] the Rev. Father Ryder on his recent Pamphlet.* London 1867

WARD, WILLIAM GEORGE. *A Second Letter to the Rev. Father Ryder.* London 1868

WARD, WILLIAM GEORGE. *A Brief Summary of the recent Controversy on Infallibility; being a reply to Rev. Father Ryder on his Postscript.* London 1868

WISEMAN, CARDINAL NICHOLAS. *Essays on Various Subjects.* 3 vols. London 1853
    Recollections of the last four Popes and of Rome in their times. London n.d.

WITSTEIN, JOHN JACOB. *Novum Testamentum Graecum.* 2 vols. Amsterdam 1751

*   *   *

Newman published the following advertisement in the front of his volume *Tracts Theological and Ecclesiastical* (1874)

ADVERTISEMENT

On collecting into one volume Tracts written at long intervals of time from each other, with the use of various libraries and of different editions of the Fathers, I have some anxiety lest, in consequence, mistakes should be found in my references, in spite of the great pains I have taken to make them accurate. However, I give here, to the best of my power, a list of the Editions I have followed:

Africanus, *apud* Routh. Relliqu. Sacr. t. ii.
Ambrosius, *Paris*. 1686, &c. ed. Benedict. seu. Maurin.
Anastasius Sinaita, *Ingolstad*. 1606, Gretser.
Athanasius, *Paris*. 1698 (Montfaucon). Maurin.
Athenagoras, *Venet*. 1747, Maurin.
Augustinus, *Paris*. 1689, &c. Maurin.
Basilius Magnus, *Paris*. 1721 &c. Maurin.
Basilius Seleuc. *Paris*. 1622, Dausque.
Bibliotheca Patrum, *Colon*. 1618.
——*Paris*. Quart. 1624.
——*Lugdun*. Max. 1677.
——*Venet*. 1765, &c. Galland.
Chrysostomus Joannes, *Paris*. 1718, &c. (Montfaucon), Maurin.
Clemens Alex. *Oxon*. 1715, Potter.
Collectanea Monumentorum, *Romae*, 1698, Zacagn.
Collectio Nova Patrum, *Paris*. 1706 (Montfaucon), Maurin.
Conciliorum Collectio Regia, *Paris*. 1715, Harduin.
Concilium Antiochenum, *ap*, Routh. *Rell. S*. t. ii.
Cyprianus, *Venet*. 1758, Maurin.
Cyrillus Alex. *Lutet*. 1638, Aubert.
Cyrillus Hieros. *Paris*. 1720, Maurin.
Damascenus Joannes, *Venet*. 1748, Lequien.
Didymus, *Bonon*. 1769, Mingarelli.
Dionysius Alex. *ap*. Athan. et Rell. S. Routh. t. iii.
Dionysius Rom. *ibid*.
Ephraëm, *ap*. Photium.
Epiphanius, *Colon*. 1682, Petav.
Epistola ad Diognetum, *ap*. Justin. Opp.
Epistolae Pontif. Roman. *Paris*. 1721 (Coustant.), Maurin.
Eulogius, *ap*. Photium.
Eusebius, Histor. Eccles ⎫
——Laud. Constant.   ⎬*Amstelod* 1695, Vales.
——Praepar.   ⎫
——Demonstr.   ⎬*Colon*. 1688.
——c. Marcell. &c.   ⎭
Euthymius, *Lips*. 1792, Matthaei.
Facundus, *ap*. Opp. Sirmondi, t. ii.
Gregorius Nazianz. *Paris*. 1778, 1840, Maurin.
Gregorius Neocaesar. (Thaumaturg.) *Paris*. 1622.
Gregorius Nyssen, Opp. *Paris*. 1615, &c.
——Antirrhet. *ap*. Collectan. Zacagn.
Hieronymus, *Venet*. 1766, Vallars.
Hilarius Pictav. *Paris*. 1693, Maurin.
Hippolytus, Opp. *Hamburg*. 1716, Fabric.
    c. Noëtum, *ap*. Opuscula, Routh.
    Elenchus, *Oxon*. 1851, Miller.
Incerti Dialogi, *ap*. Athan. Opp. t. ii.
Irenaeus, *Venet*. 1734, Maurin.
Isidorus Pelus. *Paris*. 1638
Justinus Mart. *Venet*. 1747, Maurin.
Lactantius, *Lutet*. 1748, Dufresnoi.
Leo Magnus, *Venet* 1753, &c Ballerin.
Leontius, *ap*. Bibl. P. *Colon*. et *Venet*. Galland. et Thesaur. Canis. t. i.
Malchion, *ap*. Rell. S. Routh. t. ii.
Maximus, *Paris*. 1675, Combefis.
Melito, *ap*. Rell. S. Routh. t. i.
Mercator, *Paris*. 1673, Garner.
Methodius, *ap*. Bibl. P. *Venet*. Galland. t. iii.
Novatianus, *Londini*, 1728, Jackson.

Opera Varia Sirmondi, *Venet.* 1728, La Baume.
Opuscula Eccles. *Oxon.* 1832, Routh.
Origenes, *Paris.* 1733, &c. Maurin.
Philo, *Francofurt.* 1691.
Phoebadius, *ap.* Bibl. P. *Venet.* Galland. t. v.
Photius, *Rothomag.* 1653, Schott.
Plotinus, *Oxon.* 1835, Creuzer.
Proclus, *Romae,* 1630, Riccard.
Relliquiae Sacrae Patrum, *Oxon.* 1814, &c. Routh.
Rusticus, *ap.* Bibl. P. *Colon.* t. iv.
Socrates ⎱ *Amstelod.* 1695, Vales.
Sozomenus ⎰
Tatianus, *Venet.* 1747, Maurin.
Tertullianus, *Lutet.* 1641, Rigalt.
Theodoretus, Opp. *Halae,* 1769, &c. Schulze.
——Hist. Eccl. *Amstelod.* 1695, Vales.
Theophilus, *Venet.* 1747, Maurin.
Thesaurus Eccles. Canisii, *Antverp.* 1725, Basnage.
Victorinus, *ap.* Bibl. P. *Venet.* Galland. t. viii.
Vigilius Thaps. *ap.* Bibl. P. *Lugdun.* t. viii.
Vincentius Lirin. *ap.* Bibl. P. *Venet.* Galland. t. x.
Zeno, *Veron.* 1739, Ballerin.

Index of Persons

Newman, J. H.—*contd.*
 102, 104, 118, 131, 135, 140–2, 150–6, 160
Newton, I., 4
Nicephorus, St, 96
Noe, 29, 45, 76
Norfolk, Duke of, ix
Noris, J., 136
Nun, 53

O'Mahony, T. J., 103
Origen, 6, 43, 83, 85–7, 94, 96
Orsi, Cardinal G. A., 29

Pacca, Cardinal B., 29
Palaeologus, M., 40, 43
Pallavicino, S., 11, 50–1
Papias, 17
Paul, St, 14, 17, 23–5, 29, 54–6, 58–60, 62, 64–5, 75, 85–6, 89–90, 94–6, 107, 109, 119, 132, 144, 156, 158–9
 Epistles of, 17, 23, 25, 54–6, 58, 65–6, 75, 86, 119
Paul III, 113, 135
Perrone, J., 9, 12–14, 18, 21, 78, 80–1, 103, 105–6, 110, 112, 115–16, 122–4, 126, 129–31, 136
Petavius, D., 104
Peter, St, 53–5, 58, 64, 86, 94, 107, 109–10, 116, 118–20, 127–9, 131, 139, 144–5, 148
 Epistles of, 55, 86, 119
Peter the Hermit, 95
Phaleg, 7
Philip Neri, St, 120
Philo, 90
Pius IV, 42, 113, 135
Pius V, 20
Pius VI, 118
Pius VII, 4–5
Pius IX, viii, 101, 107, 120, 126, 128, 141, 144
Plato, 106
Plutarch, 4
Polycarp, St, 66, 96, 119
Potter, J., 69
Powell, Baden, 4
Prateiolus, G., 11
Primasius, 96
Prosper of Aquitaine, St, 94
Puffendorf, S., 29
Pusey, E. B., viii, 100, 103, 111–12, 124, 142

Quetif, J., 11

Rabaudy, B., 11, 13–14, 69–70, 79, 81, 126, 128
Ranke, L. von, 29
Reithmayer, U. de G., 79

Reu, 7
Reynaud, T., 128
Rinaldi, O., 29
Rocaberti, J. T. de, 107
Ryder, G., 151
Ryder, Bishop H., 151
Ryder, H. I. D., viii, 100, 118, 142, 145–8, 151–4

Salmeron, A., 7, 17, 25, 27
Samuel, 23, 26, 53
Scavini, P., 118
Scott, Sir W., 33
Sem, 7
Sennacherib, 10
Sixtus V, 92, 148
Seynaeve, J., vii, 26, 52, 57
Sibyl, 89–90
Simon Magus, 119–20, 126
Solomon, 50
Sophocles, 4
Stapleton, T., 94
Steele, Sir R., 118
Stephen, St, 53, 76, 110, 117
Suarez, F., 81, 106, 112, 116, 120, 125–9, 136
Susanna, 92–3, 95
Svaglic, M. J., viii, 103

Tacitus, 94
Tanner, A., 120, 128
Tertullian, 85–7, 91, 93–4
Theiner, A., 103
Theodoret, 14, 85, 88, 94
Theophilus, St, 83, 85, 87, 89, 96
Thomas Aquinas, St, 15–16, 61, 64, 116, 124–7
Timothy, St, 23, 54
Tiraboschi, G., 28
Titus, St, 23
Todhunter, I., 4
Tournely, H., 41, 103, 105, 134, 147
Tracey, G., ix
Tristram, H., 151

Van Loo, B., 115–17, 121–2, 124, 130–1, 135
Vasquez, G., 120, 128, 133–4, 136
Vawter, B., vii
Vega, A., 133
Veron, F., 103, 112, 115, 131–4
Victor I, St, 110, 117
Victorinus St, 96
Vincent Ferrer, St, 62, 126, 128
Vigilius, 113, 135
Vincent of Lerins, St, 104
Vincenzi, A., 42, 78, 80, 82
Viva, D., 116, 124–6, 128–9, 131, 135, 137–8, 148

Index of Subjects and other Biblical References

INDEX OF SUBJECTS AND OTHER BIBLICAL REFERENCES

Inspiration of the Bible, vii, ix, *Part I passim*, 112, 143, 152, 156, 158
Interpretation of the Bible and Senses of Scripture, 1, 6, 16–17, 20–1, 24–6, 36–7, 46, 62–3, 68, 71, 76, 81, 83, 87, 95–7

Joel, 55
Jonas, 54–5
Josue, 53–5
Judges, 54–5

Kantian System, 146
Kings, Books of, 53, 55

Laodicea, Council of, 92, 96
Lateran, Council of, 43, 101, 134
Latrocinium, 120, 126
Leviticus, 55, 67

Maccabees, 62, 76, 82, 92, 95, 97
Malachias, 55
Manicheanism, 44
Maynooth Grant, 102
Michaeas, 55
Miracles, 8, 21
Monophysitism, 142
Montes Pietatis, 101
Moral Theology and Philosophy, 15, 18
Munich Brief, viii

Nahum, 55
Nicaea, Council and Creed of, 15–16, 19, 82–4, 96, 117, 127–8, 132
Novatianism, 101
Numbers, 53–5, 76

Osee, 55
Old and New Testaments, 6–7, 18, 25, 41–5, 49, 54–5, 59, 66, 84, 86, 91–2, 96–7

Paralipomenon, 55
Paulianists, 43
Pelagianism, 16
Priscillianists, 40, 44
Propaganda, Congregation of, viii, 3
Prophecy and Prophets, 21–3, 25, 44–5, 52–4, 58–9, 61, 64–8, 70, 72, 74, 77, 82, 84–91, 94–7, 132
Protestantism, 16, 27, 32–3, 155

Proverbs, 17, 54–5
Psalms and Psalter, 25, 50, 54–5, 61, 67, 69, 82
Purgatory, 76, 101

Rambler, The, 4, 97
Relics, 33, 127
Revelation, Divine and the Deposit of Faith, 4, 6, 15, 19, 21–2, 29, 31–2, 35, 37–8, 43, 46, 48–9, 52–3, 58–9, 65, 67–70, 72–3, 75, 79, 88, 94, 97–8, 105–16, 119–25, 127–8, 130–2, 137–9, 141–3, 145–9, 152–5, 158–9
Ruth, 55

Scandal, 4, 15, 28–9, 34, 38, 93, 102–3, 136
Sciences, Natural (*see also* Inerrancy), 4–7, 9–10, 20, 26–9, 31–2, 34–7, 49–50, 52, 69, 87, 98
Septuagint, 90–2
Society of Jesus, 120, 128
Sophonias, 55
Syllabus of Errors, viii, 101

Temporal Power of the Pope, 103, 105, 107, 113, 121, 143–4
Theologians, opinions of and school of, 9–11, 13, 16, 34, 36–9, 41, 43, 47–52, 63, 68–9, 72, 77–82, 84, 91, 93, 97, 102–3, 115, 129, 132, 135, 137–8, 146–9, 159
Tobias, 92, 95
Tradition, 12, 18, 22, 35, 41, 44–6, 52, 68–70, 92, 107, 112, 115–16, 123, 129–31, 134, 138–9, 141, 147
Trent, Council of, 9, 12, 20, 22, 40–3, 45–7, 68, 70, 78–9, 82, 93, 95, 103, 105, 115, 131, 134
Trinity, 33, 43, 57, 156–7

Ultramontanism, viii, 143

Vatican Council, vii, ix
Vulgate, 13, 55

Waldenses, 40, 44
Wisdom, 55, 76, 97

Zacharias, 55